W9-BZR-456

Steve Scott

THE MILER

OTHER BOOKS BY MARC BLOOM

Cross Country Running

The Marathon

Olympic Gold

The Runner's Bible

The *Know Your Game* Series

———

Steve Scott

THE
MILER

America's
Legendary Runner
Talks About His
Triumphs and Trials

WITH MARC BLOOM

MACMILLAN • USA

MACMILLAN
A Simon & Schuster Macmillan Company
1633 Broadway
New York, NY 10019-6785

Copyright © 1997 by Steve Scott and Marc Bloom

All rights reserved. No part of this book may be reproduced or transmitted
in any form or by any means, electronic or mechanical, including photo-
copying, recording, or by any information storage or retrieval system,
without permission in writing from the Publisher.

MACMILLAN is a trademark of Macmillan, Inc.

Library of Congress Cataloging-in-Publication Data
Scott, Steve, 1956–
    Steve Scott, the miler / Steve Scott with Marc Bloom.
        p.   cm.
    ISBN 0-02-861677-4
    1. Scott, Steve, 1956– .   2. Runners (Sports)—United States—
    –Biography.   I. Bloom, Marc, 1939– . II. Title.
    GV1061.15.S36A3 1997
    796.42'4'092—dc21
    [B]   97-18565
                                                                          CIP

DESIGN BY KEVIN HANEK

For Mom and Dad,
who trained me to reach the starting line.

ACKNOWLEDGMENTS

We appreciate the help of the following people: Steve's mother, Mary Scott, for remembering Steve's sweet and silly childhood moments; Steve's coaches Bob Loney, Len Miller, and Irv Ray, for sharing their perspective on the highs and lows of Steve's running fortunes; Dr. Kevin O'Brien, Steve's surgeon, for reviewing the chapter on the cancer that Steve beat; Ray Flynn, Steve's former mile compatriot, for his reminiscences; John Konigh, a college teammate of Steve's, for personal photographs; track statistician Jeff Hollobough, for his list of Steve's sub–4:00 miles; photographers Steve Sutton, Paul Sutton and David Madison for their generous contributions; our editors, Mary Ann Lynch and Traci Cothran, for their guidance and support; Michelle Tupper for editorial assistance when most needed; and our agent, Thomas Hart, for his faith in our collaboration. We would also like to recognize *Track & Field News, Runner's World* and *The Runner* as essential sources. Finally, we would like to thank our wives, Kim Scott and Andrea Bloom, for keeping the family afloat, in the past year and always, during the long stretches of the track circuit.

FOREWORD

I barely knew Steve Scott before we started working together on this book. While I'd covered his career and seen most of his important races, I'd never really talked with Steve other than a few words about his aspirations of running sub–4:00 at the age of 40. I'd heard he was a nice guy. Everybody in track and field knew that. I'd seen him compete like a workhorse, racing wherever the action was. Everybody knew that, too. But I knew little about Steve's lighter side—the Steve who would think nothing of slipping a live, furry animal under the sheets of your bed. Or the Steve who would wear Mickey Mouse ears during the Opening Ceremonies of the Olympic Games.

As I look back on our collaboration, which began in a hotel room off a golf course in Santee, California, in January, 1996, I feel lucky that I somehow managed to come away unscathed. In the year that we worked on the book, I was not the victim of a single Steve Scott prank. Now that he's passed 40, maybe the guy has mellowed. I won't say he's all grown up, and I think Steve would agree that his maturity is still a work-in-progress. That's one of many things we have in common.

We hit it off immediately. I found Steve utterly without pretense as we retraced his life. I also found myself feeling guilty as a journalist for not having appreciated all that he'd accomplished. But when Steve competed, he did so without fanfare or mystique; he was one of the boys. The victories were there, but the man stood in the shadows, a quiet hero.

I look at Steve as a hero—an American hero. Twenty years ago, he took the most important event in track and field—the mile—and made it his own. He did so with honesty, dignity, humor and faith, qualities he would count on again when cancer struck him in 1994. As we worked on his story, meeting at events such as the Millrose Games, Boston Marathon, and Olympic Trials, I was awed by Steve's outlook. He'd put his illness behind him and, at 40, was taking a miraculous stab at the 4-minute mile.

I know my heart will be pounding whenever Steve runs his last mile races. I also know that the next time we happen to be sharing a hotel room I'll be checking under my sheets.

MARC BLOOM
MARLBORO, NEW JERSEY
APRIL, 1997

CONTENTS

The Outer Limits

T he mile race starts on the bus ride from the hotel where you sit among your competitors and decide, based on how your season is going and how you feel that day, who you'll talk to, acknowledge, or even look at before reaching the stadium. I talk to the milers I know I can beat and avoid the others. I have power over those I can beat; I can shoot the breeze with them, even joke with them, because I have them in my pocket and they know that. Because I don't fear them, I don't worry about showing a soft side of myself or giving them the impression—not true, of course—that I could be weak or vulnerable or not up to the task of running in pain and sprinting the last one-hundred meters as though they're the last one-hundred meters of my life. As for the milers whom I'm not certain I can beat—well, I can't let my guard down with them, chat about the weather or the race in Byrkjelo or the knockwurst at the hotel. I can't give my rivals an extra edge by allowing them to think I'm not focused and fight-happy. No, I can't let that happen. So it's as if I'm two different people as I ride with my competitors to the track: nice to those I'll bury, arrogant to those who might bury me. Hey, you gotta learn to survive.

I don't want any surprises, either. I want every detail precise and under control, from the time we arrive at the stadium (where I check *in and pick up my race number), to my warmup (which is always the same routine of jogging, stretching, and strideouts), down to how many seconds it takes me to lace up my racing spikes. Everything must be kept to the bare essentials. Nothing can clutter my mind or my space. Because nothing is harder than running the mile.*

Nothing. Not the 100 meters or the 10K or even the marathon. The mile, or its metric equivalent, the 1,500 meters, demands the ultimate combination of speed and strength. In training, I run sprints till I drop and I also cover distances as far as 20 miles. I train in pain because I race in pain and if you can't tolerate pain you may as well quit. You won't be a miler.

Just because I can tolerate pain doesn't mean I don't fear it. I do. The pain is like a bad headache that travels through your entire body. Just when you need to speed up, the ache takes over and you want to slow down. Your muscles and joints, tendons and ligaments, heart and lungs all have to work overtime while lacking vital oxygen. That hurts. What I fear is whether I can, yet again, summon the will to peel back each layer of pain and still push my body farther.

My capacity is somewhere beyond my body's perceived limit. Frankly, I don't know if I've ever truly reached it. But each time I race I think I might have to. That's what running the mile is about: the outer limits.

So I sit on the bus, keep to myself, and visualize the race. In one scene, the field goes out comfortably and I have to harness my top speed for no more than the last lap. Very manageable. The pace steadily builds and builds and I'm under pressure for less than a minute. There are tactical strategies to play with, split-second decisions that may decide the race or even define my career, but that's okay.

I see myself winning. I see myself coming from behind and blowing by the leader on the home straight to win. If there's a better feeling on God's green earth, I'd like to know what it is.

In another image, the field flies impatiently from the gun. We are intent on killing each other off. This is not okay. Push too soon and you're in the outer limits with half a race still to go. Hold back too much and you risk losing everything. Someone, maybe more than one, will reach full capacity, set a record, and you won't be there. You'll be up the track when the finish tape is broken, thinking of how you'll explain that to the TV reporters.

Nearing the stadium, I think about the temperature, the humidity, the crowd, and conditions at the stadium. Wind is as important to a miler as it is to a sloop. Flags are the first thing I check when the bus arrives at the track. Still flags, at ease like a relaxed platoon, mean less resistance and a fast race. Uh-oh. I can feel the outer limits creeping up.

Before warming up, I find a patch of grass in the shade and lie down. I try to clear all the clutter out of my system. I am silent, still. At that moment, I'm inanimate. I don't exist. After fifteen minutes, I rise, jog, stretch, take my strideouts, strip off my sweats, pin on my number, lace up my spikes—the right one first as always—take some deep breaths. I am ready to race.

I want to feel as light as air, and quick. I want my uniform jersey tucked in just so, my number pinned squarely against my chest. I want a little buzz of urgency to keep me bouncy and skittish. I want everything perfect. It rarely is; usually, there's some hiccup: maybe one of your Achilles tendons feels just a wee bit unresponsive as you jog down the track to the start after racing the mile thirty-two times in thirty-two cities this particular season.

Called to take our marks, I'm happy to be given a "dreaded" outside lane on the start line. Most milers like to have an inside lane and rush off with flying elbows into an immediate rumble for the close-up positions. Let them. I like to go out at a measured pace and run two lanes wide if necessary to stay out of traffic before moving to the rail. My trademark is to hold back and come on.

The gun is up and I crouch behind the start, my left foot forward, my arms low, and my gaze pointed straight ahead, like a youngster poised for a challenge-race in the schoolyard. Crack! I let the field draw ahead as I settle toward the rear and gauge the action. I want to conserve energy, pick off one man at a time, and strike for the lead when the frontrunners begin to lose their steam.

That's me: Scottie the Miler, just a kid at heart, racing around the track, the most pure and honest form of work I know.

First Strides for Momma's Boy: High School

ompeting in the Olympics never entered my mind when I was growing up in Upland, California. I was too busy resisting attempts by my mother, a jogger herself, and the high school coach, Bob Loney, to make me take up running competitively. Not that I had any special running talent at the outset. But I was such a goofball as a kid that my mother felt the rigors of the Upland High cross-country and track squads might straighten me out.

Years later when my running took shape and I started to gain notoriety, family members expressed amazement that a cutup like me could have the focus and determination necessary to be a success. As a teenager, all I wanted was to play baseball and meet girls. Even though Upland fielded winning cross-country teams, the runners were considered geeks with no social standing. My self-image was fragile enough in a family in which my father, Gordon, was a physician and my older brother, Kendall, was a model of discipline and an outstanding medical student. Kendall, Mr. Hospital Corners, was everything I was not, and more than once I wished I could beat the crap out of him.

Upland was situated 35 miles east of Los Angeles at the base of the San Gabriel Mountains. It was the kind of conservative, white, upper-middle-class place where high school sweethearts could share sodas at the malt shop, insulated from the divisive social issues sweeping the nation. In Upland, you didn't have to lock your car, the local dairy delivered milk right to your door, and bowling was big on Friday night. If a young girl got in trouble in Upland, she had little choice but to leave town.

Far off the beaten path and in what is known as the Inland Empire, Upland, which calls itself the "City of Gracious Living," boasts orange groves, lemon groves, and grapefruit groves—and many more private schools than public schools. When I finally went out for the high school cross-country and track teams and started running through those groves, my teammates and I loved to grab whatever fruit we could and fling it at one another.

This inviting landscape had inspired my mother, Mary, an independent and adventurous woman, to begin running when the jogging movement was still in its infancy. You can't imagine what courage it took in the late 1960s for a 40-ish woman in buttoned-up Upland to venture out onto the roads in shorts and a T-shirt . . . and sweat. When Mom ran, motorists honked their horns at her. Why wasn't this middle-aged chick in the kitchen where she belonged? And cover up those legs, for God's sake!

I can remember Mom running in the summer of 1971, a year before Frank Shorter awakened our sedentary nation to the beauty of running with his Olympic marathon victory in Munich. Mom was ahead of her time all right. By then, she could knock out a steady six miles up and back Euclid Avenue, Upland's main drag, and had remade her body and psyche. In her commitment to exercise, Mom had lost weight, changed her diet, cut out hard liquor, stopped smoking, and caught the runner's high.

Aerobics guru Ken Cooper could have put Mom on a poster. Running philosopher George Sheehan could have used her as an example in his lectures. But change came slowly to Upland, and people who saw my mother run called her "The Weird Lady of Euclid Avenue." Even my dad, Gordon, a physician, thought Mom was wacky. Dad smoked and was overweight. He'd tried to run with her, but he couldn't take it and quit. Though a medical man, he could not see the lasting value in running.

Mom embodied commitment in anything she did, whether it was campaigning for a gubernatorial candidate named Ronald Reagan or caring for the Scott family in the best tradition of Donna Reed. My mother always believed that when you started something, you followed through. Eventually, I would catch on, and the perseverance I saw in Mom would also find a place in my heart.

That summer of 1971, Coach Loney knew he could count on Mom to drumbeat for the Upland cross-country team. It was essential for high school runners to train over the summer to be in shape for the fall season. I'd participated on the freshman squad and my sophomore year was coming up. Loney wanted me fit and ready, but I had already decided I wasn't running a step that summer.

My mother would not stand for that. After her morning work-out, she would come into my bedroom dripping with sweat. I was, of course, still sound asleep. She'd nudge me and say, "Steve, you better go out for your run now. It's just a glorious day, so pretty in the morning light . . ." and then I'd roll over and go back to sleep.

Upland *was* pretty in the morning, if you got up early enough. However, in the summer, after 9 o'clock or so, smog rolled in and the conditions for running were hideous. Upland sat in a bowl that trapped desert winds from the east and ocean winds from the west. That potent mix fouled the air, which was made even worse by auto emissions drifting in from L.A. and pollution from nearby Kaiser Steel.

Mom beat the smog by running at daybreak. She urged me to do the same, but it did no good. This went on week after week but she would not give up. After all, I was her baby, the youngest of three children. Kendall, my med-student brother, was four years older. Alicia, my sister, was two years older than I was. She would go into nursing. I was the playful, mischievous kid, the younger brother and baby of the family, with no apparent direction. I would become a runner.

Perhaps Mom knew even then that running would become my lifelong passion. But her habits as a devoted runner hardly made running appealing to me. She seemed like the disciple of some off-the-wall cult. She had changed her diet, started eating bran and taking vitamins. After breakfast she downed a wheat-germ drink that looked like peat moss. And she caused a family furor when she switched us all from whole milk to skim.

At 15 years old, I wanted to steer clear of that nutty regime. I hung on to my laziness; but even so, during our '71 summer vacation at Mission Beach in San Diego, Mom was still on my case. My friend and teammate Jimmy Farr was with us at the beach. Realizing that the cross-country season was just around the corner, Mom preached to both of us "to get out and start running."

Jimmy and I would say, sure, we're going out for a run right now. We would put on our running shoes, jog over to the beach out of my mother's view and proceed to play frisbee and mess around for about 45 minutes. Afterward, we splashed water on our faces to make it look like we'd worked up a sweat, sprinted back to Mom, all huffing and puffing, and reported, "Pheeeew, we just ran five miles. Man, we're beat!"

Mom fell for it. I wouldn't be brave enough to tell her the truth for another ten years. (I'm the first to admit I matured slowly.)

———————

As a lazy kid, I'd followed my brother into Little League baseball, developed into a pretty fair pitcher, and saw myself on a path toward the majors. I imagined myself as the stopper on the high school team, but Bob Loney's recruiting system for the Upland High cross-country team got in the way.

Every year, Loney organized a cross-country meet between the town's two junior high schools so he could see who had running potential and try to recruit them for the high school team. All the eighth graders had to run the junior high meet. Loney built up the rivalry into a big deal so kids would really put their hearts into it.

Pioneer, the junior high I attended, was considered the school for well-off kids. Our rival school, from the other side of Foothill Boulevard, was working class, largely Latino. To me, those kids were tough and intimidating.

The race covered a mile and a half on school grounds. I had no idea how long that was, nor how to pace myself. Wearing gym shorts and basketball sneakers, I sprinted out too fast (with the rest of the kids), died badly, and spent the race thinking, "When is this thing going to end?"

I placed somewhere around 20th out of 200. After that, Loney, who coached the track team as well as cross-country, assembled the top 30 or so finishers in a room at the school and very cleverly showcased the Upland Highlanders program. He had medals and trophies on display, including state championship awards and clippings of Upland's star, Gordon Innes, who would one day run the two-mile in track in a nationally-ranked 9:02. Then, as a dramatic climax, Loney trotted out one of his best runners wearing a team sweater bearing a varsity letter. He chose as Upland's role model a kid with long, blond hair to show that cross-country could be cool.

The sweater, of course, was a badge of honor. In fact, in the early 1970s in Upland, a high school letterman sweater was hot stuff. Loney told his audience of scrawny kids that these medals and trophies and, most particularly, that handsome kelly-green letterman sweater could be ours. All we had to do was earn them.

Boy, did I want that sweater. I saw the cool guys around the neighborhood wearing them and figured it would be a great way to attract girls. I had no idea there would be any responsibility involved in obtaining the sweater. But at that time, I had a shoot-first-and-ask-questions-later mentality.

I was in that early teen stage where I did some pretty stupid things. Only about a year before, I had pulled off the Great Smoke Bomb Caper. A friend and I made smoke bombs with matches and aluminum foil. Then we randomly picked out a neighbor's house on Laurel Street where we lived, set off the bomb, and rang the bell. When someone came to the door, we took off. Naturally, the family knew us and reported the incident. Soon after the police came calling. Of course, I denied any involvement.

When the police left and my parents questioned me, I lied at first, but soon admitted my crime. Lying was the worst thing you could do in the Scott family. My mother cut me a lot of slack, but lying was not tolerated. My father went out to the wood shack, got a stick, and beat the tar out of my rear.

Cross-country offered me the discipline I needed. The freshman racing distance was two miles, and in training we ran three to five miles a day to build endurance for competition. Loney had us do some training on the track but also gave us a lot of hills to run, a system modeled on the ideas of Mihaly Igloi, a Hungarian expatriate coaching distance runners in southern California at the

time. Igloi was considered a master. His protégés included Bob
Schul, the 1964 Olympic champion in the 5,000 meters.

Hills were part of most cross-country race courses, and every
couple of weeks Loney would arrange a specialized hill workout.
The team would jog four miles from school to the base of Mount
Baldy, where we'd run up and down a 200-meter hill ten times.
Loney, who drove to the hill in his station wagon, made a concession to us freshmen: We could ride with him to within a mile of
the hill. The shortcut appealed to me and I was among those who
took the offer.

Initially, Loney's lessons were just background noise to my
freshman daydreams. But a piece of everything he said found a
small spot in my soul, and later on I would find myself drawing
upon his advice again and again.

To earn a letter in track, you had to run two miles in under
11 minutes. I just snuck in under the 11-minute requirement and
got my letter, which Mom lovingly sewed onto the sweater; then,
a cross-country insignia—a "CC" with an arrow—was sewn onto
the letter itself. I glowed as Mom stitched the inscription and then
I proudly wore the sweater around the house to break it in.

I thought I'd be one helluva big shot at Upland High. What I
hadn't realized was that while letterman sweaters were cool, the
track letter was not. In those days attitudes toward runners were
negative, and in high school, cross-country members were viewed
as skinny, nonathletic dorks unworthy of recognition. Realizing
my cross-country emblem was almost a scarlet letter, I hardly
wore the sweater I had so coveted.

So in the spring, instead of running track, I joined the freshman baseball team. I pitched, and my friend Jimmy was my
catcher. Then the next season, as sophomores, we thought we'd
try out for football. I was always hunting for a high-status event
that would help me make an impression on girls. In junior high,

I'd gone out for football, trying to be a quarterback. Since I was incapable of memorizing the plays, on game days I had to write the plays on index cards and stuff them into my pants. Not that it mattered; I was third-string and saw little action—but at least I was on the team.

When I told my parents I might try football at Upland, they were aghast. My parents were overprotective and feared their little Stevie would get hurt. In his medical practice, Dad had treated injured football players and didn't like what he saw. For the same reason, Mom and Dad would not let me ski or ride a motorcycle. Scott kids were sheltered. Once, when my sister hitchhiked against family rules, my parents went nuts.

Mom, in particular, was impressed when Loney said I had some running promise, and she was keen on seeing that I made the most of it. My talent first became apparent when I competed in a sophomore race against Claremont High. Jimmy and a couple of my other teammates were positioned well ahead of me. When I ran past Loney on the sidelines, he called out to me to go chase down Jimmy, but I didn't respond. Loney yelled again matter-of-factly, "Go after Jimmy." Loney was very laid back, never screaming like other coaches. But something clicked in me and I flew after Jimmy, passing opponents with a finish that enabled us to win the meet. That was the first time I realized that my efforts could affect the team outcome, and it felt good.

My speed made Loney accelerate his efforts to convince me that I should give up baseball for track in the spring of '72. That Loney could talk. He would keep my dad on the phone till all hours, and I would hear my father literally snoring into the phone while Loney went on about my running potential.

Even though the baseball coach stuck me on the soph squad, a bush team for benchriders from the junior varsity, I wouldn't commit to the track team, yet. Not being a smashingly gorgeous hunk or a big, strong football player, I still considered baseball my only link to coolness.

Sports and girls were my universe. On Saturday nights, Jimmy and I would cruise around Upland in his beat-up Bonneville looking for girls and checking the action at In & Out Burger, the area hot spot. If a girl had actually responded to our calls and come up to the car window, I think I would have peed in my pants out of fear. Lucky for me, no girl ever did, but we kept cruising.

I finally got the track itch at the end of that summer while watching the 1972 Olympics on television from Munich. I could identify with the runners. Dave Wottle, the 800-meter gold medalist, inspired me most. I liked the way he came from far behind with a long sprint. Eventually, that would become my own style of racing. And I liked the way he wore a cap when he ran.

Thin, shy, and gawky, Wottle reminded me of myself. He showed me that an uncool-seeming regular guy could succeed, and even make it to the top. During the medal ceremony when the National Anthem was played, Wottle forgot to take off his cap. It was an honest slip but the media made a big deal of it and Wottle apologized profusely.

To me, Wottle's "gold medal cap" became a symbol of striking out on your own and resisting comformity. No track racer wore a cap in the Olympics; it looked goofy and was one more little thing to think about as you ran. Wottle showed me a relaxed yet courageous individuality, and I started to think I was wasting my time trying to be a ballplayer just because it was the thing to do.

Then there was Loney, who kept telling me how good a track runner I could be. I started listening because I saw that there were broad parameters of excellence in the judgment of running performances. You didn't have to win to run well; you could do your best, come in fifth, and still get a pat on the back. In baseball, however, there were rigid assessments of achievement. Strike out at bat or make an error in the field and you were scorned.

I decided I would give the track team a try the next spring in my junior year. But first I had my junior cross-country season that fall, and in every race I wore a cap, just as Dave Wottle had done.

My leap into running surprised my father, who saw how easily I'd give up on anything unpleasant, including such chores as helping out in the garden. He knew the last thing I would do was follow him into medicine. Avoiding hard work was my métier and I cringed at how hard Dad worked.

My father was a general practitioner. In Upland, a bedroom community of around 30,000 when I was growing up (68,000 today), my father served as an all-purpose country doctor. He was on call 24 hours a day and he even made house calls. He delivered thousands of babies. The phone would ring at 3 o'clock in the morning and I'd hear my father get out of bed, go into the garage, and drive off into the night.

I knew I didn't want any part of that. The only time I saw my father lose his composure was when he'd finally sit down and relax with the evening paper and the phone would ring. It was a funny act. He'd scream obscenities in frustration, then pick up the phone and answer with his best Marcus Welby bedside manner: "Hello-o-o-o . . . Dr. Scott."

My father was touchy about any affront to the medical profession. If a TV program mocked doctors in a comedy skit, Dad took it personally. He made us shut off the TV if he didn't like what he saw, and we fought over that. I was strong-willed like my father and resisted his attempt to impose his ideas on me. I also inherited his sense of humor. He'd parade around when we were young, making us laugh with silly faces or by imitating a gorilla.

Our ranch-style house on Laurel Street, where my parents still live, had a sizable backyard where Dad and I played ball and he maintained a greenhouse, his relaxation from the rigors of medicine. The grounds were orderly, the plants evenly spaced.

My father also lovingly tended to his rose garden, which I raided on certain occasions. On Mother's Day, I'd collect some of Dad's roses, write out a card with a poem, and present the gift to my mom. I had to find some way to reward her for cooking me up breakfasts of egg pancakes, a fluffy dish of egg whites, Parmesan, and butter that still makes me salivate. In later years, I'd gather Dad's roses for my high school dates, including outings with Kim Votaw, who would eventually become my wife.

At school I'd taken notice of Kim, a pretty brunette, but I was too scared to approach her. Though a freshman and two years younger than me, Kim had had a number of boyfriends and, sensing my interest, she asked me out.

A girl liked me! Kim's initiative was pretty gutsy in traditional Upland, but her forward nature made me feel at ease. Among the guys, I was a follower; with Kim, I could be the same way. Kim was vocal, confident, affectionate. She led and I followed.

Kim was very athletic and, naturally, I liked that quality. At this time, before the federal Title IX regulations took effect, most high schools did not have girls' teams. Some girls, if they had the courage and official approval, competed on boys' teams. More typically, girls with track and field interest participated in community meets as members of local track clubs, which were plentiful in southern California.

Eventually, Upland High formed a girls' track team and Kim joined. After classes, she and I would go off to our respective practices. Afterward, as in a scene from a Frankie-and-Annette beach movie, Kim and I would walk home from school holding hands and then have dinner at one home or the other. Kim's support made me feel more confident as an athlete.

When I was not with Kim, I was at home, where I shared a room with my brother, Kendall, whose perfection took me down a notch. Kendall was exceedingly quiet; though we got along fine, we barely spoke to one another. Kendall had posters of athletes on his wall. I had David Bowie. He was into science and had an extensive butterfly collection that was labeled according to genus and species. I lacked the drive to collect anything.

When we assembled model planes or monsters, it was easy to distinguish our work. Kendall painted each piece before gluing them all together, and he handled the glue like he was creating a masterpiece. His finished product was a seamless work of art while mine was a mess with the glue oozing out as though my monster had a case of the runs.

Sometimes, monsters invaded my sleep. When my mother redecorated our room, I had only one request: a dark window shade to keep out the bogeyman. Even into my teen years, I had nightmares and was a sleepwalker. I always felt as if I were being watched. My parents believed my paranoia came from watching scary movies late at night and from an overactive imagination. Mom always said that I could entertain myself—that when playing with my set of miniature army men I could vividly picture the action; she was right about that. I eventually used this imagination to my advantage. Before the idea was popularized by sport psychologists, I would visualize the details of my races in advance.

Petrified by dreams of Frankensteins and Draculas, I always wanted to sleep with the windows closed and bickered with Kendall, who wanted them open. One day, at 5 o'clock in the morning, a breeze raised the curtain, causing one of our cats to jump and knock a lamp over. When I got up, I swear to this day I could see a man peering into our window.

Nightmares, paranoia, no discipline—good grounding for a miler, right? Coping with smart-as-a-whip siblings and questionable status as a neighborhood athlete, my insecurities festered.

After five minutes of shooting baskets with Kendall I'd give up and quit. (He'd continue for hours, of course.) My attention span eventually seemed to settle in at about four minutes, or, you might say, 3:50.

I liked to make a game out of everything, from household chores to hang time with my buddies. Maybe it was growing up in a family of people who cared for the sick, but the idea of having a lot of responsibility scared me. I sensed early on that the impulses of play could keep the seriousness of life at a safe distance and I guess my running became the ultimate manifestation of that.

When I wasn't firing smoke bombs or avoiding household chores, I was climbing to the top of the Upland's Madonna of the Trails Statue on Halloween in order to plant a pumpkin on her head, or pulling other pranks. It was good, clean fun and fortunately Mom and Dad put up with it.

Mom's own running had progressed without letup and I think it gave her a more easygoing disposition. On weekends, she ran as much as ten miles at a clip and she loved the chance to compete. When the fitness movement finally took root in Upland, San Antonio Community Hospital, where we kids were all born, began sponsoring an annual 10K road race. Mom ran and took numerous prizes for winning her age division. I ran, too, and after finishing I'd wait for Mom and proudly jog the last mile with her. My mother even entered a couple of marathons. Later on, when I'd return home from college for holidays, I'd run up Euclid with Mom on Christmas morning.

Her passion for running was matched by her passion for politics. She was a true-blue conservative who'd campaigned for Barry Goldwater in '64 and served as a local campaign manager for Ronald Reagan in his successful 1972 gubernatorial bid. She always dragged me along to help distribute leaflets. When she opened Reagan's area headquarters in nearby Ontario, she enlisted me to clean the toilets. It was a filthy old place, but Mom made it shine.

Mom made everything shine. She was the epitome of the doctor's wife. Running fueled her with a sense of freedom, but she still took her dual roles of wife and mother seriously. She kept the house spotless, gussied up for my father when he came home from work, and always had dinner on the table.

What I saw in my parents' model of the Ozzie-and-Harriet relationship was what I imagined married life would hold for me one day. Mom's willingness to serve my father and the family unconditionally offered the kind of comfort and closeness that I wanted for myself later in life.

When I was older and Kendall and Alicia were in college, Mom no longer had kids to fuss over and decided to pursue nursing and go to work. From Dad's standpoint, that crossed the line. He vehemently objected: He was the breadwinner and his wife would stay home. Mom, formidable as a runner, was also formidable in the household and fought with him. This was the start of a terrible, longstanding row—the only real family conflict I can remember. In the end, Mom won. And while my father is now retired, Mom, at 67, continues to work as a nurse in a surgeon's office.

Around this time in my junior year, I entered my teenage funk period. I said little, let my hair grow to my shoulders, and grunted when spoken to. Mom had a hard time with this. She was always so bubbly and I was being such a jerk.

Remember the streaking fad of the early seventies, when people would sometimes run naked across the field during halftime of a football game? Police would apprehend them and it would make for a nifty little spot on the evening news. One time, a high school cross-country teammate and I decided to streak at a local strip mall. We went for a run and, once at our destination, took off our shorts, put them over our heads and ran past the shops like maniacs. With our identities concealed, no one knew who we were. Well . . . almost no one. There was one aghast shopper who somehow figured it out and went up to my mom and said, "I saw your son running naked. . . ." Mom laughed that one off. Guess she figured that was pretty tame for me—and at least I was running.

But there was no laughing when I got caught trying pot. In my junior year, I'd started drinking at parties. We'd get a bottle of Boone's Farm Apple Wine, I'd down the whole thing and get blitzed. Then, some friends who were not involved in sports and who had time on their hands encouraged me to try marijuana, which was widespread at school.

One guy's father found some grass in this kid's bureau drawer. The father proceeded to call me and the other guys we hung out with for an inquisition, where he suggested we'd better fess up to our parents before they found out on their own. For some reason, that made sense to me. I don't know whether it was my conscience or pure fear, but one day I simply told them, "You know, I tried marijuana a couple of times."

Oh, my God! My parents went through the roof. In their minds, I was a drug addict on heroin. They forbade me to hang out with this group of guys and monitored my coming and going; soon enough, my close friends became my running buddies on the Upland track and cross-country teams.

The fall of 1972, in my junior year, I finally made the varsity cross-country squad as fifth man. I'm convinced my Dave Wottle cap had an effect on me. In all of my races, I wore a golf cap with "Ontario National Golf Course" inscribed on it. Every time I did well the cap reinforced its symbolic value. One time I forgot the cap and in desperation had Mom rush with it to the race course minutes before the gun sounded.

That season, Upland won the state cross-country championship team title in our division. It was a big thrill being a part of that. Loney saw I had excellent speed, and that's what whet his appetite for my track participation. When we ran 200s or 400s in cross-country training, I showed what coaches call fast "turnover." My legs churned like pistons. It was a gift.

In track, we concentrated more on speedwork than long distances. I could tear down the straightaway like a sprinter. I made rapid progress in the 880 yards (or half-mile) and through the season improved my time from 2:08 to 1:58 to become the number two half-miler on the team, behind Ron Sickafoose. What really impressed Loney was my debut in the mile. Fighting a stiff wind on a slow dirt track in a meet against Pomona High, I ran 4:25. That was good, but I couldn't appreciate it since three of my teammates beat me.

I lacked confidence and Loney had to really work on me. I thought, "How can I think about being a great runner when three guys on my team run faster than I do?" Unconvinced of my ability, I went on to run only 4:30 and 4:33 in the state meet prelims.

I felt safer in the relays. There, you are not as exposed. Success is shared among four runners; so is the blame. I thrived on the team spirit, the idea that peers counted on you to come through. Relays were my kind of fun.

With my new, faster times, Mom's encouragement, Loney's faith in me, and the camaraderie of my teammates, I began to shed my fears. I was ready for any event. A couple of times, Loney threw me into the 200-yard low hurdles race, a California specialty at the time. I got chewed up by the really fast guys, but I didn't mind. I even volunteered to do the high jump and pole vault to help the team, but Loney said he didn't need me in those events.

In that junior season, I assessed my talent only in terms of our team. I could not relate at all to the '73 high school superstars, like national two-mile recordholder Craig Virgin of Illinois, 4:02 mile champion Matt Centrowitz of New York, or Mark Belger, also of New York and a junior like me, who ran the 880 in 1:50 three times that spring.

Come senior year, I became the number-one runner on the cross-country team. It was not supposed to work out that way, but Mark Sorensen, our top man, spent all of his free time playing basketball. Suddenly, I was team leader, which was a joke because I was also the team prankster. Not even our training routines were safe from attack: We did a lot of training on trails through orange groves on the north end of town. We were supposed to run outside the groves, which is precisely why we made our own paths right through them. It was harmless fun and we did no damage.

Every so often, we'd train at Mount Baldy. We'd either run from school to Baldy and negotiate the hilly trails for a total of 12 miles, or Loney would drive us to the mountain village where we'd run two and half miles up through the manzanita and oak trees to the peak at 8,600 feet, down the other side, then turn around and run back—10 miles in all.

The veterans on our team were avid trail runners who would tackle Baldy almost every weekend on their own. With the swagger of prize fighters, they ran till there was only one guy left on his feet. Each time, they challenged one another to make it farther up the mountain.

Our team's occasional antics were brought on by being dopey kids who needed to balance the rigors of distance running with humor and a challenge to stiff-necked order wherever we found it. Loney's genius was that he understood that, and gave us a long leash. Though a math teacher, Loney was not a numbers man. He spoke a lot about the mental side of running and tried to instill desire in us with a soft touch. He made goals—from varsity letters to personal bests—attainable. He wanted us to learn that consistent training would produce results. More than anything, he wanted us to believe in ourselves.

We were impressionable young runners, eager to soak up any convincing lesson delivered by Loney. Yes, we could excel, we could run faster, we could be proud. At the same time, we were too raw to truly understand the intricacies of success. Loney was the key: believe in what he said and you could move mountains.

Loney relied on a time-honored coaching device to hasten that belief. He used our race times on hilly cross-country courses to show us how we'd run during the track season. With excitement, he'd tell someone, "You just ran 10:30 at Palos Verdes. That's a 9:30 two-mile." It didn't matter whether Loney's analysis was accurate. You believed him, and you knew he believed in you.

After one meet, Loney took me aside, put his arm around my shoulder, and said softly but emphatically that I had just run 30 seconds faster than he expected. He told me I was underestimating my ability. To which I said, "You really think so?"

During the fall of my senior year, Upland won almost every cross-country meet. But we were not your typical harriers. We were a ragtag mob. We had long hair and wore colorful boxer shorts under our racing shorts, with the boxers hanging out. Some of our guys arrived at meets shirtless. Before competition, while schools from San Bernadino warmed up with military precision, we tossed a frisbee. We looked as if we were going to a rock concert, but I think other teams that were committed to their marching orders envied us.

Back then, California high schools turned out droves of great distancemen, but few of them continued their success in college; most kids were burnt out from excessive running before they could possibly reach their potential. In high school, they trained upwards of 15 miles a day, wringing every ounce of strength from their young legs. Coaches, seduced by the high mileage that was given credence by professional marathon runners, either didn't know any better or didn't care.

I doubt I ever ran more than 40 miles a week at Upland. Loney knew what was right and did not want to push his runners to their breaking points. I trace my longevity in this sport to not being a teenage phenom on the fast track from the get-go.

Out of this melange of sound training and California nonchalance, I was finally moved to run on some weekends. Teammates would come calling and drag me out. I guess I wanted them to. We always went to the mountains. I lagged behind, but not too far behind. I'd heard that guys who got lost would end up running 20 miles in the darkness to find their way back. The Mt. Baldy bogeyman was my incentive to keep up.

In competition, I still lacked racing savvy, and mere survival instincts carried me to third place in the state cross-country meet, then a two-mile event, behind a pair of runners from Lompoc High, which had one of the greatest distance squads ever. The runners who defeated me, Jim Schankel and Roger Fabian, were the Mantle-and-Maris of high school cross-country. In track, they could better 4:10 for the mile. Loney used to say, "Lompoc rules the world!"

In my senior track season at Upland in 1974, I reaffirmed Loney's faith in me in the first meet, against Chaffey High. I won the 880 and mile and was then put on the anchor leg of the mile relay. We needed a victory to win the meet. I received the baton 40 yards behind and ran with everything I had left, blind to the fact that I should have been too tired to make it all the way. I made up 39 yards, but we still lost.

I went up to Loney and apologized. He was not upset; in fact, he was ecstatic. He told me my 440 split time was 49.9. It was windy and we had run on a slow dirt track. Loney said under better conditions I would have run 47-and-change. He told me, "You're going to the state meet."

Loney, the master psychologist, pulled a fast one and it worked. Years later, I realized my split was probably closer to 51, but on that day I felt like a million bucks. Even if Loney was jumping the gun, I had run well and that meet was an awakening.

All that spring, everything clicked for me. I had the essentials—greater physical strength from mountain training, a growing confidence, and a sharper focus on the state championship meet, the big season-end goal. In March, I ran a 1:54.8 880 at a home meet and turned in a 1:52.4 anchor 880 on a sprint medley relay team event at Chino. I even ran well in 220-yard legs on sprint relays, but I injured my knee and was sidelined for three weeks. My strength came back in no time and I looked forward to anchoring Upland in the high-powered Mount San Antonio College (Mt. SAC) Relays at the end of April.

Mt. SAC proved to be a turning point. On Friday evening, I came from seventh place to second on the anchor mile of the distance medley, running a 4:15.4 split. On Saturday, in the two-mile relay, again I got the baton in seventh and raced to second with a 1:51.4 880. I gunned down people like Ralph Serna, the great little runner from Loara High who ran a 4:07 mile that year and who would become my teammate in college. After the race, Serna asked me what event I planned to run in the state meet. When I told him the 880, he sighed with relief. He'd be running the mile.

When the state meet finally came around, I was still scared. Loney told me over and over, "You can run. You can compete."

The state championship was held in Bakersfield. My family came up and stayed in a little motel off the airport. I told Kim not to come because I felt she'd be a distraction. I didn't think I could handle a girlfriend and state meet all at once. Understandably, she took offense at that.

On the eve of the meet, I sat in my motel room trying to let Loney's faith in me sink in. It was one thing to understand Loney's rallying words on an intellectual level, quite another to let them touch my soul and spur me on. I thought about my season, how I'd surprised myself over and over, and I woke up the next day a more secure athlete.

In the 800 qualifying round, I won my heat in 1:52.0, my best high school performance in an individual race. John Musich of Burbank High, the favorite, won his heat in 1:51.7. The stage was set for Musich and me to race for the gold medal in state championship final. It was our own little Olympics.

In the final, Musich took off in the lead. Positioned in lane one, I got jostled and boxed in and fell way back. Musich's first quarter was 54.8. He was gone. Every time I'd try to move, I'd get boxed in. Finally, on the home straight, I shot through on the inside of the track to place second. Musich ran 1:51.0. My time was 1:52.4 and I was ecstatic. Loney's reaction was understated, on the order of: "Hey, I knew you could do it."

Thanks to Loney's good sense, my potential had barely been tapped. Musich, on the other hand, had trained 100 miles a week under the guidance of a coach who ran ultramarathons and was known for his running obsession. Musich's college running never amounted to anything whereas my legs were full of life.

But my senior track season was not over. I qualified to compete in the U.S. junior championships in Gainesville, Florida, and the Golden West Invitational in Sacramento, considered the high school national championship. In both meets, I ran the 800 meters against New York's Mark Belger, the best high school half-miler in the country.

To compete in Gainesville, I had to give up Grad Night at Upland, an annual ritual in which everyone goes to Disneyland and spends the night. It turned out to be a questionable sacrifice.

I took sixth in 1:52.4. Belger ran second behind Ohio State fresh-man Tom Byers, who would later become a mile rival of mine. At Sacramento, I was fifth in 1:54.0 as Belger triumphed in 1:50.4. Belger and I got to see a lot of each other over the years and nowa-days we occasionally bump into one another and reminisce since he, too, lives in the San Diego area.

One shared memory that frequently comes up occurred at the Gainesville junior meet. Mark and I had a lot in common: we lacked discretion, did not embarrass easily, and, once racing was over, yearned for female companionship. In Gainesville, after the 800 final, we actually talked a couple of female runners from the meet into coming to the track at midnight to run a naked relay.

We recruited two other guys to participate. Unfortunately, once at the track, the girls chickened out. Not that I blame them. But since we had been so bold in arranging the rendezvous, we felt that we could not back out, too. "Who's going first?" someone said sheepishly.

The four of us stripped to our running shoes. We surveyed the grandstand to make sure no one else was around. A breeze picked up and we looked at each other, wondering what we'd gotten ourselves into. Standing in the altogether in a locker room was one thing. Even streaking, with its who-was-that? disappearing act, had its cover. But, now, uh. . . . Okay, it was time to be men about it.

Mark led off, the other two guys followed and I anchored. Meanwhile, the two girls, laughing on the infield, timed us. We ran pretty hard. It felt . . . well . . . free. At the end of the adventure, neither young lady ended up in a compromising position. Give them credit for good taste.

In retrospect, I think my performances suffered at both the Gainesville and Sacramento meets because they were post-season events and I was no longer representing my team. Drawing on the camaraderie of my teammates, whether tackling the hills of

Mount Baldy or running relays on the track, is what drove me to those initial breakthroughs. It would take time and maturity before I'd learn to run for myself.

My state-meet second place produced college scholarship offers from places like UCLA, Long Beach State, Brigham Young, and the University of Idaho. I was not much of a student and had been thinking about attending Chaffey Junior College in nearby Alta Loma.

The one coach who had been recruiting me all season was Len Miller of the University of California at Irvine. Previously, he'd coached at high schools in the area; he knew Loney, and had taken a liking to me. Miller was a great salesman, and my parents liked his disciplined style, which they felt I sorely needed.

In one season I'd gone from obscurity to state runnerup. Heralded runners like Ralph Serna were talking about me as a top college prospect. College coaches were calling. Suddenly, I was contemplating life away from home: living in a dorm without Mom's cooking, or Loney's arm around my shoulder, or Kim's hand as we walked down Euclid.

Everything seemed to have happened so quickly. My mother told me to run. My coach gave me my goals. My teammates had coaxed me out to the mountains. This was my foundation as I began to think about making a name for myself in track and field.

But when I imagined college life, I didn't think of winning races or becoming an Olympic candidate. I certainly didn't think of taking to heart the opportunity for higher learning or paving the way for a career. I thought about calling home when I needed assurance and coming home to see Kim, who would be entering her junior year at Upland. Kim was proud to have a college "man" as a boyfriend, and we sat down and planned my trips back home.

I could have gotten a full ride at most schools, but I valued Miller's commitment and chose Irvine, even though it had a measly budget and gave me a one-sixth scholarship worth only $624 a year. I went off to college to run. Before long, I wanted to quit.

CHAPTER TWO

Tough Love Yields Victories: College

I arrived on the University of California at Irvine campus in August of 1974. The school was about an hour's drive from home. I considered myself an 800-meter runner who used the fall cross-country season as routine conditioning. Since I'd trained 5 or 6 miles a day in high school, I figured we'd run 8 to 10 miles a day at Irvine. How tough could that be? In college, the cross-country racing distance for men was 6 miles. That was long for me, but since I did not consider myself a distance runner I anticipated cross-country races as good buildup for the track season when I would concentrate on developing my speed.

I settled into the pleasant suburban campus, surveyed the surroundings where we'd probably do our distance running, met the 15 or so members of the "Anteaters" cross-country squad—and had no inkling of the torturous experience to follow.

Len Miller, the Irvine coach, had a ritual designed to quickly rid the team of incoming runners too soft to complete the program. It was expedient, and it was brutal. Before classes even began, he ran us into the ground. None of us was prepared for what Miller threw at us: workouts morning and evening, 15 to 20 miles a day, complete with boot camp calisthenics, in the heat and up in the mountains. This initiation for the cross-country season went on for two weeks on campus, then a week more at a training camp in the Sierras.

It was overwhelming, but who could complain? I was a green kid, barely wet behind the ears, whose ill-defined talent had earned him eleventh-hour high school accolades. I could have taken some plush full ride at UCLA or Long Beach State but instead, for an entitlement of $624 a year, found myself under the thumb of a sweet-talking warden who had talked my parents into believing he could make me into a miler.

At the outset, I hated Miller. All of the Anteaters hated Miller. We hated getting up at 6 o'clock in the morning to be ready at 6:30 for the sun-up workout. For the first few weeks of training, Miller arranged for team members to stay with families in the area. I think I slept on somebody's floor.

At 6:30 A.M., after brushing your teeth, you had to be ready to run as far as 15 miles. Fifteen miles! I had never run 15 miles, or even 10 miles, all at once. At 6:30 in the morning, I had never done anything other than lie still.

It was almost unheard of for college runners, especially freshmen, to train 15 or 20 miles a day. Before we ran, Miller had us do situps, pushups, drills, and jog for our warmup. The warmup alone took an hour. Then we ran. That took close to two hours. Then, in the afternoon, maybe we had some weight training, and after that we had a workbook with training concepts to study. Then we collapsed. I would just about pass out after getting something to eat, sleeping until the evening workout when my muscles were so sore I could not fathom any more exercise. But Miller would dish out another five to seven miles. And on it went every day.

Sprawled out limp on the campus grounds, I commiserated with freshmen teammates John Konigh, Ron Sickafoose, and

Ed Ahlmeyer. We considered Miller the enemy; if only we had the strength to plot ways to get back at him. I kept thinking of my comforting high school experience under Bob Loney. Oh, did I miss that guy. He had a sweet disposition and held the philosophy that running was what you decided to make of it.

Whenever I spoke with Kim, I must have sounded like a wounded soldier. She gave me her sympathy and that helped, but I needed a lot more than sympathy. I felt I needed either a new pair of legs or to get the hell out of Irvine.

Later that season, I would realize that Miller knew what he was doing. This was not the reckless slave-driving of an unschooled coach. Miller knew he would kill off some people, and that's what he wanted.

In Miller's mind, anyone who couldn't hack it at the outset did not deserve membership on the University of California at Irvine cross-country and track teams. Miller also knew that those who survived his regimen would form a select group, a kind of "dirty dozen." We would be highly fit, ready to perform, and through our travail we would forge close emotional bonds. You can't beat that if you want a team to run through walls toward a national championship.

Training mileage is an important issue on the American running scene. In the 1960s and 1970s, when the United States seemed to be on the cutting edge, we produced Olympic champions Bob Schul (5,000 meters), Billy Mills (10,000 meters), and Frank Shorter (marathon). At his peak, Shorter trained three times a day, upwards of 150 miles a week. But in the last 20 years American men's distance success has been spotty, and some people in the sport believe we just don't train hard enough.

Miller would probably agree with that. He had coached successfully for 15 years at various high schools in California before coming to Irvine the year before I did. One of his protégés had been Eric Hulst, who at 15 ran an amazing 9:04 in the two-mile to set a national high school record for freshmen that still stands. Hulst would eventually join me at Irvine. So would Ralph Serna, the top high school miler of 1975. Miller, actually the assistant coach, set out to build a powerhouse at Irvine, then an NCAA Division II school. Bill Toomey, the 1968 Olympic decathlon champion, was head coach. But Toomey was really a figurehead while Miller did the coaching.

Those first few days at Irvine I would have preferred Toomey. Even as a former decathlete, he could not possibly have been as tyrannical as Miller. One morning before practice I had to be dragged out of bed and propped up by a teammate. I was in such a daze I started running without tying my shoelaces. While burning more calories than a marathoner, my appetite was poor. After three days, I called my mother. I was crying and wanted to come home.

I did not get much sympathy from Mom. As a runner herself, she understood what hard training was about and was all for it. She also felt I was a loose cannon who needed discipline. My mother listened to my pleas in exasperation, then told me, "You made a commitment. Stick it out for a year and after that, if you're still unhappy, you can come home."

With no other options, I stayed. Each week of the indoctrination was hell. I could not finish the first few long runs and had to be scooped up by Miller in his car. It was like the sag wagon for the wounded in a bicycle race. Thank God I was not alone. Other guys couldn't finish either and we sat in stony silence wondering how we could possibly survive the college team.

Our off-campus training camp was held in Westwood, a remote logging town north of Sacramento at an altitude of about 6,000 feet. We stayed in a large house that belonged to a friend of Miller's. The house was situated on the edge of town, and the local girls, who didn't have much to do, got a big kick out of seeing us run down the main drag shirtless in our skimpy shorts.

Naturally, we took advantage of that. Despite Miller's warning, we bought beer and coaxed the girls into the house when Len wasn't around. Miller loved poker and found a game in a neighboring town. But he could sense we were up to no good. When he confronted us, one straight arrow came clean and admitted he had taken "three sips of beer." Life got even harder for him after that.

We did our running, twice a day, on trails through the woods. We hiked and fished for trout, which Miller cooked for dinner. As a group, we had a daredevil mentality. When the Santa Fe Railroad came rumbling by, we hopped on and off the car ladders, seeing who had the nerve to remain on board the longest before the train picked up speed and left town.

Toward the end of summer, I was still so angry about Miller's regimen that in an attempt to get hurt and have an excuse not to run I played pickup basketball. It didn't work. Running or otherwise, I never got injured at Irvine; very few Irvine runners did. I guess Miller's system weeded out the softies, and we survivors were made of steel.

When freshman classes began at Irvine, I chose social ecology as my major. I was interested in detective work and a social ecology program could be used for a career in law enforcement. I took courses in psychology and sociology; social ecology was one of the easier majors. I had rejected any major having to do with math, science, or writing long papers. A few years later, in a *Track & Field News* story, I was praised for my broad interests including social ecology. I think the writer assumed "social ecology" meant saving the world, or at least the whales. For me, I guess that was somewhat the case. At the time, I saw myself with an FBI badge hunting down terrorists. But first I had my own survival at stake.

As the season went on, Len Miller continued to murder us. Warmups included 125 situps and 125 pushups. Workout staples were repeated fast runs of a half-mile or mile. We did 20 halves in

2:25 each with a two-minute jog between runs. We did 10 one-mile runs in 4:45 each with four-minute jogs. By now, I was completing every workout and getting as strong as an ox. My greatest talent as a runner may have been my ability to tolerate hard training. Though I was not the kind of kid who could take initiative, I could follow orders, and Miller capitalized on this. In training, I was the fighter still on his feet at the final bell.

As a group, we were unified in our loathing for Miller. We needed to find some clever, risk-free way to get back at him. We started calling Miller "P.B.," which we told him meant Pretty Boy. Miller always dressed sharply and combed his wavy hair. He didn't mind us calling him P.B.—he didn't know that it really meant Pubic Brain.

By mid-season, my confidence was growing and I did the unthinkable. Len Miller wouldn't tolerate tardiness. One afternoon, Ed Ahlmeyer, my roommate, came late to the track because of an exam. Miller jumped all over him. When I stuck up for Ed, Miller chewed me out, too.

As we embarked on a five-mile run from campus to a canyon location for hill training, I was fuming. We all were. When we got to the hill, Miller was at the top. The hill was about a half-mile long—long enough, I'd thought, to tell Miller where to get off without him hearing me. At the base of the hill, I yelled Miller's name followed by an obscenity.

It was quiet in the canyon and Miller heard my cry. When the bunch of us reached the crest, Miller asked who'd cursed him. Everybody kind of looked at me, and I raised my hand. Miller promptly kicked me off the team.

As Miller ordered, I went back to the lockers to shower and wait for him. I sat nervously outside his office trying to justify in my mind what I'd done. To cope with Miller's program, we Anteaters had become as close as inmates in a POW camp and I couldn't stand the idea of missing that closeness.

Waiting, I felt that my pride, as well as my running future, were on the line. I told myself that I would have to make some concession to Miller to get out of this bind and remain on the squad. I felt like a new recruit in the army succumbing to authority. I'd attempted to buck the regime and it hadn't worked.

I reviewed the scene again and again in my mind: the run, what I'd said, the inquisition, my admission of guilt. I was still not shrewd enough to appreciate Miller's psyche and figured I'd have to appeal to him purely for pragmatic reasons: I wanted back in.

Len Miller finally arrived and we went into his office. The first thing I noticed was a novelty sign on his wall that read: "A Freshman Is the Dumbest Animal on the Face of the Earth." Maybe Len was right, but this was a time for me to try and save face.

Miller and I talked and had a good conversation. He told me he respected me as a person who would stick up for a teammate, and I told him I respected him as the man in control who had a system we had to follow. It proved to be a turning point in our relationship. On the one hand, my ego deserved to be taken down a notch and no coach would tolerate an insurrection; on the other, I'm sure Len saw that my strong will was an asset and that it should not be shattered beyond repair. After all, if I was to be the caliber of runner he expected, I would need a streak of toughness. He put me back on the team and our relationship improved after that.

Our cross-country squad was too inexperienced to achieve anything that fall season, but in track in the spring of '75, I won the NCAA Division II mile in Sacramento in 4:09.7. In a style that would become my trademark, I charged to the lead on the backstretch of the bell lap. But because it was Division II, my first national title drew little notice and I put little stock in it myself.

My college goal was an NCAA Division I track title. As a Division II champion, I was eligible to compete in the Division I meet, but Len said I wasn't ready for the big boys yet. "Your time will come," he told me. "You'll know when you're ready."

Imagining that time gave me goosebumps. I would lie awake at night envisioning myself in the NCAA and thinking of the big races I'd seen on television. One was the '73 NCAA mile won by my first role model, Olympic 800 champion Dave Wottle of Bowling Green State in Ohio. Rallying from behind, Wottle sprinted the last lap in a blistering 53.3 seconds to win. That's how I wanted to win it: blowing by the field from behind.

To me, an NCAA gold medal was even more prestigious than an Upland High School letterman sweater. My race was on. . . .

———

In the summer, we repeated Len Miller's boot camp and had a magnificent cross-country team in my soph season. We were a team of young dynamos—all freshmen and sophomores—led by incoming star recruit Ralph Serna. It was quite a coup for Miller to land Serna, who'd run a near-record 8:46 two-mile in high school and was sought by numerous Division I colleges.

There was so much talent on campus that fall of '75, I was concerned about simply making the seven-man varsity team, much less winning anything. But I had acquired more strength than I realized and was able to hang on to our top guys in competition.

At the All-California meet in Santa Barbara, Serna and team-mate Brian Hunsaker tied for first, I was 13 seconds behind in fourth, and we won the team title handily over Cal-Davis. The tie, decided when the two men were well ahead and felt no need of racing one another to the limit, showed solidarity. It was also a sign of the times. The running boom was gathering steam and in the selfless spirit of distance running, victorious athletes in cross-country or road events would sometimes finish holding hands. Since this act of communion was technically against the Amateur Athletic Union (AAU) rules, it could result in a disqualification.

Serna was distinctly the class of our team, and in the NCAA Division II Cross Country Championship, held on our home course at the Irvine Coast Country Club, there was no way Hunsaker or any other Anteater could match him. It was a clear day with temperatures in the 70s. And, despite having been stung by a bee moments before the race, Serna won the 5-miler in 23:41 to become the event's first freshman champion. I ran a clutch race in fourth (24:06) while Hunsaker placed 11th (24:24) and Irvine captured the team title.

Afterward, Miller told the press, "For a young team that was inexperienced, how could a team have a better effort?" There was talk of an Irvine dynasty. "Great expectations are warranted," beamed *Track & Field News*. I was happy earning all-American status for making the top 25, even happier being thrown with the guys into a water hazard on the course by celebrating Irvine fans.

I had lost the urge to call Mom and cry to come home. I was having too much fun.

Mooning was big college recreation then and on trips to meets, we would hang B.A.s (Bare Asses) out the car window. Usually, we took two carloads of runners to a cross-country meet. I always tried to avoid riding with Len. So did John Konigh. We were two peas in a pod. John had the mooning record: 69 miles without letup. My best was about 15 miles.

Our motto was: The harder we ran, the harder we played. Our team dorm rooms were "action central," with girls drifting in and out and an ample supply of beer. We'd drive around Irvine in a pickup truck collecting street signs to decorate our rooms. One time, during Christmas break, a cop caught us with the goods. Because of the holiday, the court was closed and he let us off. Otherwise, I think we would have spent a day in the slammer. I would have had some time explaining a rap sheet to my folks.

Yeah, we felt if Miller was going to run us to the limit, we had to find some way to enjoy it. One of Miller's staples was a hill workout in which we'd have to run out and back from a hill (total: 10 miles)—as well as up the hill, about 150 yards long—30 or 40 times. One time, a bunch of us decided to do the last repetition with our running shorts in hand. Len didn't seem to mind. When we reached the crest, he said, "Great workout," and drove off.

Pranksters are seldom content: We wanted more. A private gated community in nearby Newport Beach caught our attention that day. A big American flag hung at the entrance, and we thought that flag would sure look neat back at the dorms. When the security guard was asleep, we grabbed it. It didn't take long for the authorities to track us down. We were showering back at school after the workout when Miller came into the locker room, opened Konigh's locker, and found the flag. That really pissed Len off and he started to become more vigilant about keeping us in line.

After our cross-country success, we continued to shine. In the spring, at Slippery Rock, Pennsylvania, I repeated as NCAA II champion, this time at the 1,500-meter distance (about 100 yards short of a mile). This was 1976, an Olympic year, when many meets switched from linear to metric distances, and the 1,500 meters was run in place of the mile. My winning time was 3:46.4, equal to a 4:04 mile. Serna took second. We both came back in the 5,000, with Serna second and me fifth. That was a respectable double for a mile-type like myself and proved to me those hill workouts were paying off. Best of all, Irvine scored in other events and we won the team championship, giving us a sweep of NCAA II honors for the year.

Now a high school senior, Kim came to cheer me on at UCLA where I completed in the 1,500 meters at the '76 AAU Nationals. I returned the favor, watching her compete on the Upland girls' sprint relay team at the California state meet.

Kim and I spoke almost daily and saw each other often, either in Upland or on campus. We took camping trips and spent a weekend on Catalina Island. I went back to Upland for Kim's school dances. Each time, I couldn't wait to see her.

When I'd left for Irvine, Kim and I had agreed to be true to one another, but since she was still in high school, I felt uneasy that she might get involved with other guys. I knew that some in her crowd were sexually active and I always wondered what might be going on. Whenever Kim came to one of my meets, I felt more confident—athletically and otherwise.

In my AAU qualifying heat at UCLA, I ran second to make the final in 3:41.9, the equivalent of a 3:59 mile, my first "sub–4:00." Though it would be another year before I'd break 4:00 in a full-length mile, I was ecstatic. To go within weeks from the NCAA II meet and into the AAU final was a huge leap.

In the final, I ran sixth in a blanket finish in which a mere second separated the first seven finishers. My time was 3:43.2. Villanova's Eamonn Coghlan, aiming to become the first Irishman to win the AAU 1,500, achieved his goal in 3:42.1. This was my first race with Eamonn in what would become a colorful rivalry. But at this time I was a nobody to Eamonn and he didn't say a word to me.

I detected a certain edge to Coghlan, a take-no-prisoners demeanor he could project at will. I began to understand the role of psychological gamesmanship in racing strategy. I could not be a sweetheart to my opposition; I needed to be feared like Eamonn was feared.

Each success and each improved time reminded me of Len's promise that I would become a mile to reckon with. Since the half-mile had brought me success in high school, I'd balked when Len told me the mile was my best event. I hated to admit Len was right, but as my faith in Len grew I began to train more seriously, shape my goals, and look toward the future.

John Walker was my hero, and he had been a major influence on my life as an athlete. When I was a high school senior, in 1974, he was ranked the number one miler in the world.

In college, I had looked for writeups of Walker's races and studied the pictures. Walker wore beads. I wore beads. John liked the ladies, drank beer. Me, too. I cut his picture from the papers. I thought John was the coolest guy in the world. He was outspoken and very "politically incorrect." In New York for the Millrose Games, he had the audacity to say in an interview: "American runners are crackpots. Running's all they talk about. They're a bunch of bores."

From the first, Walker struck me as a free spirit, a rebel, his own man. Considering the rigid conventions of American runners, Walker was a miler and a rock star all in one, as ultra-cool as David Bowie.

When Walker set the world mile record of 3:49.4 in 1975, the first time 3:50 had been broken, I laminated the newspaper photograph and hung it on the wall of my dorm for inspiration. Walker did it in Goteberg, Sweden. But he didn't just do it: He announced to the media he would break the world record, then did it. And he did it essentially by himself since the designated "rabbit" faltered by not running fast enough. Rabbits are second-level runners assigned to set the pace for the first portion of a race (then leave the track) so the favorites can measure their efforts from behind.

That year, Walker won almost all of his races and was named worldwide *Track & Field News* Athlete of the Year. He was favored to win the 1976 Olympic 1,500 in Montreal and early that spring of '76 who should appear at the Irvine track to work out: Walker.

He was passing through southern California for treatment on an injured Achilles tendon. We watched him train. Then, while he'd sit in the whirlpool nursing his foot, my teammates and I would stand around gawking. What do you do when your hero literally comes knocking on your door?

You ask him if, well, you know, is drinking beer really part of your training?

Sitting in the Irvine whirlpool, John was a captive audience. He was standoffish and barely tolerated our stupid questions. John was not a gracious man, not at first glance. He hated when reporters grilled him about his training. Feats that others might have considered extraordinary he considered mundane. Like the time he jumped into a marathon unannounced, built a big lead after 23 miles, and then dropped out.

In later years, when John and I became good friends, sportswriters would use me to get to John. On the surface, John was gruff, intimidating. He would give off the signal: Leave me alone. Journalists would come up to me and wonder, "Do you think it would be okay to talk with John?" I'd say, "Sure, just start talking about horses, something he's interested in, and he'll melt."

Walker's 1976 visit to Irvine had liberated me. I'd felt constricted by the accepted standard of the successful middle-distance runner as clean-cut and straight-laced. Jim Ryun, the Kansan with the crewcut, was considered the icon, on and off the track. My high school coach, Bob Loney, had encouraged me to read Ryun's book. I respected Ryun's running, but he did not appeal to me as a personality.

Walker validated my anti-Ryun persona. He enabled me to resolve the inner conflict between the disciplined athlete and off-the-track maverick. I was not comfortable adhering to the belief that to be a serious runner you had to be an all-American boy. I was not at ease with the idea that I would have to live up to some idealized image of a miler in order to succeed. Walker showed me I could try to be a good runner and be my own person as well.

That spring season, I set out to do both—especially in the first of three races outside the collegiate ranks that proved to be turning points in my career.

The 1976 U.S. Olympic Trials were in Eugene, Oregon, "Track Town, USA." I hoped to compete, and Len really wanted me in there. Two problems: I had not run the qualifying time, and my brother Kendall's wedding, in Upland, was scheduled for the day of the 1,500 final. With his gift for salesmanship, Miller got around the first problem. At the conclusion of the AAU Nationals at UCLA the week before, Miller convinced officials to let me into the Trials. Unlike the sprints, where the number of lanes dictates the precise number of competitors, in the 1,500 you can add a runner without consequence.

Kendall's wedding was all set for that Sunday. I was the best man. But with the final for the 1,500 also Sunday, not only did I have the race to worry about, but I also had to resolve this family commitment. I spoke with Kendall and my parents and they were good about it. They agreed the Trials were an opportunity I could not miss and gave me their blessing to run. What chance did I have to make the final anyway? To cover all options, my father purchased airline tickets for me for all three days of the 1,500. Some vote of confidence.

Len came with me to Eugene. He tried to convince me I could make the Olympic team. He kept prodding me, "You can run with these guys." Going into the first round, I felt lucky to be there. The track setting, at Hayward Field on the University of Oregon campus, was inspiring. No fans were more knowledgeable or appreciative. Here I was, a mere college sophomore.

After I made it through the heats and semis into the final, my attitude changed. I started to think, these guys are not that far ahead of me. In thinking about Sunday's final, I realized that my attitude had changed. I now felt that I could kick with anybody. In my semi, I'd run stride for stride with Matt Centrowitz, Rick Wohlhuter, and Mike Durkin, the favorites. My time, in fourth, was 3:40.4, then a personal record, the equivalent of a 3:58 mile.

The wedding was out the window, but my family still supported me. Mom, with her runner's impulses, was thrilled with my success and wished she could be with me to witness it; Kendall proceeded with an alternate best man; Dad gave me his blessing but with some equivocation. He didn't quite understand this running thing. Even years later, when I'd come home from a summer on the European circuit, he'd say: "How are you making a living? When are you going to get a job?"

Dad had grown up in the Depression, worked his way through medical school under the GI Bill, and served in the military. He had one son who was a doctor and about to get married. He had a daughter who was a nurse. I was, as always, out of sync, and Dad found that difficult to accept. Kendall's wedding was the perfect metaphor for the Scotts. The entire family was getting together for a major event and I was off running.

I grew excited about my chances and Len tried to keep me loose. Oregon had not quite shed its 1960s sensibility, and between the semi and the final, Len took me outside Eugene to see a commune where people walked around naked. Len didn't want me hanging around the motel fussing over the race. He wanted my mind on something else and the commune was as good a diversion as any. I think it calmed Len down, too.

The top contenders, Wohlhuter and Durkin, were midwest-erners long out of college and representing the University of Chicago Track Club. Centrowitz, who grew up in the Bronx, was the hometown favorite in Eugene. After a sensational high school career in which he'd run a 4:02.7 mile to lead the nation, he attended Manhattan College as a freshman, then transferred to Oregon. Now a senior, he'd run a 1,500 in 3:37.3. Running in close quarters with these three veterans, drawing on their native aggres-sion like a transfusion, made me feel like I belonged. I'm sure they ran the semi with just enough effort to advance to the final. I pushed harder, feeling I had to in order to keep up.

Physically, I was ready for the final. Miller's training had pre-pared me for the three-race schedule. I was also ready mentally. Miller's sidetrip had settled my mind. The night before the race, however, the peace was broken. And on race day, everything blew up in my face. Both times, the same man was responsible: a reck-less nut case, Tom Byers of Ohio State.

On the eve of the final, at the dorms where the athletes stayed, Byers was literally bouncing off the walls. He had just missed qualifying in his semi for the final and had been fouled. Now he had learned that officials ruled in his favor on an appeal to run the final. In an instant, he went from depression to exultation. He was flying. I had never seen such a hyperactive guy in my life.

I was trying to ignore him. All I could think of was: Get away from me—I have a race to run. Tom was impossible to ignore. Still seething over the foul issue, Tom said something about getting revenge in the final, but I let his remark pass.

I was focused on what was to come. Running three 1,500s in three days, whether in the Olympic Trials or Olympic Games, is not something to be taken for granted. Some top runners cannot handle the rounds. This is especially true on the college level where—after cross-country, indoor, and outdoor track—it's easy to run out of gas at the end of the long season. In my case, the

Trials seemed easy compared to the training I'd done. I found myself getting stronger with each round. And three races in three days was nothing compared to the three races in three hours—one a 5,000—that I had run in our conference championship.

When we lined up for the final, the fragrance of Oregon timber was in the air. I felt free as a bird. No one expected me to make the team. I felt no self-imposed pressure. I was 20 years old. There would be other Olympic years.

In the tradition of Olympic qualifiers, a sit-and-kick race was expected. Good. That would play to my strength.

Abruptly, like some suicide bomber, Byers, seemingly intent on exacting revenge, took off like a freaking maniac, and the whole pack went with him. I should have realized I could back off and catch people dying later, but I got dragged along. Byers hit the 400 in 53.6 and the 800 in 1:51.3, ridiculously fast. The bastard. Centrowitz was second in 1:52.8, still way too fast. I was sucking wind around 1:55 and thinking, I'm a dog, there's no way I can hang on.

Most of the nine-man field swarmed by me. "Just get me to the finish," I repeated to myself. "Just get me to the finish." When I arrived, I was seventh with a paltry 3:48.9.

Wohlhuter, the class of the field running his sixth race in nine days (he'd also qualified in the 800), won in 3:36.5. (At the Montreal Games, he would take Olympic silver in the 800 and a sixth in the 1,500.) It was very close for the three Olympic berths. Centrowitz was second in a 3:36.7 personal record. Durkin ran the same time in third for the final spot on the team.

And Byers? He collapsed worse than I did and was destroyed in last place. His final 400 was a jog-like 73.5, embarrassing at the Olympic Trials, or any meet for that matter.

Everybody had had it with Byers. Mike Slack, who took fifth, was about ready to strangle him. Slack, in his 30s, was a kicker. This had been his last shot at the Olympic team. Byers's self-destructive bent had ruined Slack's race plan. Some of us went out for pizza later, and Slack was still fuming. He said if Byers had been there in the pizza joint he would have killed him.

Any runner has a right to run any way he chooses, but there appeared to be malice in Byers's foolishness. Obviously, he was not capable of winning or even coming close to making the team off that pace. All he could hope to accomplish was to screw up the race for all but the three lucky souls who had something in reserve at the end.

Miller let me off easy. He may have been a taskmaster, but he was also sensitive. He told me there would be other opportunities and I should learn from the experience.

And I did. The race itself was only half of it. The day after the meet, I noticed droves of runners who'd just competed like me going out to run. They were distance stars like Frank Shorter and Craig Virgin but also many of the 1,500 guys. Some came up to me said, "We're going out for 10 miles. Want to come along?"

I looked at them like they were sick and thought, "What are you, completely crazy?"

What I witnessed in Eugene was stunning to me: single-minded dedication of runners to excel no matter what it took. All around me were athletes who saw a long-term connection between effort and success.

I'd made the Olympic Trials final just sailing along, not doing anything extra. I was still not running in the mornings, and I was not running on weekends, holidays, or summer vacation. Up to that point, through my sophomore year in college, I had shown I could do what my parents and coaches prescribed. In Eugene, the dedication of my peers made an impression on me and I wondered, What would happen if I really became a dedicated runner? Could I take any initiative of my own? I realized then that greatness required more than what I had given.

CHAPTER THREE

"Masked Man" Makes Breakthrough: Turning Points

That summer of '76, instead of handing out at the beach, I trained. I got a job as a camp counselor in Irvine, teaching sports to kids. I lived in the college dorms and ran 10 miles a day. I ran in the morning and I ran in the evening. When school resumed in the fall for my junior year, I continued two-a-days. On weekends, I did long runs. I became more diligent in the weight room.

My newfound dedication was reinforced by Irvine teammates Eric Hulst and Ralph Serna, the nation's hottest distance recruits out of high school the past two years. Serna had become the U.C. Irvine Anteaters' leading cross-country runner. Hulst, the most heralded high school distance prospect in the nation, would be his equal. Together, Serna and Hulst gave us potentially the best distance tandem—among Americans—in the collegiate ranks. Their training habits rubbed off on me and soon we became a threesome.

That fall of '76, Serna and Hulst were so strong they led our training sessions, and I was relieved about that. Now that I was an upperclassman with some credentials, I was counted on by some of the guys for team leadership. But in cross-country workouts I could cede that role to Serna and Hulst, whose dedication forced everyone, including me, to push even harder.

There were times when I was so wiped out from training I'd literally fall asleep in class. Mondays were the worst. That's when we did the week's most hellacious training—neverending repetitions of 800s or miles. I would have just enough time to drag myself from practice to the commons for a bite to eat before an evening class. Afterward, I'd conk out in my dorm without even having the strength to call Kim.

I still felt insecure about our separation. Kim was now in college herself, a freshman at Mount San Antonio College, a two-year school, in Walnut, California. I had a few dates at Irvine, but mostly I remained loyal to Kim. Besides, any girl who came into my dorm could see I was already taken. Kim had sewn me a bedspread as a birthday gift and embroidered a heart on it with our names and the date we'd met.

So I was stunned one day that semester when Kim proposed a trial separation. Kim suggested we go our separate ways as an experiment to see if we really cared for one another. She thought that we'd either strike up other relationships or get back together. I got scared and said no. I didn't want to risk losing her.

Whenever my link to Kim was strained, I relied more on the team for emotional sustenance. We Anteaters breezed through the '76 cross-country season, and at the NCAA II meet, held in Springfield, Missouri, on a 10,000-meter course, Serna and Hulst, the pure distance runners, were very generous to me, the miler. Confident of victory, they held back their pace so I could keep up with them and we could finish together. We ran three abreast practically the whole way and crossed the finish sweeping to a virtual tie in 29:42, 15 seconds ahead of the fourth-place man from Southwest Missouri State. Meet officials declared Serna the winner with Hulst second and myself third as Irvine captured the team trophy.

Photos of the three of us approaching the tape, which ran in *The Harrier* and other journals, gave us the aura of invincibility on the running scene. It was cold and we all wore leggings, long-sleeved jerseys, gloves, and matching hats along with our UCI singlets. The race was held on a golf course and as the three of us strode in unison from one fairway to the next, I could hear expressions of awe from spectators who'd probably never seen anything like it.

Serna and Hulst showed no signs of distress. It was as if they'd gone out for a jog. Their strides were mirror images. I, on the other hand, looked a little stressed. Out of gas, I was trying desperately to fall in sync with their rhythm so we could tie as planned. Len had given me a pep talk about keeping up. He had an ulterior motive; he didn't want Serna and Hulst expending unnecessary energy racing each other since their one-two finish was virtually assured.

Though united as athletes, the three of us had little in common out of uniform. Eric was straight-laced, wholesome, and always toed the line. Ralph was creative, an artist who painted landscapes and saw the beauty in running. I was the long-haired "party animal," an affront to authority. Our differences helped us get along because we were not competing for the same identity on the team.

This was still Division II—small time, I thought. Next year, with our entire team intact, Irvine would be moving up in rank to NCAA Division I. And Miller, never one to softpedal his views, was encouraging us with comments like, "We're going to stick it to the Kenyans."

The Kenyan distance runners had begun to have a profound impact on collegiate running. The University of Texas at El Paso (UTEP), with a mostly Kenyan squad, was the reigning NCAA Division I cross-country champion. Coaches like UTEP's Ted Banks recruited Kenyans, many of whom had ready-made strength from living at high altitude and undergoing the rigors of running many miles to school. There were no yellow schoolbuses in the Rift Valley of Kenya. Some of the Kenyans were also older than our American college boys. The Kenyans were pliable recruits. How could they turn down the opportunity to come to America, get a free college education, have facilities they could only dream of, train for the Olympics, and ultimately be in a position to earn a living on the international track circuit? At this time, there was only one regulation running track in all of Kenya.

Some people felt the Kenyans were taking scholarships away from American youth, but I took the long view. My college track-team experience led me to believe that the Kenyans' presence would raise the level of competition and benefit American distance running. Also, the experience of running against the foreigners on home turf would mean less of an adjustment when venturing abroad to the snakepit of the international circuit.

Stick it to the Kenyans? We got our chance that same fall season of '76, since the top six individual finishers in the NCAA II meet were eligible for the next week's NCAA I championship—the real NCAA—in Denton, Texas. That meant Serna, Hulst, and I could run. I was so naive I thought we could dominate there, too, maybe all make the top ten. My mother and sister surprised me by coming out to Denton to cheer us on.

Miller told us we had to get out fast—the time-honored cross-country admonition in a big field of more than 300 runners—to be in position to stick with the leaders. Miller's aggressive strategy was unwise for someone like me, a grinder most comfortable coming from behind. We all listened to Miller and went out hard. But this was not Springfield, Missouri.

The leader was Henry Rono, a Kenyan from Washington State. Rono was a 24-year-old freshman in his first NCAA meet. Few people knew who he was; I certainly didn't. Up front with Rono were two other Washington State Kenyans, Samson Kimobwa and Josh Kimeto. And Washington State wasn't even the team favorite. Clinging to the Kenyans like a boy among men was the pride of the Big Ten, America's own Craig Virgin of the University of Illinois.

Rono hit the first mile in a sizzling 4:17. Serna hung on for dear life around 20th. Hulst was farther back. I was slipping backwards through the field, heading for oblivion. When the damage was complete, Hulst placed 34th (decent for a freshman), Serna was 74th and me . . . 187th. I was back with the walk-ons.

In a performance that signaled a new era in collegiate distance running, Rono won convincingly as Kenyans took seven of the top 15; foreign athletes took seven of the top ten as all-Kenyan UTEP repeated as team champion with Washington State in third place. Rono would go on to light up the track world with four world records in 1978.

Virgin, a 21-year-old senior who would go on to win two world cross-country titles, placed 20 seconds behind Rono in third. Normally easygoing, he was stunned and angry. "There's no way I'll believe anything Chaplin says about their ages," fumed Virgin, referring to Washington State coach John Chaplin. "I've talked to coaches from Kenya. They [runners] measure their ages by taking the distance from their nose to their elbow."

Chaplin, always a charmer with a stump speech on any subject, fielded criticism of his recruiting techniques by saying he was at a disadvantage attracting American runners to the remote Washington State campus in Spokane. "We're a cowtown," he would say. "American kids don't want to come to a cowtown."

My strength from cross-country running in the fall of 1976 carried me into the 1977 indoor season. After I ran my first sub–4-minute mile, a third-place 3:59.7, at the Sunkist meet in Los Angeles, Miller felt I was ready to run with the big boys. He talked Al Franken, director of the Jack-in-the-Box meet in San Diego, into letting me into the field. I would have the chance to race Wilson Waigwa of Kenya, Eamonn Coghlan, and my hero, John Walker, who had won the Olympic gold medal in the 1,500 the previous summer in Montreal.

Less than a year before, I was asking Walker dumb questions while he soaked in an Irvine whirlpool; now, I would be racing him. Not too many people knew I was in the race. All the pre-meet commotion centered around Coghlan and Walker. Franken told the media there would be a world record attempt on the 3:55.4 run by Irishman Niall O'Shaughnessy in Columbia, Missouri three weeks before. But from what I could tell, no one in the Sunkist field really had records in mind.

Meet directors were notorious for building up the mile and promising records, inflating the public and media with expectations that were unrealistic. I think this hurt the sport because when the records (inevitably) were not broken, people were disappointed and races were considered failures.

Ultimately, these publicity hypes and promises of new records introduced a greater reliance on rabbits to set a recordbreaking pace; instead of pure and exciting competitions, many miles became dull as few records were broken and fans lost interest. Hype was destroying a wonderful sport. To my mind, one great miler against another was all you needed.

With Walker, Coghlan, and Waigwa, the Jack-in-the-Box Mile had a terrific lineup. As always, Miller had to convince me that I belonged. He devised a race plan for me with winning in mind. We figured the pace would be slow, with Coghlan and Walker measuring one another. But we could not allow the pace to dawdle all the way to the last lap. As good as my kick was, these guys could destroy me—especially Waigwa. Miller told me to make my move early.

The mile was billed as the marquee event of the meet, which also featured Frank Shorter and Rod Dixon in the two-mile, Mike Boit in the 1,000, Dwight Stones in the high jump, and Francie Larrieu in the women's mile. Reporters bit on Franken's world-record promo—the track was considered fast—and a packed house of more than 12,000 track fans filled the San Diego Sports Arena. There was great anticipation for the mile. Not only was Walker the Olympic champion, but Coghlan, considered the far superior indoor runner, had placed an agonizing fourth in the Olympic 1,500, missing the bronze medal on a lean at the finish. It was payback time.

When the field was introduced, the announcer got my name wrong. He stumbled over it, first saying "Scott—" then, kind of like, oh yeah, the guy from Irvine with the scraggly long hair— "Steve Scott." I made a point of saying hello to Walker, something awestruck like, "Remember me . . . it's great to have this opportunity . . ." He stared right through me.

My Irvine teammate and buddy, John Konigh, was the rabbit. His job was to help Coghlan and Walker. He did. Konigh raced through the quarter in 58.3 and the half in 1:59.6, certainly not world-record pace, then stepped off the track. Walker was second and Coghlan third. Coghlan, thinking Walker was in great shape, sat on him. I hung back near the rear behind Waigwa.

With Konigh's job finished, the pace sagged and the field bunched momentarily. No one wanted the lead. I maintained my speed, which propelled me all the way to the front. Suddenly I was like a pitcher making his first start in the majors and firing his first fastballs at 98 miles an hour. I felt a tremendous surge of power. When no one immediately challenged me, I started to think maybe Len was right, maybe I could win. The crowd was in a frenzy as people smelled an upset.

I hit the three-quarter in three minutes even. Waigwa had pulled into second while Coghlan and Walker stuck on each other from behind. I built a small gap on Waigwa, but on the last lap he shot by me with the pickup of a sprinter to win in 3:55.7—awfully close to the world indoor record, as it turned out. I took second in 3:56.5, slashing my best time by over three seconds, and outran Coghlan and Walker who ended up third (3:57.9) and fifth (3:59.2), respectively. Less than one second out of first, I had joined the fraternity of the world-class.

Afterward, most of the attention was still on Coghlan and Walker. Why had Coghlan, the "chairman of the boards" who'd come into the race with 13 straight indoor victories, made such a tactical blunder? What happened to Walker, the Olympic champion, supposedly in 3:53 shape? His countryman, Rod Dixon, second to Shorter in the two-mile, answered that one. He told reporters that he and John had made a quick trip to Las Vegas, where they spent hours working the slot machines. "Didn't you see that powerful action in his outside arm?" joked Dixon.

My success was heralded in *Track & Field News,* which ran a story about me with the headline, "Who Was That Masked Man?" Miller was quoted as saying I would eventually break the world record, and I was quoted as saying "Everything Len predicts for me comes true."

That was the race that made me a "professional." I earned my first official prize of sorts. Though AAU officials tended to look the other way when athletes like Coghlan or Walker were slipped post-race envelopes, the NCAA was feared by U.S. meet promoters and the rules against payments to college athletes (still in effect today) were usually upheld. This seemed hypocritical to me. An athletic scholarship is a form of payment, isn't it? And nowadays, that can be worth upwards of $125,000 for four years.

Miller got Franken to give him $100 to buy me a gift. I could not receive the money itself. I told Len to buy me a down jacket I could wear when I went camping.

The Kenyans continued their onslaught during the 1977 indoor track season, and with my 3:56.5 at Sunkist, I had established myself as an NCAA contender. No other goal entered my dreams. For a college runner, an NCAA title was like an Olympic gold medal.

Apparently, I was still no match for Henry Rono. At the NCAA indoor in Detroit, I knew how Craig Virgin must have felt, facing Rono in Denton. The team duel pitted the Kenyans of the University of Texas at El Paso versus the Kenyans of Washington State, and the mile was a pivotal event with both Waigwa (of UTEP) and Rono (of Washington) competing. Less than an hour before the mile, Rono had won the two-mile in meet record time (8:24.8).

Since Irvine had a meet elsewhere that weekend, I went to Detroit myself, without Len or teammates at my side. As an athlete moving up, I had to develop some independence and learn to compete without a coach to lean on. I was the baby chick flying from the nest and during the meet, my immaturity showed.

The pace crawled through the first quarter of the mile. Rono took over and led at the half. I sat in third. Waigwa, meanwhile, ran last, seeming unconcerned. Just past the three-quarter, in his signature slingshot surge, Waigwa bolted all the way to the front and raced to victory in 3:59.0. Without Len's exhortations to spur me on, I was content to be the first American, no more. Rono outran me for third as I took fourth. Rono wasn't even a miler, but his gutty last lap on the back end of a double enabled Washington State to defeat UTEP, 25½ to 25, and deny the Miners a fourth straight team title.

So, I was the first American miler, but not first at the finish line. I still lacked competitive savvy. When would I ever win the NCAA title?

The only runner I saw then who had the toughness of a Waigwa or Rono was an 18-year-old girl named Mary Decker. The California teenager with braces and pigtails had already made a name for herself in the middle distances. She was staying with her mother in Orange County and that winter would drive over to Irvine to train with our guys. I could not believe how she handled Miller's killer workouts—Mary was an animal on the track. We were all in awe of her.

Mary seemed to be impressed with me, too. In the evening, she would come back to campus with a girlfriend and park near my dorm so she could peek into my room. If I came out, she'd peel away. Mary was a terrific athlete and had an appealing charm, but I kept my vow to Kim, and nothing beyond teenage teasing became of my relationship with Mary.

———

These indoor races, with their Olympic-level fields, aura of importance, and my improving sub–4:00 performances, increasingly endeared me to the mile. I've always been drawn to both the structure and complexity of the mile. As a precise, tidy standard, the four-minute measure provides me with a defined framework I need. Even when I could run sub–4:00 by rote, it was comforting to know there was always an historical context with which to assess my effort. Whether I ran 3:48 or 3:58, I could apply four minutes, first achieved by Britain's Roger Bannister in 1954, as a guiding force.

Bannister's run of 3:59.4, on a breezy spring day in Oxford, England, is track's most recognized performance. I was charmed by the history behind Bannister's saga and proud of the identity it gave the mile. Champions in the mile, more so than in any other track and field event including the 100 meters, were remembered. Who could forget Bannister, Herb Elliot, Ron Delany, Jim Ryun, Kip Keino, Sebastian Coe, Coghlan, and Walker?

The mile suited my temperament. The rush of the 800 was over too soon for me, and my natural speed was not fast enough for it. I never had the attention span for the 12½ laps of the 5,000. The mile permitted no physical or psychic weakness and served up a full plate of strategies to keep your mind working overtime. Each mile was different and new. Each field offered opponents of different talents. It's quite a challenge to draw out your best while tangling with frontrunners and kickers, guys with sharp speed and others with sharp elbows. I thrived on the drama. It made winning feel transcendent. It was a feeling I could not find anywhere else.

Something about the mile gave the race an immaculate quality. In requiring equal parts speed, strength, and cunning, the mile seemed to distill the essence of running. And it had produced inspirational athletes, people like Bannister, the Oxford student who became a physician, and, soon after, Elliot, the Australian who retired undefeated.

Turning 21 in the spring of 1977, I felt like I was starting to taste that glory. My next breakthrough performance came on a trip that was as much a vacation as a race. The San Diego mile earned me an invitation to the 1977 Jamaica Invitational meet May 13 in Kingston, where I would run the 1,500 against Filbert Bayi of Tanzania, the world recordholder in both the 1,500 and mile. I had never traveled outside the United States and this would be my first international race.

Since the meet provided two plane tickets, I took Kim. Traveling together made me feel Kim and I were solidifying our relationship and that we would ultimately be married. Turning 21 and finishing my junior year, I felt like an army recruit stationed overseas who is insecure about his girl back home and wants to tie the knot. Any way to snatch Kim from her crowd of friends in Upland appealed to me, and as we ventured to the Caribbean the race itself became secondary.

Len was generous to let me compete. Irvine was in the midst of its season, with the conference and NCAA championships coming up. (The spring semester was over, so I wasn't thinking about classes.) Without Len, Kim became my surrogate coach and Len told her to keep me relaxed. "Stay loose," he instructed me, "and race hard."

The first thing we did upon arriving in Kingston was get into bed. Then, everything else fell into place. We lounged on the balcony of our room, munching on guavas and blissfully watching the bay. We shopped and fell in step with the seductive island culture. "Man, have a good time," was the mantra of the weekend.

Track was Jamaica's major sport. It's considered so important that several high school teams from Jamaica travel to the Penn Relays in Philadelphia every year and oftentimes sweep the boys and girls featured events. Penn is their Final Four. It was a revelation and a treat to see how a big meet could be the talk of the town. Unfortunately, that rarely happens in the United States.

A crowd of 35,000 filled Kingston's National Stadium for an event organized by the Jamaican government. They came for the sprints. Jamaica's reigning Olympic 200-meter gold medalist from

Montreal, Don Quarrie, would be running the 100 and 200 against Olympic-caliber fields. In the Caribbean, track seemed an outgrowth of the communal beat, a festival with island pride at stake like a summer basketball league in Harlem. Trinidad had its Olympic 100-meter champion going up against Quarrie. The 100 was dubbed the "Super Century." That's what you heard in the Kingston air: "Super Century, Man."

In the 400, the Bahamas had its best runner, the beefy Mike Sands, a Penn State graduate who'd gone to high school in Brooklyn. With the charm and good looks of a Sidney Poitier, Sands was known as much for his romantic conquests as for his 400-meter running. The American delegation was led by 1976 Olympic 400 hurdles champion Edwin Moses, one of track's all-time greats and among the most esteemed figures in the sport. At this time, Moses, who would collect his second Olympic gold in '84, was in the early stages of a 10-year streak that would ultimately total 107 straight victories.

It's funny how little things stick in your mind, but the athlete I remember most from Kingston is Canadian high jumper Debbie Brill, one of the first athletes to wear the skintight "bunhugger" shorts. It was hard to keep your eyes off her. Brill's body language was a good diversion since I began to feel wound up as the race approached. Some athletes like to be psyched up for a big race. I learned early in my career that being "psyched down" suited me better. Being loosey-goosey helped me adhere to my race plan of starting out modestly and coming on strong.

To stay calm, I needed as much diversion as possible so before leaving the hotel for the meet, Kim and I hit the sack. We'd done the same before the Jack-in-the-Box meet in San Diego. I've always felt sex a few hours before competition relaxed me and contributed to a good performance. I know other athletes agree. And from what I saw going on around the hotel, the positive effects were obvious.

The stadium was a sea of black faces. It seemed all of Jamaica had turned out, with many Kingstonians dressed in their holiday finery. American track journalists made the trip, as did Dave Wottle, the 1972 Olympic 800 champion, as CBS's commentator.

We were on Jamaica time, which meant there was no real time schedule. Meet officials chatted and socialized as athletes waited patiently for their call to race. The mile was delayed and my psyching down worked so well I fell asleep with my head in Kim's lap in the infield. Finally, we were ushered to our marks.

Bayi was given the inside lane. On his right was another Tanzanian, Suleiman Nyambui, a rangy runner who would gobble up NCAA titles at Texas-El Paso and take the 1980 Olympic silver medal in the 5,000. The nine-man field also had Americans Ken Schappert and Paul Cummings; Steve Ovett, an up-and-comer like myself from Great Britain; a pair of Czechs; and the rabbit, Sylvan Barrett of Jamaica.

I had heard of Bayi, who set the world mile record of 3:51.0 two years before in Kingston, when the meet was called the Martin Luther King Games. Bayi's 1,500 record was 3:32.2, equivalent to a 3:49-and-change mile. Bayi was boyish-looking while his countryman, Nyambui, had the countenance of a village elder. Bayi was quiet, Nyambui gregarious. Bayi was also a notorious frontrunner, but his sharpness was questionable and the experts wondered if he was ready to take the pace.

I had never heard of Steve Ovett. He was 21 years old and had run a 4:04.0 in Brighton two weeks earlier. I'd prepped for Kingston with a 3:55.1, second at the Penn Relays behind Wilson Waigwa. I doubt Ovett or anyone in the field other than the Americans knew who I was. If anyone had asked Waigwa about me, he would have had good reason to tell him how easy I was to beat.

Wottle, doing commentary for CBS, didn't think so. He kept repeating that "We should keep an eye on Steve Scott." Viewing the tape later, it was funny to find Wottle identifying me as the

Irvine runner in blue "trunks," as though I were a prizefighter. I guess the shorts I happened to pack were a little baggy; usually I prefer a snug, contoured fit, which makes me feel light and fast.

American runners had a history of the baggy look. The 1972 Olympic uniforms in Munich were so loose and ill-fitting that marathon champion Frank Shorter had shorts flown to him from home; then he sewed on the USA emblem. Since in high school I'd been moved by Wottle's '72 Olympic victory and copied his style of running with a cap, there was a certain symmetry in Wottle's TV role for my coming out party on the international circuit.

I had shoulder-length, curly, reddish-blond hair and a beat-up college singlet about as stylish as a high school football jersey. I had Californian written all over me. And American success had become the theme of the meet: Steve Williams had taken the Super Century over Hazley Crawford (fourth) and Quarrie (fifth); Edwin Moses had won not only the 400 hurdles but also the 110 hurdles over Cuban star Alberto Casanas. It was up to me to sustain U.S. success.

Barrett, the rabbit, shot out to the lead with Bayi in tow and Ovett third, hugging the inside. I settled into fourth. The first 200 went in 29.90. Nyambui moved up ahead of Bayi into second and then into the lead as Barrett fell away after only one lap. The first quarter split was a piddling 61.16.

Nyambui led the next lap with Bayi second and Ovett third. I hung back in sixth, for some reason drifting into the outside of the second lane, wasting yardage. Bayi regained the lead as Cummings, a Brigham Young University graduate from Utah, moved up on his shoulder. Bayi looked smooth while Cummings had to work at it. The pace was still unimpressive and the half went in 2:01.48. Perfect for me.

Bayi and Cummings held position with Nyambui third and Schappert now fourth ahead of me. Schappert had come up through New York City's Catholic high schools league, a wellspring of middle-distance talent. I still had not found the track's inside line, but I was bursting with power so it didn't matter.

Bayi hit the three-quarter in 2:59.20, and then the final lap was signaled with a beep that sounded like a train whistle. Nyambui went after Bayi. With 200 to go, Bayi had two strides on the field but began to glance back, a sign of weakness. I started my kick on the far turn, angling from the outside and onto Bayi's shoulder at the top of the home straight. Ovett came charging with me from behind. Nyambui and Cummings fell back.

It was Bayi on the inside, me in the middle, and Ovett on my right as the three of us sprinted for the tape. Bayi's form grew ragged and he glanced back twice within seconds—he was finished.

In the course of a race, I experience two levels of consciousness. In all but the final sprint, I am tuned in to my surroundings. Should I move up or stay put, do I have space or feel boxed in? I am aware of the crowd, hear Kim calling from the sidelines. I feel no strain in my body. Despite the competition, I tried to re-create the sensation of running a routine dual meet against San Diego State. I didn't frame the run in terms of Bayi's presence. I thought: just run and kick, my version of "Don't worry, be happy."

The final 100 meters was another zone entirely. My vision narrowed to a pinpoint. I heard nothing. I was barely aware of Ovett flying in tandem. Everything was me. I was in my last gear. It was a 15-second time warp. If it's hot, you don't feel the heat. If your heart pounds, you don't hear the beat. If your breathing is labored, you don't sense the strain. All of your senses are encapsulated into one brief and powerful out-of-body whoooooosh.

I drove hard on the balls of my feet. My arms cut up and back, punching the air. I have noticeably erect running form and when I sprint I'm very upright, if not arched slightly. This is not ideal in a close race because you have to lean at the finish and for me that takes an extra few hundredths-of-a-second. It also throws off your center of gravity.

I derived my speed from strength. A lot of milers, Ovett included, did speed drills in training. Miller's stock-in-trade was longer and deeper work, such as half-mile repetitions and hills. I had the strength to sustain whatever speed I possessed but could not switch to sprint form and a long stride on the final straight. Someone like Ovett, on the other hand, could open up.

With the finish looming as both reward and relief, Ovett and I both went for it, two 21-year-old newcomers getting our first taste of the big time. Though spent, I felt no pain. I doubt Ovett did. My thick torso and Ovett's wiry frame leaned across the line as one. I had him by inches. It was so close we were given the same time: 3:39.8.

Then, it hurt.

I embraced Kim, waved to the cheering crowd, shook a few hands, got some pats on the back and bent over with hands resting on knees. I heard my heart pound, felt my breaths heave. Bayi came rushing in third in 3:39.9 with Nyambui a big stride back in fourth. When I could straighten up, I embraced Kim again and as we walked it off down the track, she happened to have her hand resting firmly on my rear. That innocent touch showed up on TV and everybody back home couldn't wait to tell me they'd seen it.

My victory confirmed Wottle's credibility. The CBS anchorman, Don Criqui, told the American audience, "This Steve Scott is quite a story . . . a relative unknown. . . ." I had little exchange with Ovett, who ran undefeated the rest of the season to earn his first number-one world ranking.

But this was my day and it was euphoric. I celebrated by calling Len with the news and resuming my romantic holiday with Kim. Amid the excitement, I started to think of myself as an international runner with Olympic goals. Within one year, from the spring of 1976 to the spring of 1977, I had added psychological tools to my running. Until this period, I was a purely physical athlete, enduring punishing training to gain strength but lacking commitment. Now I understood how direction, desire, and drive—the three D's as I called them—were essential in making me a complete athlete with a chance for success on the world circuit. I knew what I had to do. The real fun had only just begun.

———

In the spring of '77, I picked up a couple more NCAA II titles, in the 800 and 1,500. While these races were little more than workouts for me, the victories advanced me into the NCAA Division I Championship in Champaign, Illinois, where I faced Wilson Waigwa again in the 1,500. Len reminded me that Waigwa liked to hide in last place until the last lap. Len told me I could beat him, and I told myself I could beat him.

Damned if Waigwa didn't nail me. I foolishly allowed a sedate pace and found myself boxed in with a lap to go when Waigwa unleashed his big move. He sprinted the final 400 in 52.5, earning a well-deserved fifth victory over me. I had yet to score one over him.

When we both went on to the AAU Nationals at UCLA. I was thinking, "What do I have to do to beat this guy?" Waigwa was a sweet, soft-spoken athlete with no pretensions. While his running style, with its swift force from deep in the pack, was keen strategy, Waigwa played no head games. He took the line and ran.

UCLA was like my home track. With the crowd behind me, I ran in midpack through a modest first two laps. Mike Boit, another veteran Kenyan who had won the 1972 Olympic bronze medal in the 800 and was a Ph.D candidate, took the lead with

600 to go, hitting the three-quarter in 2:57.3. I was third, holding back. I wanted to make sure I was the first American. Waigwa owned me, and the wily Boit had great range.

On the backstretch, improving miler Mike Slack, a University of Chicago graduate, took the lead as Boit faltered. Around the last bend, I poured it on, drew even with Slack, and waited for Waigwa. He sprinted his heart out and we leaned for the tape. It was anybody's race.

I took it. My momentum pushed me forward while Waigwa, his body contorted in the intensity, seemed to scream out at me in our moment of lunge. His eyes glared with concession; mine were almost closed in acceptance. I won by about an inch. We were both credited with a 3:37.3, my best time to date. I don't think I'd really figured out how to beat Wilson Waigwa, but at least the next time I would know it was possible.

As the American champion, I was now entitled to compete abroad on the European summer circuit, the essence of international track and field. Track was very big in Europe; in most countries, it was second in popularity only to soccer. This is where a young athlete like myself could gain experience, make connections, pick up some money, learn to trade elbows on the track, and endure the hardships of hopping from race to race with little rest and strange food. The circuit was a culture unto itself, and a rather primitive one at that.

Miller could not afford to make the trip himself that summer, so he arranged for me to hook up with Arnie Robinson, the 1976 Olympic long-jump champion, and hurdlers James King and Wes Williams. All three men were black, which was a new cultural experience for me. At Irvine, the black and white athletes on the team did not mingle that much. During my first swing through Europe, which was aborted after nine days, I roomed with King and the four of us hung out together. Robinson, also competing, was in charge. He was a very open guy who had not let the Olympic gold medal go to his head. He arranged our travel and got me into races.

I competed first in Mainz, Germany, then in Helsinki, Dusseldorf, and Stockholm. I was badly out of sorts from my first dose of jet lag. I felt sorry for myself, was homesick, and missed Kim. I drove myself crazy thinking she'd found another guy. Despite everything, I took third in the 1,500 in Helsinki and fifth in the mile at Stockholm, running 3:56.0, top-notch for an American collegian. In both those races, Waigwa (of course) was ahead of me, but he ran second both times. Eamonn Coghlan won at Helsinki while Josef Plachy, a Czech, took Stockholm.

I felt sorry for Iron Curtain athletes like Plachy, who seemed overly protected. Soviet bloc athletes were restricted by their countries' track officials, did not mingle with other athletes, rarely spoke to the media, seemed spiritless and in desperate need of a good laugh. Everything they did had an aura of state secrecy.

I was like a colt, and Robinson had the task of breaking me in. He told me how often I should race, what event I should run. He negotiated my race fee, which was only a few hundred dollars, and picked it up afterward. Athletes got paid to show up and run, and could receive bonus money for their place or time.

Track and field was still technically an amateur sport as dictated by international rules, and if you were caught receiving payments the authorities could make an example of you and bar you from competition. Then you'd be finished. Still, more and more athletes insisted on at least token (under-the-table) payments from meet promoters, who filled stadiums, attracted corporate sponsors, and made a pretty good business off the backs (and the legs) of the runners.

The preceding year, in testimony before a congressional hearing of the President's Commission on Olympic Sports, the marathoner Frank Shorter had explained the system of under-the-table payments, the bedrock foundation of the sport. For his honesty, Shorter almost lost his amateur standing with the U.S. track and field bureaucrats, who felt threatened by any expression of an individual athlete's assertiveness.

The system in Europe was for all money to be distributed in cash in a hotel room. Athletes, or their coaches or agents, waited in line to collect from meet officials. Most agreements were informal and there was a lot of haggling. The whole process was crude and unsavory. And at some meets that are part of the lesser circuits, it's not much different today.

I made about a thousand dollars for my four races. This meant I was guilty on two counts: for accepting money as an "amateur" athlete and for violating NCAA rules, which strictly prohibited such payments. In Europe, though, as opposed to the United States, I didn't notice any other collegians adhering to those rules, either.

I thought I was rich. In Stockholm, I spread the bills out on my hotel bed like precious gems. But I still missed home, and my newfound bounty meant I could afford to skip a few meets and go back. So, instead of staying the whole summer as planned, I went back to Upland for a few weeks. When I returned to Europe, I stayed for five weeks, again with Robinson's group, and competed in Britain, Italy, Tunisia, Belgium, France, and Germany. I probably raced too much, but then I always would.

Seeing the world opened me up and also hardened me. In the classier meets, we stayed in decent hotels, ate good food, and got paid on time. On the "B" circuit, everything was up for grabs. In Viareggio, Italy, you got no pickup at the airport, you had truck-stop accommodations, and the meet promoter would chisel you down to pennies. It was hard to get any sleep because your neighbor's late-night carousing could be heard through the paper-thin motel walls.

My only victory of the summer came, strangely enough, at an African meet in Tunis, where I improved my best 1,500 time to 3:36.1. That time made me the fourth-fastest 1,500 man in the world that year. All the traveling drained me, but I was happy having finished a season in Europe ranked as the number-nine miler in the world, a notch ahead of Eamonn Coghlan. I began my senior year at Irvine with one burning goal: the NCAA title.

In 1977, I jumped right into fall cross-country training without a break from the summer circuit. It was crazy, but I seemed able to take it. I needed to regain my strength anyway. Racing through Europe, you can't train much. The cycle of the internationalist consisted of up to 100 miles of training per week in the fall, then speedwork and racing toward a peak for the summer international season.

To be primed for summer racing abroad, a progressive ten-month program was necessary. It was similar to building a house. In the fall and winter, I developed a foundation of strength with long, steady running. In the spring, I emphasized speed, sharpening my ability to kick the last lap of a mile wth gusto.

My relationship with Len was growing closer and I could see how his demanding system was driving me ahead. I was starting to believe his claim that one day I would break the American record in the mile. But not everyone shared our conviction. One local sportswriter, aware tht I'd yet to win an NCAA title, wrote, "If Steve Scott ever breaks the American record in the mile, I'll run the 3,000 steeplechase with my hands tied behind my back." We used that quote as motivation.

Irvine was now an NCAA I school, and Ralph Serna remained our number-one cross-country runner. Irvine was ranked sixth nationally, but again we couldn't get it together for the NCAA championship, held in John Chaplin's "cowtown" of Spokane. Rono repeated his victory on his home course; foreign runners took six of the top seven. Serna was our top man in 59th position, and Irvine placed 15th out of 29 teams.

After my success abroad, I was anxious to be "one of the guys" again. I think people were watching to see if my new reputation had turned me into a jerk. To prove it had not, I led the apple-throwing assault from the tenth-floor window from our hotel room in Spokane. Fruit rained down on innocent Spokanians and splattered everywhere. We were joined in our offensive by runners from other teams. Our victims had no idea that these hooligans were the NCAA contenders they had read about in the *Spokesman-Review*.

That silliness helped me guard against a new kind of pressure: the pressure of expectation. Up to now, I had a relaxed attitude. I was considered up-and-coming. Thus, almost anything I achieved was notable.

But now I began to think, "I gotta win this race." I started measuring up the other competitors, feeling a lot of pressure as the "American Hope." In meet after meet on the indoor circuit, I'd line up against a Kenyan (Wilson Waigwa), a German (Thomas Wessinghage), an Irishman (Eamonn Coghlan), a New Zealander (John Walker), and a Tanzanian (Filbert Bayi). I felt I had to win for the American crowd.

Though I couldn't buy an indoor victory that winter, I was in such good shape for the '78 outdoor campaign of my senior year that I promised the press a fast time in my first spring meet. That was unlike me, but I was feeling good, the meet was at home, and I had no competition. I tore a 3:53.9 mile. It was a big personal record (PR) and unheard of for a solo run, a season opener yet. I considered the performance a wakeup call to my opposition. Now I was a real threat for the NCAA.

But then I got sick. We were scheduled to run the Drake Relays in Des Moines. Our goal was to show the midwest how California kids could run, and the fans expected a sub–4:00 out of me. Even at that time, in 1978, no one had broken four minutes in the individual mile at Drake. I woke up the day of the race with 103 fever. I had to withdraw, but I went to the stadium and on the P.A. system apologized to the crowd of 19,000 with the promise that I would come back next year and break 4:00 for sure.

With the NCAA coming up, I was in bed for a week. This was my last chance to win the NCAA and the illness struck me with fear. The most important race of my life, for which I was now the favorite, was in jeopardy. As I lay around, I thought that if I lost and had to explain that I'd been sick, people would say I was making excuses. I hated when other athletes did that, and I couldn't bear to think I might be in that position myself.

Despite my weakened state, I had little chance to rest. Miller was trying to balance team goals with my individual needs. At our conference meet, the Pacific Coast Athletic Association, the team counted on me for winning points in the 800, 1,500, and 5,000. It was brutally hot, and the triple took place over a four-hour time stretch. After winning the 1,500 and taking 2nd in the 800, I died in the 5,000 and came in seventh, but Irvine still won.

For my last NCAA, held at Hayward Field in track-mad Eugene, Oregon, I competed at about 80 percent of full strength in the 1,500. Concerned about a lack of late-race speed, I adjusted my plan and decided to push the pace at the halfway point and rely on my base strength. Actually, I took the lead sooner, at 450 meters, and held off a bid by Oregon senior Matt Centrowitz, a streetwise New Yorker running his last race in a Ducks jersey, to move ahead. Centrowitz stuck to my shoulder, but faded with a lap to go. Ray Flynn, an Irishman from East Tennessee State who would become a close friend, drove hard to catch me, but I won by a body length in 3:37.6 for the 1978 NCAA crown.

Man, that felt good. All season I had dreamed of taking that victory lap in the mile at Hayward Field, and as I toured the track waving and smiling to the crowd I felt blissful, relaxed, as though I'd not been ill at all. As the favorite, I didn't want to appear too excited a winner; in Eugene, where they knew their track, that could have come off as showboating.

Realizing this long-term goal and at last winning the NCAA title as a miler remains one of the greatest rewards of my career. But despite my success, the media, especially in the East, did not seem to have a high regard for me. When they weren't lamenting the passing of the mile's glory days from the Jim Ryun/Marty Liquori era in the late '60s and early '70s, they were building up Villanova runners Mark Belger and Don Paige as the next great American middle-distance hopes. It disturbed me that the 1,500— certainly a marquee event—was not included in ABC's telecast of the NCAA meet.

The East-West schism was part of track's upholstery. The week after the NCAA, when I defended my AAU national 1,500 title at UCLA, I got the sense that reporters were pulling for Villanova freshman Sydney Maree, the black South African who spoke out against apartheid and eventually became a U.S. citizen. Maree had run fifth in the NCAA 1,500.

At UCLA, I narrowly defeated Maree to become only the second miler (after Jim Ryun) to successfully defend the AAU title in the last 25 years. My races were close because I was rarely concerned with time. I was perfectly happy rallying from behind to win by inches, the time be damned.

As America's new mile leader with two straight AAU titles plus the NCAA crown, I went back to the European circuit. Again I traveled with Arnie Robinson, James King, and Wes Williams. I guess they didn't mind having a token white guy hanging around.

By this time I was a college graduate. I had not attended graduation exercises at Irvine as a protest against an athletic administration that had begun to cut funding to the track program. These changes put Len in conflict with school officials and his days at Irvine were numbered.

Seeing this unfortunate development at Irvine gave me a keener sense of track and field realities and the use of power. Opportunity in Europe was all about leverage and power. It was about how important you were to the meet promoter, who needed to satisfy sponsors, attract TV coverage, and fill seats. And it was about what back-room deals could be worked out. Arnie used his leverage as Olympic champion to make sure I was given a spot in meets. It was the old piggyback routine: When Carl Lewis became the biggest draw in the sport, his lesser Santa Monica Track Club teammates were ensured entry into Grand Prix events. You want Carl, you take everyone. Now it was you want Arnie, you take Steve Scott.

In my first race at the fabled Bislett Games in Oslo, where the small, homey stadium rocks with energy and anticipation, I ran a close third in the "Dream Mile," behind Waigwa (him again) and Filbert Bayi of Tanzania. Although I was tired from the trip, I still lowered my best time to 3:53.8. The next day I had a commitment to compete in Helsinki, but when I arrived the promoter refused to let me run. He would not even give me a hotel room and I had to sleep on the floor in a friend's room. He'd lied to me. The reason for my rejection was simple: The locals wanted a Finn to win. And indeed, Antti Loikkanen, the Finnish national champion, won.

For the first time, I was a man without a meet in a foreign country. But soon, I found a 1,500 in a small town, Vasteras, outside Helsinki, courtesy of two New Zealanders, Rod Dixon and Dick Quax. Dixon, the 1972 Olympic 1,500 silver medalist, was past his prime in the middle distances and five years away from winning the New York City Marathon. Quax was a former world recordholder in the 5,000. They took me under their wing. I defeated Dixon at Vasteras and he collected my prize for me of a couple of hundred bucks.

With college running now behind me and no team goals at stake, it was not always easy for me to marshal a killer instinct. Miller, still my coach, had tried to implant that instinct in me during training. He would say, "I want you to dig down deep now." Or he would challenge me toward the end of a workout: "I want a 51 out of you for this quarter." I needed more grooming for the instinct to take root and become a permanent part of me.

Britain's Steve Ovett already had it. Undefeated and ranked number one in the world in 1978, Ovett beat me in Dublin, Oslo, Malmo, Turku, and Tokyo. At least I was getting close. In Oslo, Ovett outran me by only a stride as I improved my 1,500 to 3:36.0, second-best American time ever.

I was catching on, making adjustments, adding options to my come-from-behind racing strategy. I realized it was impossible for me to outkick Ovett in a pure sprint. He could run a flat-out 200 in under 22 seconds. I would have to take the lead earlier than usual and try to sustain a long, drawn-out kick in stages from 600 meters out.

In one of my last races of the summer, a mile in Berlin, I moved ahead as early as the half mile but was caught by Thomas Wessinghage of Germany, who won in 3:55.4 to my 3:55.7. I derived some satisfaction by edging Waigwa, who ran third at 3:55.8.

The Steve Scott "stock" had risen and I was now earning $500 to $1,000 in under-the-table payments at the marquee races. But it would still be years before a professional athlete like me could earn a living unencumbered by some restriction or another.

So, there I was: a college graduate with a B.A. in social ecology, a 3:53 mile, several national titles, and innumerable losses to Wilson Waigwa. My track earnings were about $5,000 a year, and Kim and I were starting to talk about marriage. I wanted to train for the 1980 Olympics, which were two years away.

I had clear goals. The question was: How would I achieve them?

It was obvious I needed some kind of job that gave me the time to train. I couldn't go into detective work because Kim (now a graduate of Mount San Antonio College) refused to marry a cop. She didn't want to live with the constant worry that her husband's life was on the line. That was fine with me. It was not as if I had my heart set on law enforcement, anyway.

But my heart was set on the Olympics. I turned to teaching, which would allow time for running, and obtained a substitute teacher's certificate in Irvine. At college, I had served in the Education Motivation Program, tutoring needy youngsters. The idea of working with kids appealed to me, but I was soon to learn that substituting in a junior high was like parachuting into a war zone. The kids were unruly, abusive, vulgar, and particularly eager to take advantage of a substitute teacher. They didn't listen to a thing I said, and in one shop class I was afraid they'd electrocute one another or set the place on fire.

After two weeks, I'd had enough, and feeling that I was escaping with my life, I quit. Now what? I had to run, but I had to eat, too. I decided to take the gamble of racing for my daily bread. I saw milers like John Walker doing it. Of course, Walker was an Olympic champion and world recordholder. But along the way he had been an apprentice like me with the same fears and dreams. I took Walker's example and in 1978 set out to make mile racing a way of life.

Cruel Games of Pain: 1980 Olympics

By fall 1979, I was a year out of college, had three seasons of international track under my belt, and had won three straight U.S. national titles at the 1,500 or mile. In European meets that summer, I was victorious in Stockholm, Dublin, London, and Lausanne. I improved my best mile to 3:51.11 while placing second at Oslo behind Sebastian Coe of Great Britain, whose 3:48.95 that day set a world record.

I was earning my living as a runner and ready to commit to my other great passion in life—Kim. She and I were married in November, 1979.

We had a church wedding with over 300 guests including many of my college teammates. Naturally, I couldn't adhere to every convention. On the morning of the wedding, I ran a 10,000-meter cross-country race in Orange. I had organized a cross-country squad and we needed some racing under our belts before going on to compete two weeks later in the AAU cross-country nationals.

The race was held in the morning, and the wedding was at 2 o'clock. Plenty of time, I assured Kim. I won the race and was back in Upland by 11 to shower, get dressed, and take pictures. I neglected only one of Kim's requests—to get a haircut. I still had my shaggy orange locks at picture time.

I'm a romantic at heart. For our wedding night, I thought it would be cozy to be in the mountains where it's crisp and cold, to get a fireplace roaring and cuddle up. To that end, I reserved a thirty-dollar cabin with a fireplace at Mount Baldy. Unfortunately, in November, it's freezing at night. The room had no heater and only thin blankets. I kept waking up to throw more wood on the fire. But Kim and I got our money's worth and looked forward to thawing out on a ten-day honeymoon in the South Pacific.

We vacationed at a Club Med resort in the Tahitian Islands and it was glorious. We had a hut on pontoons jutting out into the bay. Although my European trips had already made me a man of the world, I spoke no French, the language of Tahiti. This proved to be a handicap when Kim fell ill with food poisoning. We rushed to the nearest doctor—a man with a shack for an office and no credentials on his wall who, of course, spoke no English. We had to communicate through sign language. With Kim expelling everything from her system front and back, it became a comic scene. The doctor gave her two shots of something and eventually she got better. But I never did learn to speak French.

Honeymoon notwithstanding, I continued my running without letup. The Moscow Olympics were only 244 days away. On Bora Bora, I ran the circumference of the island as Kim biked at my side. We'd been told it was 12 miles around; it turned out to be 17. Kim was very athletic and, enjoying the breeze on the seat of her bike, handled her assignment with ease. I just about died in the heat, yet the day after we returned home I ran the cross-country nationals in Raleigh, North Carolina, groundwork for the 1980 Olympics. Against a field of 10,000-meter runners, I placed seventh and just missed qualifying for the world cross-country championships in Paris.

It felt like the world was ours.

At the time of our wedding, the '79 world rankings came out and I was rated the number-three miler in the world. Coe was number one. His countryman, Steve Ovett, was number two.

I was 23 years old and on top of the world. I was collecting $1,000 or more per race on the European circuit, and had just signed a $10,000-a-year shoe contract with New Balance and another $10,000 promotional contract with the Sub–4 clothing firm. Sponsorships for track runners were modest and I took what I could get. I was thrilled to be able to run for a living as I entered the next stage of life as a married man.

For New Balance, all I had to do was wear the company product on my feet. For Sub–4, which was trying to make inroads in the running apparel business, I wore the uniform, spread goodwill, and enlisted top runners like my buddy John Walker to join the Sub–4 Track Club. Sub–4 got a lot of play out of pictures in running magazines of Walker, me, and others with "Sub–4" emblazoned on our chests, snapping finish tapes in triumph.

Meanwhile, I set my sights on Coe, Ovett, and the 1980 Moscow Olympics. Every runner dreams of making the Olympic team and winning a medal, the peak achievement in track and field. As the leading American miler, I felt nothing could stop me from meeting Coe and Ovett in Moscow and racing for the honor of being called the world's best.

When my coach, Len Miller, left Cal-Irvine to take the coaching position at Arizona State that fall, Kim and I followed Len to Arizona and rented a two-bedroom apartment in Mesa, not far from the University. Kim got a job in her field, respiratory therapy, and spent time in the summers traveling to Europe with me. We talked about having a family, but decided to wait. In the meantime, we adopted a mutt from the pound and named him Tiggers. Everything seemed tidy, manageable, and just right.

Though Len continued to train me hard, he treated me with more respect now that I was a post-collegiate professional athlete, and we became good friends. We made a lot of decisions jointly and I pretty much decided my racing schedule on my own.

As I went forward to fulfill my Olympic dreams, I felt energized by what I viewed as "Team Scott": Len, Kim, and me—all in this thing together.

It wasn't easy leaving California and our families behind. Kim was very close to her family, and Mesa was a six-hour drive from Upland. On occasion, we would meet Kim's dad, Bill, and her brother, Rick, on their hunting trips to the Arizona desert. Bill introduced us to hunting and while Kim abstained I fell in love with it. Our clan would stay in a trailer off the Colorado River, hunt quail, and cook our prize for dinner.

I needed this kind of recreation to balance the hard training and anchor me at home since my line of work required traveling almost every weekend to races. I think at times Kim would have preferred that I work a regular 9-to-5 job like other husbands. Immediately after our honeymoon, I had dashed off to Raleigh for the cross-country event, and that upset her. Kim had to adjust to being alone for days at a time, which was hard on her.

We quickly outgrew our little apartment and early in 1980 bought our first home in Tempe, taking pride in fixing it up together. We purchased furniture and shared in the painting and wallpapering. I was the dreamer, spurred by images of Olympic titles and world records; Kim was pragmatic, concerned about the house, paying the bills, having food in the fridge. In our early years together, Kim was my grounding wire, keeping my feet in my boots as I extended my youth with a career in running.

Every so often, when the insecurities of being a track wife got to her, Kim would make an offhand comment like, "Why don't you get a real job?" I understood how she felt. What kind of life, what kind of career, was track and field? I had no guarantees for the future. I was merely working my body to the limit without injury, dependent on Len's coaching and the whims of sponsors and meet promoters with little tolerance for poor performance.

And I was gone a lot. On the road, I would usually catch the first flight home, leaving my buddies and sometimes an irked sponsor wondering why I was in such a hurry. Sometimes, instead of phoning home as promised, I'd be out with the guys while Kim wondered where I was.

At the time, there was little money to be made in running, even by the superstars. To the public, track and field was considered a minor sport. Was there really any future in it, especially in the American market where so many other sports grabbed the headlines and television revenue? It was disillusioning to see how someone like John Walker, an Olympic champion and world recordholder, struggled to make six figures a year, while some second-tier golfer could clean up in any weekend tournament.

But at 23 I didn't let the pay scale get to me; all I wanted was to run under the stars in the Arizona desert, and race Coe and Ovett in Moscow.

To beat the heat, I had to run early and late. I did my morning road work along canal paths and my evening track work at the Arizona State stadium. When the heat was really bad, I had to wait until 10 P.M. to hit the track, and even then it was around 100 degrees. In the dry, dark stillness of the huge stadium, I'd run my laps while Len stood there, finger on stopwatch, as the rest of Arizona was heading for bed. It was invigorating.

But Kim paid a price because our lives revolved around my running and we were oftentimes out of sync in our daily routines. I did a morning 10-mile run and then was home most of the day while Kim was at work. We rarely had dinner together because I could not eat before my evening track sessions, which required composure, focus, and a body tuned like new skis before the first snow. I'd eat late, have a few beers, and conk out at 2 o'clock in the morning.

Because racing the mile demands the strength of a distance runner plus the speed of a sprinter, on many days I trained myself dizzy with exhaustion. After my morning distance run, the rest of my day was calculated to marshal the energy, fortitude, and peace of mind to confront the unmerciful nightly track work.

Other than time spent on my Sub–4 duties, I'd spend my days hanging around, playing golf with Len, taking naps—and waiting. Waiting to go to the track with hunger and fear. I couldn't wait to put my body through greater and greater exertion so I could feel the pride in accomplishment; but I harbored doubts that I could rise up and do it.

Sitting around the house in late afternoon, I could almost taste the exhilaration to come that night. I would sit quietly and think about the workout and how fit I was. I would think about beating Coe and Ovett and the races I'd win in Europe.

Once in a while, Kim would come to the track at night to watch. Sometimes, I'd have a training partner like Ray Wicksell or Pete Heesen, friends who did some of my road training with me. But usually, it was just Len and me and the stars.

Believing as Len did that I needed to be as strong as an ox, I typically logged close to 100 miles a week, probably more training volume than any other miler in the world. If Coe and Ovett were running 90 miles a week, I'd do 100. If they were doing track training twice a week, I'd do it three times.

My evening track sessions began at dusk with a warmup 5-mile run from home to the stadium. Then I stretched, ran a few strides, and procrastinated with anxiety before the first hard repetition of the track. Shaking out my legs as I stood on the brick-red track, I'd feel both powerful and scared at once as Len said, "Time to get started."

One of Len's toughest assignments was three sets of 800, 400, 800. I'd run the 800s in 1:56 and the 400s in 55 with jogs between the runs and 5-minute, full recovery breaks between sets. Some nights, I could barely lift my legs; other nights, in a groove, I'd find myself touring the track in a trance, running in rote, mechanical fashion, not feeling a thing. I liked to pulverize the final repetition and, when I could coolly rip off a fast lap, Len would give me a look of affirmation and maybe say something like, "You know, you're ready to run 3:48."

I could take that to the bank, but it was hard to take it home because by the time I'd run the five miles back as a cooldown and walk in the door at 11 o'clock, Kim would be asleep. We learned to exist in our own orbits and do the best we could.

With time to kill, I worked on my golf game, my third passion in life. My dad introduced my brother and me to golf when I was around 12 or 13 years old. We played a small 9-hole course in Ontario, California, or hit balls at a driving range.

At college, I became a legitimate player because Len played as did my roommate, Ed Ahlmayer, a scratch golfer. In Arizona, Len, ever the wheeler-dealer, got a company to sponsor us so we could golf for free at a country club in Scottsdale. Len and I were close in ability, shooting in the mid-80s, and we'd have a ball making side bets. In the languorous heat of the afternoon, we took our time, spending four hours out on the course.

Four hours? How about playing a round of golf in a half-hour?

Late in 1979, shortly after settling in Arizona, I got hooked into a golf scheme that would result in more notoriety than any of my record-breaking running performances. Sub–4 was sponsoring a road race in the San Diego area and wanted to drum up publicity. The head of the company organizing the race, Dennis Caldwell, was also a runner who loved golf. He did a little research and discovered an achievement listed in the Guinness Book of World Records: the fastest time playing an 18-hole round of golf. It was about 30 minutes.

That's us! Dennis set up an event that today would probably have ESPN drooling. He checked the rules, gathered six officials who would follow us in two golf carts, and notified the media. As pure fun, I dove into it. Run, golf . . . if you could hunt quail at the same time it would have been my vision of Heaven.

The idea was to run as fast as you could from one hole to next, take a deep breath, and play. The rules required that your ball come to a dead stop before you could take a swing. You couldn't shovel the ball like a hockey puck. Obviously, the better you played, the faster you'd cover the course.

We were allowed to have balls set up on all the tees. The two carts accompanying us were for verification and also to provide clubs in an emergency, like a bike van servicing a flat tire in the Tour de France. The course layout in Anaheim was over 6,000 yards, but with all the back-and-forth coverage I'd end up running over five miles.

I played well and ran well. And the running wasn't easy either! Heaving, I would have to hold my breath for a second at each shot to steady myself. I was like a swimmer sprinting to the wall without taking a breath. I finished exhausted and still beat the Guinness record with a time of 29:30.

No media had come out. After our feat, Dennis made some calls and a few reporters and TV people showed. The first thing they said to us was, "Sorry we missed it. Can you do it again?" We did not even get credit for the record. Guinness required one of its own people to observe and verify the performance. Dennis had not known that.

No matter, word spread. Wacky Steve Scott, the unruly, long-haired runner from California, had done it again. The wires picked it up and the story made the papers everywhere. *Golf Digest* ran a story. That really made it official. When I returned to the track circuit, reporters peppered me with questions about the "golf thing." I'd be at a press conference in Stockholm and the Scandinavians would pipe up with, "Tell us about the golf. . . ." Hey! Didn't anybody want to know about my records in the mile?

———————

With the Moscow Olympics coming up, I had less time to indulge my golf fantasies. I was the American challenger to Coe and Ovett, who'd captivated the track public abroad with their fast times and their efforts to avoid competing against each other. In the summer of '79, when they'd led the world's milers, the two Brits had not competed together on the same track once.

While Ovett had not raced against Coe that season, I had.

I first showed I was ready for Coe with my performance against Don Paige in the '79 AAU national 1,500 at Mt. SAC. A Villanova junior, Paige was coming off an 800-1,500 double victory at the NCAA Championships—the first middle-distance sweep in 21 years—and the media was building him up. It was not just his victories. Paige looked like Jim Ryun and he ran like Ryun: head bobbing, all limbs, explosive kick. When the eastern media called Paige "the next king of the mile," I wondered: Had they forgotten about me?

At Mt. SAC, I relished the chance to prove once again who should wear the 1,500 and mile crown in the United States. Len Miller was an excellent tactician. The way he saw it, if the pace was slow all the way to the final kick, Paige could outsprint me in a full-out 200. We hoped the pace would be around 2:01 for the half. Then Miller wanted me to take the lead and quicken the pace every succeeding 100 meters to gradually take the sting out of Paige. That's exactly how it transpired.

An out-of-shape Dick Buerkle led through the 800 in 2:01.0. I charged ahead on the third lap with Paige chasing me. Through each 100, I accelerated a little more . . . a little more. . . . My third 400 was 54.9 and Paige was still there. But what did he have left?

At the top of the homestretch, Paige hung to my right shoulder, but he strained and his neck muscles tightened like the roots of a tree. With a smile to myself, I outran Paige to win decisively in 3:36.4, breaking my meet record.

Fueling for my showdown with Coe, I was dismissed in Europe, where I was "the American," considered marginal in the shadows of Coe and Ovett. The track community in Europe was rampant with anti-American sentiment. For the same reasons that the French or English envied American power but disdained American culture, international track promoters and media liked nothing more than for Americans to be cut down to size. The press always baited me to try and manufacture some controversy for tabloid headlines.

My race with Coe took place in Oslo in July, and catapulted me into 1980 Olympic contention. Twelve days before, on the same

Oslo track, Coe had set a world 800-meter record of 1:42.4. Now, against me, he would attempt the mile record, John Walker's 3:49.4.

I was hungry to race Coe; apparently, Ovett was not. Asked about his absence from the Oslo mile, Ovett was quoted as saying, "It'll be a hollow victory for the winner. It's high time the runners come to meet me where I will run." This kind of crap went on for years.

Actually, Coe was a neophyte in the mile. He'd been seen as a 400 runner moving up to the 800, and even with his world 800 record some considered the 1,500 a reach for him. Coe himself, who always knew the right thing to say, suggested he lacked sufficient training for a world record and hoped he could run 3:53.

Miller and I saw Coe as we had Paige: I would need to put the pressure on early. I could not match his natural speed off a tentative pace. Even if Coe beat me, I felt I had a chance at Jim Ryun's American record, 3:51.1, which had stood since 1967.

The rabbit was Steve Lacy, who did his job for two laps. I took the third quarter and pushed hard, but it wasn't hard enough. Coe went by me with ease to shatter Walker's record with a 3:48.95. I ran my heart out but eased up a tick through the finish to hit 3:51.11, a heartbreaking hair off Ryun's mark. That performance began Coe's reign of sainthood. "Sebastian Coe Joins the Immortals" crowned *Track & Field News.* Coe maintained an understated posture. He said he still felt he was not yet a blue-blooded miler but thought he could entertain the possibility of attempting an 800-1,500 double at the Moscow Olympics.

I thought that was just fine. I was inching my way closer to being the best. I wanted to race Coe again and again. I wanted to race Ovett. I wanted so badly to race them both, the three of us on the track together, no rabbits, no backroom deals, just flat-out racing for the Olympic gold medal in Moscow. That would have been something.

Every runner is ingrained with the Olympic ideal. It involves purity and brotherhood, the concept of sport for sport's sake. It suggests a communal spirit in which all athletes are linked in their quest to stand on the victory podium with gold medals around their necks. The Olympic vision may be naive, but it holds. As track and field athlete, especially in America, you are defined by the Olympic Games. There would be little public awareness of track if not for the Games. No matter what the year or track season, a runner is, in a sense, always in training for the Olympics.

When 1980 dawned, I felt invincible. I had mastered the art of running a mile on a Friday night, hopping a plane, traveling across the country, and running a mile on a Saturday night. The U.S. and Canadian indoor circuit was like a traveling circus, with many more meets than exist today. I survived these grinding, back-to-back doubles with some creative psychology. For the second race, I felt I had a built-in excuse with no right to expect anything big. This lifted the burden and relaxed me. The more relaxed I felt, the better I ran.

One weekend in February seemed to set the tone for the disillusionment that would come later in the year. President Carter had already announced the threat of a U.S. Olympic boycott of the Moscow Games because of Soviet aggression in Afghanistan. As a condition for U.S. Olympic participation, Carter insisted that the Soviets stop their incursion. I was stunned but in a state of denial. A boycott could not really happen, could it? I was trained to run, not interpret global politics. I had a mile to run, two in fact. First, the Sunkist meet in Los Angeles on Friday night, then the Brooks meet in Houston on Saturday.

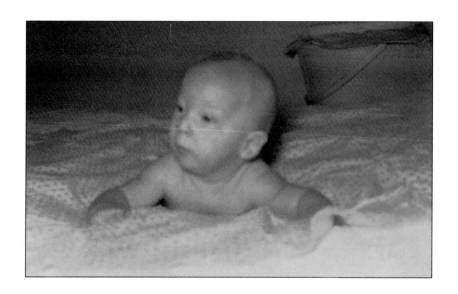

TOP
Baby Stevie, 2½ months, July 31, 1956.

ABOVE LEFT
Little Steve, 1957.

ABOVE RIGHT
Cowboy Steve, 1958.

RIGHT
The Scott kids: Alicia,
Steve, Kendall, 1963.

RIGHT
Baseball days, 1968.

RIGHT
Upland High School, 1974.

BELOW
*Steve (2nd from left), 1974,
takes second in the boys'
880 yard run.*

ABOVE
Upland High School, 1974.

ABOVE
Steve gets a hug from his Mom, Mary (left), and Kim, U.C. Irvine cross-country race, 1975.

LEFT
High school senior yearbook, 1974.

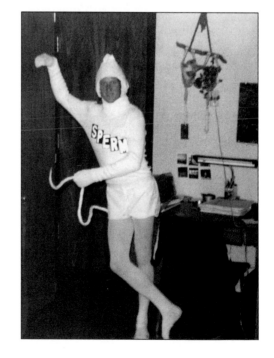

ABOVE
The Cal-Irvine cross-country team celebrates victory. Coach Len Miller holds the plaque, Steve right behind it.

RIGHT
Halloween, 1976.

TOP *Steve just about to win the 1500 meters, Cal. State Northridge vs. USC vs. Irvine; Ralph Serna to his left.*

BOTTOM *Irvine runners Ralph Serna, Eric Hulst (center), and Steve (left) crossing the finish line, 1976 NCAA Division II Cross Country Championships. He placed 3rd.*

ABOVE AND RIGHT
Irvine Meet of Champions,
1977.

TOP *Irvine Meet of Champions, 1977. (Photo by Bill Leung, Jr.)*

BOTTOM *Steve leads the pack in the 1977 Penn Relays.*

ABOVE
Meet of Champions, 1977, Irvine.

ABOVE
Steve (center) and UCI cross-country teammates, 1978.

LEFT
NCAA Indoor Championship, Detroit, Michigan, March 1977.

NCAA Indoor Championship, Detroit, Michigan, March 1977.

TOP
1978 AAU Championships.

ABOVE LEFT
College roommate Ed Ahlmeyer (left) and Steve in Arizona, 1978.

ABOVE RIGHT
Sweethearts Kim and Steve, UCI Banquet, 1978.

*1979 AAU 1500 meters. Steve third from right, settling into position
at the first lap— he will come from behind to win.*

ABOVE
First race with Sebastian Coe (in the lead), Oslo, 1979.

*1979, Kim and Steve's wedding portrait. Steve ran a 10,000 meter
cross-country race in Orange that morning.*

In L.A., I faced Eamonn Coghlan, who was undefeated and racing doubles almost every weekend, along with Filbert Bayi, Steve Lacy, and Thomas Wessinghage. For me, Sunkist was a home meet and I put pressure on myself. L.A. was one of the few places where people always rooted for me and I didn't want to disappoint them.

I was ready for Eamonn. That winter, I'd already broken Steve Prefontaine's U.S. indoor 3,000 record in 7:45.2. I'd run some 3,000s for variety and also for the added strength it gave my miles. In Tempe, Miller continued to feed me the strength training of a distance runner: I'd run a mile, three-quarter, 800 and 440, all at 63-second lap pace, then repeat the set. At Sunkist, after Lacy led at the three-quarter in 2:57.1, it remained for Eamonn and me to sprint for the win. Eamonn held me off, running 3:52.9 to just miss his world indoor record, while my 3:53.0 earned me my first American record.

The Brooks meet promoter, Ron Stanko, had promised Eamonn and me he'd have a Lear jet waiting in L.A. to whisk us to Houston. We'd agreed to compete in Stanko's meet on that basis. While the meet was Saturday evening, Stanko scheduled the mile—by itself—for the afternoon to get a $20,000 rights fee from CBS to telecast the race live. We needed to get a decent night's sleep before the event.

When we got to the L.A. airport after midnight, there was no private plane waiting for us and we were furious. Eamonn called Stanko and told him to shove it. But I was game for a race under any conditions and decided to try and make the trip. With few flights available and bad weather, by the time I got to Houston I barely had time for a shower and a quick nap before racetime.

Stanko was a good salesman and talked Coghlan into coming; when Eamonn did show up he ran halfheartedly and finished last. Needless to say, I was exhausted but had to face Don Paige, John

Walker, and Ray Flynn, all of whom were fresh. The made-for-TV event was a joke. It was held in the Astrodome, but since it was run as a solitary event apart from the meet there were no spectators to see it. We ran in the quiet of the huge arena, which had a five-laps-to-a-mile track. Times were fast but did not count in the record book because the oval was considered "oversized" for indoor purposes. But it got on TV and Stanko got his twenty grand. I got a victory in 3:54.2 as Paige ran second and Walker third.

When the circuit moved outdoors, I won my first three mile races leading up to the Olympic Trials in Eugene. The Trials meant nothing. The track landscape was dominated by the U.S. Olympic boycott, which now seemed virtually assured. It was a terrible time to be a runner. Not only were we denied the Olympic opportunity, but most of us could not speak out against the boycott. Washington did a masterful job of snowing the public and the media and it was considered un-American for athletes to question U.S. policy.

Most reporters and athletic officials characterized Olympians as one-dimensional jocks who should stick with their sport, mind their own business, and feel privileged to be athletes in the first place. As athletes, we'd been groomed to respect authority, compete blindly, and be optimistic. We were perfect pawns for President Carter's flawed policy against the USSR. It was sad to see how the United States continued to trade with the Soviets and provided them abundant grain from America's heartland while using athletes as leverage in a political dispute. We were considered expendable, we were not unified, and could be manipulated without public outcry.

I felt pummeled to the ground. I had trained my heart out at considerable sacrifice with the Olympics as my goal. Almost every TV interviewer who ever put a mike in my face would say something like, "So what are your plans for the Olympics?"

The boycott would take away the opportunity to improve my meager earnings. Companies that sponsored athletes—Nike, Adidas, or Sub–4—offered bonuses for making the Olympic team and winning a medal. An Olympic medal also elevated your appeal and fees on the European circuit afterward and gave you greater bargaining power with sponsors and meet promoters in the years to come.

But it was not the lost income that hurt the most. Only the Olympics brought the world's best runners together. I wanted the chance to find out what kind of runner I really was.

The irony of the athletes' plight was overwhelming. Track authorities from the AAU (at this time called The Athletics Congress) always tried to keep us in our place by using the Olympics as a weapon. Whenever athletes rumbled with rebellion over an issue such as restrictions on race payments, officials would hold the ultimate carrot over our heads: Olympic eligibility. If we didn't play ball, we could lose our "amateur" standing and be finished.

Track officials also pressured us into competing on U.S. national teams in dual meets against other countries. The bureaucrats made it seem as if patriotism was the issue, but it was really about power—about our rights as athletes to determine our own destiny. Oftentimes, these meets—U.S. vs. Britain or U.S. vs. Germany—disrupted our personal racing schedules and resulted in a loss of earnings and prestige. Pressure was greatest for the U.S.-Soviet meet, a Cold War creation held almost every year since 1958.

Now, as the Moscow Games loomed, the United States and Soviet Union were deadlocked and no race could settle the standoff. No Olympics for America? It was as if someone had canceled the World Series.

It would be some time before American athletes, at least in track and field, would rebel against our sport's "leadership." Unlike baseball, football, and basketball, which have developed strong players' unions, track has no such unity, and even today we are a fractured society beholden to penthouse authorities. For example, it's taken over a decade for prize money to be authorized for the World Track and Field Championships, while more than $100 million in TV revenue for the event has gone into the coffers of the sport's international governing body.

I wanted to speak out against the 1980 boycott but couldn't dare. I was still a newcomer to the international arena. I was only 24, two years out of college, and felt great pressure to toe the line. I received no guidance from track officials or the U.S. Olympic Committee and learned what I could of the issues from reading the papers.

I imagined a public lynching if I stepped out of the pack and took a bold stand. I also feared reprisals from the track authorities. So I kept my mouth shut or, when asked, played the game. I even lied. After one race, I told reporters, "I'm in favor of a boycott. But there's always the chance we'll still go. The whole thing is mentally trying, always that little seed of doubt."

It was a very confusing time. Conflicting signals were everywhere. There was incessant posturing. Every day, there was some new Administration plan to pat us on our heads for our sacrifice. Most of us lapped it up like puppies. Some athletes, veterans like Francie Larrieu Smith and Dwight Stones, courageously spoke out against the Carter boycott and were put down for it by the media, the public, and even by other athletes.

The only way to survive those months was to narrow your focus, push the boycott to the periphery of your consciousness, and run. I was naive enough to think that the Russians might retreat from Afghanistan, or the United States might come up with a real political solution, and we still could go to the Games.

In late May, The Athletics Congress stuck with its plan to hold the Olympic Marathon Trial in Buffalo, New York. This was done to show we could still go on with our important events as though everything were normal, and also because the marathoners, after all, had trained months for the race and needed to run it as a form of closure. Oddly, most of the marathon was run in Canada since a ready-made course was available from another marathon. The winner was a medical student, Tony Sandoval, who showed the strength and poise of a legitimate Olympic gold medal contender.

Bill Rodgers, winner of four New York City and four Boston Marathons, waged his own personal protest against the boycott and did not compete. Rodgers was at the peak of his powers and angry at his missed opportunity. His anti-boycott sentiment drew charges from some reporters and running fans that he was unpatriotic and out of his league. Instead, Bill should have been lauded by everyone for his courageous stand. We may have been mere athletes, unschooled in the fine art of international diplomacy, but we were smart enough to know we'd been taken. Out of expediency and political gain, President Carter had picked on the most helpless, powerless group of all: athletes. Some of us were not even old enough to vote. It became apparent soon enough that the situation was hopeless. The Senate and House supported the President's position. The U.S. Olympic Committee voted in favor of the boycott. The International Olympic Committee refused to move the Games from Moscow. The Soviets remained in Afghanistan and, amid the old Cold War strains, polls showed as many as 75 percent of Americans supported the boycott.

From then on, the media show focused on those nations joining the boycott and those who planned to snub the United States and go to Moscow; the transparent concept of an "alternative Olympics" for Americans and our supporters; and putting on the track and field Olympic Trials, which were being held to show that everything was still okay. There were also attempts to pacify the athletes by inviting a delegation to the White House to meet with the President and his aides.

The Olympic Trials were still being held in Eugene. As with the marathon in Buffalo, U.S. track and field needed to showcase its stars in the face of trauma and go through with the exercise of naming a 1980 "Olympic Team."

The Oregon track fans, the best anywhere, filled Hayward Field to honor us. They understood the conflicts we faced as athletes seeking peak performance without the fulfillment of promised rewards. It was a celebration tinged with sadness. Len Miller helped me take a pragmatic approach and keep the emotions of the boycott off the track. I was fit and rested and won my first Olympic Trial 1,500 in 3:35.15, a fast time on a windy day.

Since I was young and would have other Olympic opportunities, I felt even more pain for others, the veterans who'd pinned their last Olympic hopes on the 1980 season. People like 34-year-old Dick Buerkle, who made the team in the 5,000, and 36-year-old Greg Fredericks, who made it in the 10,000.

A Hollywood film crew showed up in Eugene that year to film scenes for the movie *Personal Best* starring Mariel Hemingway. Ironically, even as track athletes were being dismissed by the government, we were being placed in the Hollywood spotlight. America has never known quite what to do with us professional amateurs.

The biggest joke of all came two weeks after the Trials. The grand master plan for a "separate" Games was reduced to the Liberty Bell Classic in Philadelphia, a hastily arranged meet with athletes from 30 nations. The competition was weak and meaningless, but as a Trials winner I felt an obligation to be there. I'd already gone to Europe, winning the mile in Stockholm but running an awful seventh in the 1,500 at Oslo behind Steve Ovett, who tied Seb Coe's world-record of 3:32.1. Ovett had broken Coe's world mile record on the same track two weeks before with a 3:48.8. In Britain, Olympic authorities had been given the autonomy to make their own decision about the Games. They would go.

Coe and Ovett were going to Moscow.

I was going to Washington.

After the Oslo meet, I rushed home to win the 1,500 in Philadelphia, then joined other members of the 1980 "team" in a grandstanding public relations visit to the White House. The President presented all the Olympians with gold medals. We were entertained, treated to a Rose Garden picnic, and told how patriotic we were.

I don't know if I would have won a medal in Moscow. But it was the void—of missing out on the Olympic experience—that cost me later on. I would be back in the Olympic picture in 1984, but, without the feel for the grandeur and scope of the Games, I would come in cold.

The Moscow Olympics went on in mid-summer during our presidential visit. In the end, 72 nations, including Great Britain, Italy, France, and Spain, took part while 49 nations joined the United States (according to the Carter administration) in the boycott. The headline news centered on the Coe-Ovett showdown. Since NBC had canceled its coverage, I kept tabs on the races via radio reports, like someone in the forties listening hard for the latest War news.

The results were surprising. Coe, considered the better 800 man, took second behind Ovett in that event. Ovett, more esteemed in the 1,500 at the time, ran third as Coe won that race. Go figure.

Hoping to race them in the balance of the European season, I trained hard to be ready. I spent a week in Boston running 100 miles in seven days and two road races (a 5-miler and a 10K) on successive days. At one point that season, I even ventured into a half-marathon. I had heard that Ovett had run one in 64 minutes, so I thought I'd try it. I managed to run 63 and a half minutes. That's not exactly the way to sharpen up for the mile, but I always had feelings of immortality when it came to my running.

Now in August, my schedule called for 1,500s or miles, in Zurich, Nice, Brussels, London, Dublin, and Rieti, Italy. I would run six races in 19 days and was glad to have Kim along with me. Kim never got caught up in the meets themselves, but she'd go sight-seeing, come to the stadium to see me race, and jog with me when I worked out at the practice track. When I became preoccupied with my events, Kim spent time with other track wives like John Walker's wife, Helen.

Kim was uncomfortable seeing the transient nature of a track athlete's life. The way athletes mixed socially to wile away the hours and lend one another support made her suspect that I'd find myself in compromising situations. When I traveled while Kim was at home, I surrounded myself with track buddies, women included, an alliance that would become a divisive issue in our marriage.

Despite the camaraderie, it was easy to feel vulnerable in the clutches of European meet promoters. Many of the meets on the Continent were controlled by Britain's Andy Norman, for years one of the sport's most powerful figures. Norman was an agent hired to line up fields and negotiate athletes' fees for meets; since he also represented individual athletes like Ovett, he was criticized for having conflicts of interest.

Usually, he treated me well. But there were times when I knew that Ovett was getting something in the neighborhood of $10,000 to run while I was getting $2,000, even though the two of us had almost the same marquee value. One year, at a meet in Paris that

Norman managed, rumor circulated that the meet hadn't brought in enough money and some of the athletes wouldn't be paid. Andy's gofer overheard a bunch of us plotting to confront Andy if we didn't get our due. Later, Andy came storming into my room, threw the cash on the bed, and told me I'd never run in Europe again. I wasn't worried because by then I was familiar with Norman's bluster and, as nearly the number-one miler in the world, I had some leverage of my own.

But in Zurich, in the post-Olympic summer of 1980, Coe was the golden boy and it was written all over him. I was told that after his 800 defeat in Moscow, Coe was publicly berated by his father, Peter, who coached him. To me, it seemed unhealthy for a world-class runner to have his father as coach. In that kind of relationship, feelings of love and power could be tangled.

Considering the way Len gave me my space on the circuit, I wondered how Peter Coe appeared to dictate Seb's every move. Details of Seb's workouts made their way through the track grapevine, intimidating some of Seb's competitors. The workouts, truth or exaggeration, were beyond what any other miler had done, and I noticed some of the runners whispering about them in awe.

With the Games over, Coe and Ovett went their separate ways in pursuit of world records. In Zurich, I ran the 1,500 in 3:33.33, my fastest to date, but all it got me was a distant second behind Coe, who just missed the world mark. I wanted to compete in Lausanne two days later, but Ovett called the shots in Europe and didn't want any serious competition in his attempt at the 1,500 world mark. He won, but did not threaten the record.

Coe and Ovett had a perfect chance to elevate track with head-to-head running following the Games. But as gold medalists, they were desperate to preserve their standing in England, where track is a major sport. Star athletes are treated at once like royalty and garbage by the uniquely fickle and consuming British press. The media built up champions to the point of hero worship, only to revel in bashing them down. Many journalists followed the athletes tabloid-style, seeking any morsel of information, any speck of dirt, that could win the day's headlines.

Ovett feared Coe more than Coe feared him. Ovett lacked confidence. He could be in world record shape and still back away from Coe. I ran in Nice, winning the mile, then faced Ovett in Brussels and London. He beat me decisively both times. What could I say? He beat everybody in five straight victories after the Olympics. Everyone but Coe, who ended his season early, claiming a bad back.

Ovett's three-meet tear, from Brussels to London to Koblenz, culminated in a world 1,500 record of 3:31.36 for Ovett, with two others—Germans Thomas Wessinghage and Harald Hudak—also under the old record. Before 44,000 fans in Brussels, I tied with John Walker for second in the mile in 3:52.7 as Ovett triumphed in 3:51.6. The field was ridiculously large with 18 men. Walker got knocked around, losing ground at the start. At London, in a race dubbed the Golden Mile, I got closer to Ovett, running 3:52.92 to Ovett's 3:52.84.

After the race, Ovett did not show for interviews—even though it was his own country. He had done this before and gotten away with it. Ironically, as hungry as the British press was for access to Ovett, they seemed to accept his disappearance without a fuss. That irked me. I also didn't care for Ovett's showboating as he crossed the finish and waved to the crowd. Who did he think he was—a sprinter?

My London performance showed I was literally on Ovett's heels and that I might finally nail him in Koblenz. But I would not have that chance. Andy Norman saw to that. First, he made sure the Koblenz budget left a mere pittance for me. And since he handled the meet in Dublin, he offered me a decent sum, $3,000, to race there on the same night.

I took the money and won, returning home to Arizona with cash in my pocket. Soon our lives changed dramatically when Kim found out our first child was on the way. Track life is not made for young families and in the next few years, while my running flourished, my personal life began to unravel.

CHAPTER FIVE

Record Racing in Europe: 1981 and 1982

B eing a miler is a selfish existence. You think only about yourself. You sacrifice normal life. You will do anything to fulfill your potential in track and field, a sport that at its heart seems less and less in sync with American culture.

In the early 1980s, track began to lose its cachet on the United States sports landscape. The vacuum created by the 1980 Olympic boycott certainly contributed to this. But while other sports like football, basketball, and tennis captivated the public with whiz-bang, in-your-face marketing, complacent track officials did not catch on. Few corporate sponsors came our way, and track lost some of its audience.

People no longer had the patience for track's deliberate pace. Meets went on for hours, there was plenty of dead time between events, and distance races produced few heroes. Even the mile seemed to ask too much of viewers' shrinking attention spans.

American sports fans were bombarded with thrill-a-minute events like the souped-up "Final Four" college basketball tournament. The more sports became pure entertainment and were worshiped for the big money and big stars, the more track, never packaged very effectively, suffered.

But you persevere. You are a miler, not a quarterback or a point guard. Your specialty is running four laps around the track, fundamentally a rather amateur endeavor. Everything you know is compressed into four minutes—hopefully a little less—that leave you empty of all resources and, preferably, a little happy. Your happiness is based on these four minutes. You can't screw up.

After my lost Olympic opportunity in 1980, I set my long-range sights on the 1984 Olympics and my more immediate goals on running faster, breaking records, and becoming the best miler in the world. I wanted nothing more than to race Sebastian Coe and Steve Ovett at my best. But I felt I would need another year of grooming and, when the time came, just the right setting—like the Bislett Games in Oslo, which always drew a handpicked field and worldwide TV for what was considered the most prestigious meet on the European circuit.

My hopes and dreams were based mainly on what would take place during a few short weeks in Europe at the height of the summer's international track season. I had to think like a European, live like a European. The big races were on their turf: Stockholm, Lausanne, Zurich, Brussels, and, of course, Oslo.

There was no place like Oslo. No matter where I was, I could close my eyes and inhale the intoxicating aroma of the Scandinavian summer. I could envision the humble track at Bislett Stadium, its pristine air, the midnight twilight, the rhythmic chant of the Norwegians to run, run, run. At that time, running on that track mattered to me more than anything else in the world.

At the end of 1980, as I looked ahead, I gauged that with greater athletic maturity I would start to reach my peak in 1982. I imagined my best-in-the-world chances would come that summer in Oslo, which had two meets within a week and a half—the

Oslo Games in addition to the more famous Bislett Games, both held at Bislett Stadium. Almost ten years of running would give me the instincts to seize this fleeting opportunity for exultation and make it mine.

However, in December of 1980, my miler's singleminded existence was hit with a surprise when Kim found out she was pregnant. We felt blessed to be having our first child, but it would mean a new kind of life for Kim and me—a life with long periods of separation. While I traveled the world competing, Kim would have to remain home most of the time caring for our child.

I didn't know a single miler competing in Europe who traveled with a child in tow. When Kim and I got married, I assumed we would share in the vagabond lifestyle of the track circuit. I needed Kim for support and had seen how other athletes' wives joined them. But even at the outset, track life was a stretch for Kim. Her frame of reference for a happy marriage was her parents, who worked standard hours, stayed home, and were rarely apart. Still, Kim wanted to share in my experiences. Suddenly, with a child on the way, our future plans were in jeopardy.

In 1981, armed with the speed of a sprinter and the strength of a distance runner—both qualities fused to my system like DNA— I began my climb to the top, itching to let loose. While setting American indoor records that winter in the mile (3:51.8) and 2,000 meters (4:58.6) and winning most of my races in the United States that spring, I began taking Lamaze classes with Kim in preparation for helping with the delivery of our newborn, due in August.

The classes gave me a warm and excited feeling as I listened to the stirring of the fetus and anticipated helping in the delivery. But I must admit my thoughts drifted to Europe, where that summer I would run 14 races. I worried whether Kim's delivery would affect my racing schedule.

The European season had two distinct groupings of events. The first series of meets ran from late June through late July. Then there was a gap of a couple of weeks before resumption of major competition in mid-August, which was exactly when the baby was due.

It was too hot to train in Arizona in the summer, so in June we went back to our hometown of Upland, California, to stay with Kim's parents. When I left for Europe, Kim was in good hands, but I fretted over how the birth would play out with the heart of my season coming up.

In July, I ran 3:49.68 to set an American record for the mile and become the first American under 3:50. I was less than a second off Steve Ovett's world record. I could taste even greater success.

As Kim closed in on her ninth month, I kept tabs on her progress from Europe. It was very hot in Upland that summer, and Kim was especially uncomfortable because her parents didn't have an air conditioner. In mid-July, I left Dublin to return home to California, brush up on my Lamaze lessons, and be at Kim's side during her final weeks of pregnancy.

I was consumed by the coming of my next race, a mile in Zurich on August 19. Zurich was just a notch below Oslo in importance and I had to be there. My performance would almost certainly affect my world ranking for the year.

With my career poised to take off, Kim and I had agreed, with the doctor's approval, that labor would be induced if she was not yet ready to deliver by the time I had to leave for Zurich. The doctor was sympathetic to my plight. We were all in harmony on the plan.

Sure enough, that's what transpired.

The birth was a natural delivery in the Alternative Birthing Unit of Upland's San Antonio Community Hospital, the same hospital where I was born. Labor was induced on August 14, and it was a difficult labor, lasting 18 hours. The baby was not positioned properly, and because of the delicate nature of the delivery I was not allowed to assist. It was a painful ordeal for Kim, and I stood by to help her maintain the required breathing rhythm. At times, I was overwhelmed with emotion and walked outside the hospital room to ask God for everything to be all right.

Finally, on August 15, our son, Corey, was born. Thankfully, everything was fine. I cut the umbilical cord and helped with the afterbirth. With the situation under control, my emotions quickly turned to Europe, where I had to run, earn a living, and make my mark.

Kim showed amazing strength. An hour after Corey was born, she was up and around saying, "I can do that again."

On August 17, two days later, I hopped a plane to Europe. I staggered into Zurich on the 18th, and the next night placed a paltry eighth as Sebastian Coe triumphed about half a track ahead of me. It was the only race all year in which I was not even a contender for victory.

In Upland, Kim wasn't faring much better. Corey was colicky and only content when nursing. He wouldn't take a bottle. If Corey wasn't sleeping, he was either crying or nursing. Kim didn't get much reprieve.

With six more races in 13 days, neither did I. But I was able to regroup and come away with two more American records— a 3:31.96 1,500 meters in Koblenz, Germany, and a 7:36.69 3,000 meters in Ingleheim, Germany. All told, I lost three times to Coe and twice to Ovett. But my 1,500 at Koblenz was just six-tenths-of-a-second off Ovett's world record. I was coming. Next year would be different—I'd be ready.

With my growing family far away, in Europe I grew close to other milers like John Walker, my mentor from New Zealand, and

Ray Flynn of Ireland. When I boasted to some of the guys that I had been with Kim in the delivery room, they didn't believe it. This practice apparently was unheard of in their countries.

I felt closer to my family than ever before, but having to be away so much was putting a strain on my marriage. We had a new baby to care for, and much of the time I couldn't be there. Kim began to resent my "separate" track life and even to be concerned about the fact that there were a number of women in our runner's fraternity. All I could do was reassure her that nothing was going on, and it wasn't.

Meanwhile, I was almost giddy with my running prowess. When I returned home in early September, the fourth-ranked miler in the world, I plunged right back into distance work.

Just when Kim really needed me as a full-time husband and father, my track career vied for my attention. I had to train or I would never keep up. Build, build, build. Coe and Ovett (ranked number one and two) were building; I was building. Few American milers ran cross-country or road races. I did. I felt that distance events of 5,000 and 10,000 meters gave me added strength. I ran five 10,000s in succession, improving my best time to 28:28, and showed at one 10K in San Diego in December that I could hold up even when I felt as if my head would explode.

My favorite Polynesian restaurant in San Diego County served a sumptuous dish, "Chicken of the Gods," which I hungered for. As an athlete, I had two states of mind: uncompromising devotion to excellence on the track, and a childlike, risk-taking, disdainful, live-for-the-moment attitude off the track. Somehow the two went together.

At dinner the night before the 10K, I got drunk on mai tais and beer and afterward could not hold down the Chicken of the Gods. It was one fine mess that lasted till 3 o'clock in the morning. The race was at 8 A.M., and I was in no condition to run, but somehow I managed to win. This showed me I was bulletproof. No one could touch me. It seemed it would last forever.

Finally, I was beginning to think I could be the miler that my coach Len Miller had predicted.

———————

Len continued training me on the track at Arizona State with boot-camp tenacity. I welcomed his rigorous workouts. The harder, the better. I would run through brick walls to become the best miler I could.

We were now living in Scottsdale, 15 miles from Tempe, having bought a bigger house in a better neighborhood. I went for long solo runs in the open desert on the nearby Pima Indian reservation. I trained under a sun that baked me redder than I already was.

The body had to be punished to strengthen and I accepted that. I also knew that while being whipped into a higher level of fitness I would find that precious moment of passage from struggle to conquest and feel great.

Milers typically trained on the track with repeated fast one-lap runs, covering 400 meters each. Two factors were critical in measuring the success of the workout. The speed of each run, of course, but also the amount of rest time taken between each run. This respite was called the "interval." That's why speed training is oftentimes referred to as "interval work."

The shorter the interval time, the harder the workout. Less rest made each succeeding run that much more difficult. Between each hard run, it was important for your pounding heart to ease back closer to a resting state. Most milers needed about two minutes' rest between fast 400-meter laps to sustain a workout like this. Len gave me one minute and asked me to run the laps in 58 to 59 seconds. My training usually was more stressful than the actual racing. But that was the point: Punish the body now and in competition you'll feel like you can fly.

To handle 20 fast laps with only 60-second rest periods, I had to come up with mental strategies. In my mind, I would break up the 20 laps into four segments of five sets. Anticipating a set of five hard runs was manageable; 20 was too much to bear at once.

After several runs, I'd fall into a rhythm, and it was uncanny to see how I'd hit my precise time goal, down to the tenth of a second, on every lap. If I ever strayed and ran, say, a 60.8 instead of 59.8, Len would say evenly, "C'mon, now, you have to dig down. . . ."

Len didn't have to holler or gesticulate. At this point in my career, I needed little convincing, especially when Len would call out, "Coe's on your shoulder, pick it up."

By the 15th or 16th lap, I was already thinking of the last run, salivating at how strong I felt and the anticipation of blasting number twenty to show I could run with anyone. I would see myself in Oslo leading Coe and Ovett and bursting with power and joy. And I would run my twentieth 400 in 52 seconds—the kind of speed necessary to triumph in Europe.

As 1982 began, instead of running a full indoor season during the U.S. winter season, I went to Australia and New Zealand for a month-long training-and-racing tour of six cities: Adelaide, Melbourne, Sydney, Christchurch, Hamilton, and Auckland. Down Under, it was summer, and the ideal running conditions were a magnet for European runners anxious to escape their dreary winters. A few other Americans also came down.

Kim and Corey, now five months old, came with me, and we recruited Kim's mom, Nancy, to join us and help with child care. We schlepped an entire nursery of baby paraphernalia onto the plane.

Down Under, I hung out with John Walker, by now my closest friend on the track circuit. It was Walker who'd urged me to make the trip. He'd organized the race series and recruited the athletes. He proselytized on the benefits of running in this remote corner of the earth that had bred some of the world's greatest milers. An entire gospel had been spun around Olympic champions like Herb Elliot (Australia) and Peter Snell (New Zealand) and coaches like Percy Cerutty (Australia) and Arthur Lydiard (New Zealand). John said running Down Under offered an excellent foundation for success in Europe. Who was I to say no?

I enjoyed my time in Australia and New Zealand and found the two nations similar to the America of the 1950s. Life was simple and unpretentious. People were friendly and did not lock their cars. There was an endearing pioneering spirit and a belief that hard work paid off. As visitors, we had time to enjoy the countryside, and one day I threw caution to the wind and went jet-boating on a fast, shallow river in Christchurch.

You'd never find Coe or Ovett doing something so rash as jet-boating. Coe was a dilettante who rarely associated with the other athletes. Ovett was more one of the boys, but he was also a momma's boy. From what I'd heard, Ovett, who lacked confidence, called his mum for sustenance from the track circuit. At least when I cried to my mother, I was still in college.

To be sure, Coe and Ovett had to be more circumspect than I. The British press covered their every move. In the United States, no one much cared what I did. I could go jet-boating, even break my leg, and only a handful of track nuts would give a damn.

In Australia and New Zealand, track enjoyed a comfortable happy medium. There was a cultural imperative to produce great runners—to gain strength from the land and do something with it. In New Zealand, Walker was a national hero, but unlike Coe and Ovett, he was given the space to stray from convention and not have to pay for it. Every Kiwi kid in an athletics club wanted to be John Walker, a track and field star. Walker was like Mickey Mantle. The Golden Boy.

With Coe and Ovett in my thoughts, I tagged along with Walker, who taught me a lot about the mile and how to race under pressure. Walker liked to race a lot, and we shared that passion. The two of us were sometimes criticized in the media for our frequent racing, but we did what we loved.

Still, there were risks. Walker told me that milers who raced often in Europe did not get enough rest and their performances suffered. With as many as six or seven races scheduled during a two-week span, Walker said it was essential for milers not to train hard between races but instead to merely jog. Walker also introduced me to the idea of doing long training runs, like a marathon runner, to rebuild strength after the summer season. On a fall Sunday, I'd run for two hours, covering close to 20 miles.

Walker had inherited these concepts from his predecessors. He'd set the world record in 1975, the year before winning his Olympic 1,500 title. That was the kind of sustained peak I hoped to reach in the period leading up to the next Olympics in Los Angeles.

The inspiring landscape Down Under put my early 1982 season in perfect pitch. I won five races: three 1-miles, a 1,500 meters, and a 2-mile. I ran easily and my times were good. In four of the meets, Walker ran a close second. My only loss came at 1,000 meters, short for me.

———————————

Though fatigued when I returned to the United States that February, I carried my strength into the Millrose Games at New York's Madison Square Garden. I'd never won the Wanamaker Mile, the featured Millrose event and the biggest American cup race of all.

I am not a natural indoor runner; my erect running style is incompatible with the tight, banked turns. Whereas someone like Eamonn Coghlan, the world indoor recordholder, ran low and hugged the bends, I bounced around with considerable slippage. An indoor race for me was like a workout in which you sprinted the straightaways and jogged the turns. But with Coghlan injured and not competing, I felt I had a chance to win my first Wanamaker Mile.

At some indoor races, I would feel pressure and tighten up, worsening my vulnerability on the boards. But this time at Millrose, the 75th running, I was loose. Not having to worry about Eamonn helped. Even when I could deliver an auspicious indoor showing, it seemed Eamonn was always a step ahead. The previous year, when I'd set the American indoor record of 3:51.8 (which still stood going into 1998), it was a second-place run behind Eamonn's world record, 3:50.6.

Now at Millrose, my challenge would come from Tom Byers, one of the flakiest athletes in track. He could go out at a desperate pace and die, or he could go out at a desperate pace and win. You never knew what Tom would pull. At the previous year's Bislett Games in Oslo, Byers was the designated rabbit in the 1,500. As assigned, Byers set a swift pace; then, instead of dropping back, he shockingly maintained his lead to steal the victory.

Byers had long hair and cobalt eyes, looked like a rock star, and tried to present himself as Johnny Cool. But inside, he raged, and it didn't take much to set him off. In a period of a couple of years, Tom had moved about five times to find the right running terrain, right coach, right weather, right zen.

One time in Phoenix we agreed to play golf together. When I called Tom to check on our date, his wife told me he hadn't slept all night and had gone out at 6 A.M. to hit balls for two hours at a driving range.

By the time we started our game, Tom was a mess. He kept saying how he hit beautifully at the driving range, but now nothing was going right for him. After one especially poor shot, he got so frustrated he took his driver—he'd just purchased a new set of clubs—and threw it into the lake. He raced the same way: uptight and out of control, his own worst enemy.

Though I could criticize Byers the miler for his lack of discipline, off the track it was easy to be friends, especially since I knew I was the superior runner. I found it more comfortable to pal around with the guys I could beat. That's why Eamonn Coghlan and I had a schizophrenic relationship. During the winter, when he ruled the indoor circuit, I kept my distance, fearful of letting my guard down. In the summer, when I prevailed on the outdoor tracks, I would often invite him out for a beer.

I could always be that at ease with Byers. But, while he was unpredictable, Byers was an 800 runner as well as a miler, and he had an explosive sprint-kick as a final surge in a race. At Millrose, I had to make sure he could not use it as a weapon against me. My kick, especially indoors, was more gradual. The Wanamaker Mile was the one indoor race above all I wanted to win. Its status as the pearl of the winter season was well deserved. The meet director, Howard Schmertz, was rare for the breed: a decent, honest man athletes could trust.

The Wanamaker Mile always started at 10 P.M. sharp with the Garden lights dimmed and dramatic introductions of the field. I received a healthy, respectful cheer from the New York crowd, 18,000 strong, but as the race got under way the pace was uncharacteristically slow and the fans booed their disapproval. I responded by taking the lead to keep the pace honest, but the first two split times were still slow: 61.4 for the quarter and 2:00.7 for the half.

Byers hung on my shoulder. I picked up the pace some more but at three-quarters the time was 2:59.3, still modest. It would come down to a kick over the last quarter, less than three laps. On the backstretch of the last lap, Byers made a bid to pass me, but I held him off to win in 3:55.37, the world's fastest indoor time to date that season. Only inches behind, Byers ran 3:55.41, his best ever, while John Walker ran a close third in 3:55.62.

That winter, track took a big stride forward as a burgeoning professional sport with prize-money payments to athletes via a new indoor Grand Prix circuit in the United States and Canada sponsored by Mobil. The precedent eventually led to a more lucrative Mobil outdoor Grand Prix—held in conjunction with the International Amateur Athletic Federation, track's world governing organization—and helped fully professionalize the sport.

With my limited indoor season, I was not collecting too many dividends that winter. When the offer came to return to Auckland in April for a bizarre downhill road mile, I bit. I received only a few thousand dollars to take part, but the freaky nature of the event appealed to my playful sensibility. A downhill mile! How ridiculous. Where do I sign up?

John Walker was in on the plans, of course. Though a rancher with a laid-back persona, Walker was an enterprising man with excellent marketing sense. He'd run the inaugural Fifth Avenue Mile in New York in the fall of 1980 (a Fred Lebow creation won by Sydney Maree in a "world record" 3:47.52) and felt a Queens Street Mile, downhill in downtown Auckland, could be a big hit.

So in April, between the indoor and outdoor seasons, I found myself back in New Zealand; frankly, it was not the smartest detour for me. While Coe and Ovett were methodically building their prowess for the track, I was making another exhausting trip to run a meaningless race that had injury written all over it. Downhill racing was murder on your legs and back. If you walked such a course, you'd have to lean backwards to stop yourself from falling. But I was game—I wanted to enjoy track on my own terms.

It looked as if all of Auckland had turned out for the event. There were New Zealanders on rooftops, balconies, and lining the streets so tightly that we had to run single file, like cyclists slicing the cordon of fans on mountain peaks in the Tour de France. World-class milers typically ran the first quarter-mile in about 58 seconds, but this route was so steep we did it in 42 seconds.

We weren't milers, we were boulders pushed down a mountain. We hit the half in 1:40. With the adventurous spirit in New Zealand, the hard-drinking crowds ate up the daredevil nature of the race. Amid the Mardi Gras atmosphere, the course finally flattened out into a commercial district near the bay, we came flying to the finish, and I won in 3:31. I was just relieved that my body was still intact.

Everybody in New Zealand called it a world record. The media had a lot of fun with it, but when Steve Ovett heard about it he didn't pick up on the lighthearted humor. He said, "Well, I could probably do that, too, jumping off the cliffs of Dover." Funny guy, that Ovett.

With my advanced survival skills, I took a break from competition and went off with Walker to hunt, fish, and train. New Zealand is noted for its trout fishing and John set up an excursion to Solitaire Lodge. He even hired a chef to prepare native dishes. When we were out on the lake catching seven-pound trout, a million miles from everywhere, the mile seemed irrelevant.

There were several runners in our party and most everyone hated training with me. I ran too hard: I'd go and routinely belt out 10 miles in 55 minutes. That's how I got strong. I ran 90 or more miles a week—hard. I ran hills, fast repetitions on the track, long runs, short runs with abrupt pace changes. Hard training, downhill miles, heavy travel. Just pile it on, I could take it. I hated the idea of being treated like a prima donna. Let Coe and Ovett swim in that pool.

Back in the States in mid-April with Oslo three months away, I continued my all-out running with Len in Arizona and competed without tapering off before races. Though fatigued, I did not question Len. I knew his system was working. I won all four of my mile and 1,500 races comfortably—at the Bruce Jenner meet in San Jose, the Pepsi Invitational at UCLA, Kinney Classic in Berkeley, and the U.S. Nationals in Knoxville.

I could do no wrong. At Jenner, I ran my last 200 like a sprinter in 23 seconds to defeat Ray Flynn. At Pepsi, I ran my last 400 like a sprinter in 52 seconds to defeat Don Paige and Jim Spivey in 3:52.68. At Kinney, I ran 3:54.1 to defeat Walker and Flynn.

Because of all the travel and nonstop training, I was tired. But once the race got under way, it seemed the fatigue left me like some exorcised demon and I could pump out a roaring last lap. "God, I'm flying," I'd tell myself in disbelief.

Each string of successes reinforced my feeling of invincibility and at practice I nearly levitated with joy. I couldn't wait to get up in the morning and run. I couldn't wait to go to the track in the evening for speed. I allowed nothing to disrupt my focus. When Corey, now nine months old, got up in the middle of the night, I slept while Kim tended to him. When I came home from training at night, Kim was already collapsed and sleeping. As I said, being a miler was a selfish existence.

As summer approached and the Oslo races neared, the track world's heart skipped a beat: Coe and Ovett agreed to duel in a three-race series: a 3,000 in London, 800 in Nice, and climactic mile in Eugene, Oregon, in late September. I could join them in London and Nice, but I was not invited to compete in Eugene for the mile. The reason was obvious: I could spoil the show.

Frankly, this was track at its worst. Late September was far too late for a big mile. Athletes accustomed to peaking six weeks earlier were tired and burnt out by then. Agents, starting to become influential in the sport, got their hands on this one. The International Management Group handled Coe; Andy Norman, the bullying European agent, handled Ovett. I told the media the series would backfire and the mile, in particular, would be an embarrassment. I felt neither Coe nor Ovett, despite the thunderous publicity, would win. An American would.

A better strategy, especially on American soil, would have designed the mile as a U.S./Britain showdown: Don Paige, Sydney Maree and me vs. Coe and Ovett. Throw in Tom Byers, the neurotic matinee idol, just for spice. Run earlier in the season. That would have been something. But the people with money and power who were massaging Coe and Ovett had convoluted self-interests to satisfy.

My final tuneup race for the European season was the 1,500 at the U.S. Nationals in Knoxville. I was a three-time American titlist, but Sydney Maree, the South African in the process of becoming an American citizen, had beaten me the previous year. I was still training hard without letup. The way my season had been going, I felt confident of winning but wanted a brisk time as a going-away boost. My first European race would be six days with the first of the two Oslo meets—the Bislett Games.

I tailed the frontrunner, Mark Fricker, who covered the first three laps in 58.3, 1:56.2, and 2:54.4: a good pace. I took over and raced home clear of Maree and the rest of the field in 3:34.92, a meet record and the equivalent of a 3:52 mile. It felt easy, too, maybe an 80 percent effort. I was ready for Oslo.

Around this time, the grand Coe and Ovett scheme and their six-figure deal began to fall apart. It seemed Coe was injured and Ovett was . . . what? The series was eventually canceled and I would face neither man at Oslo, where the mile was billed for the first time as "The Dream Mile."

Ovett did compete in Oslo, but he ran the 3,000 instead of the mile and placed second. He claimed he bypassed the mile because his leg was "sore." In my opinion, Ovett had a winning streak to protect in the 1,500 and mile and simply would not face me. My 3:34 in the U.S. Nationals scared him. I should not have been surprised by Ovett's event switch. He had pulled the same thing on me the previous year in Koblenz, Germany. I was supposed to race Ovett in the 1,500, but he had the meet director set up a mile for him against second-string opposition. I won my race and Ovett, following his personal rabbit, won his.

What did surprise me about Ovett was how insecure he was. In the hotel before a meet, you'd hear him say, "I'm so tired, I don't think I have it in me. . . ." For some athletes, those sentiments were a ruse. For Ovett, they were real—and he was the world record-holder!

Ovett's excuses would go unchallenged by the British press, who did not want to risk being on Andy Norman's bad side. Years later, when one journalist, the highly respected Cliff Temple of the *Sunday Times* of London, criticized Norman for conflict of interest, Norman (according to the British press) allegedly spread rumors that Temple had been sexually involved with one of the female athletes he advised. After Temple committed suicide in 1994, his friends, including many in the media, said the untrue accusations contributed to Temple's death.

In 1982, I got $2,500 to run the Bislett Games in Oslo. My manager at the time was Joe Douglas of the Santa Monica Track Club. Though I was not a Santa Monica member, Joe did me the favor of arranging my fees and picking up my money after the races. He wouldn't even take a cut. Later, when Carl Lewis emerged as track's leading figure and joined Santa Monica, Douglas was to become one of the sport's most powerful agents.

But in earlier years Douglas was a doormat for European meet promoters, who made him beg to get journeymen runners into their meets. I saw what Joe had to go through on behalf of his athletes. One time, when a leading meet promoter refused to pay me the money he owed me and fell into a drunken stupor, Joe barged into his hotel room in the middle of the night and demanded the fee. He got it, too.

With Lewis subsequently joined to Joe's hip, it was payback time and Joe would revel in it. For all the criticism they've taken for demanding high fees, Lewis and Douglas were responsible for elevating the pay scale of elite track and field athletes and helping to professionalize the sport.

Athletes new to the sport today may not realize that before the Carl Lewis era, the agent game was still a mom-and-pop operation. At times, I even had to get a fellow athlete like John Walker, who knew everyone and had leverage, to help me convince a promoter to give me a few bucks.

Bislett Stadium in Oslo was an intimate arena with the feel of a high school track. It was noted for its 48 world records, mostly in the distance events. Bislett held almost 7,000 people, plus a few thousand standees, and every one of them knew the skinny on each athlete, especially those in the mile.

Conditions were perfect: I thought of it as the warm-and-fuzzy. Typical for Europe, the mile would go off near midnight, when it was medium-cool with a whispery breeze. I could take a deep breath and, like energy harnessed from a dam, oxygen-rich air from the nearby forest would fill my lungs.

We were staying in spartan quarters on a lake. Outside my window, there were smooth dirt running paths and access to forest trails. It was pure and serene and glorious, and a perfect environment for running. I didn't mind the cafeteria-style meals. And I certainly didn't mind the stunning blond Norwegian women who sunbathed topless in the parks. On the eve of the meet, the promoter, Svein Arne Hansen, held his annual strawberry party with champagne, Scandinavian delicacies, strawberries the size of lemons, and many of those same stunning blond women from the park parading around in little else but their tan lines.

If you can't run your best in Oslo, you need to find another sport.

I lined up for the mile in a state of utter tranquillity. I surveyed the field and felt I could win. Fast times were never my primary motivation; winning was. Maree and Walker were running. So was Ray Flynn, my roommate in Oslo, and Briton Dave Moorcroft, a 5,000-meter runner so hot he was considered a threat in the mile.

There were 15 men in the field. The track was small with only six lanes and when the gun sounded we had to funnel from a crowded start for position. I always ran most comfortably sitting back where I could pace myself, see everyone, and calculate the best expenditure of my kick. Because I am not a physical athlete, I feel encumbered if there are too many arms and legs violating my turf. If there are two runners blocking my path, I prefer going around them rather than through them.

After the rabbits led us through a fast opening quarter in 55.6 and a fast half-mile in 1:52.4, the pack was still in close formation. Every time I tried to move up I was bumped or cut off. On the third lap, I was unnerved when Flynn was shoved and his leg darted into my left thigh. But nothing could deter me this night. At the sound of the bell signaling the last lap, I held second behind Maree, ready to take him. With 200 meters to go, there were still six men in contention.

In the crowded stadium, we were urged on by fans who leaned from the front-row seats over the guardrail and pounded the tinny advertising signs lining the fence. This sound, traditional Norwegian pace music during a Bislett Games distance race, accompanied our every stride. The ringing, a plea of faith and devotion, helped you to run faster. You had to.

I waited until the last turn to make my move. I came wide around Maree and cut him down on the home straight. But he wouldn't let go. I could see his shadow down the track as I triumphed by a stride in 3:48.53, to better my American record by a more than a second. Maree's time was 3:48.85; only Coe (3:47.33) and Ovett (3:48.40) had run faster. Moorcroft and Walker also broke 3:50 with Flynn just shy. It was the deepest mile ever.

One down, one to go. Leaving the stadium at 1 A.M., in the dreamy half-light of the Norwegian summer, I jogged with Walker and Flynn the four miles back to our quarters. In eleven days, I'd return to Bislett for the second meet, the Oslo Games.

The Oslo crowd loved my race but not with the full force of their passion. They had been spoiled by world records, and we didn't produce one. It was disappointing to see track fans of this caliber hung up on time. Was a searing, competitive race no longer enough?

I must admit, though, I was bitten by the possibilities myself. "You can break the world record in the mile," Walker had told me. Now, with American records to my credit in both the 1,500 and mile, I wanted the world record. It was time. I wanted the recognition I felt I deserved. Plus, it was getting hard to take the continuing slights of the Coe and Ovett public relations machines. There had been sparse television coverage of my mile victory in the States. . . . After all, neither Coe nor Ovett was running.

Coe-and-Ovett continued to enthrall the British press, which exploited the class differences between the two men. It was Charles-and-Di, good cop-bad cop, the monarchy against the ruffians. Coe—charming, handsome, educated, and articulate—was like the royal family; Ovett was a commoner. Coe rarely ate or slept in the same place with the other athletes. He stayed in finer hotels and dined with the meet promoter or sponsor. Ovett mixed with the "regular folk" but was sullen and said little.

———————

The Brits' obsession with class seemed to extend to the Kenyan runners, who were becoming more dominant by the week in distance events the world over. I detected a subtle condescension toward Kenya, formerly a British colony. White rule and jungle stereotypes seemed to die hard in the minds of many.

Ironically, Kenyan runners were subject to the worst abuse from their own people. Every country had a regulatory track and field federation that ruled the sport and fell under the umbrella of the international body, the IAAF. As athletes' assertiveness grew, conflicts with the federations were common.

Now, at the 1982 Bislett meet, a dispute between Kenyan runners and their federation escalated until the Norwegian officials capitulated to the authorities and did not allow the Kenyans to compete. Kenyan officials, whose corruption would eventually be disclosed, claimed they wanted Kenyan runners representing Kenya at a meet involving African athletes that same weekend in North Carolina.

That in itself was an infringement on athletes' rights: Athletes should be able to choose where they want to compete. In truth, however, Kenyan track officials, seeing their athletes partake of Western prize money, flexed their muscles as punishment against their own stars who now refused to give them a piece of the action.

One Kenyan dissident in Oslo was Mike Boit, a middle-distance runner and 1972 Olympic bronze medalist in the 800. The "Dream Mile" was delayed when, despite orders to the contrary, he took the starting line. Although the Norwegian meet official stripped Boit of his race number, he ran anyway and finished in the pack, but his performance was never recorded. We runners owed Boit a lot for his bold stand and for refusing to bend.

At the time, American runners also were fighting hard for financial freedom. Even though The Athletics Congress, track's obstinate ruling body, feared our potential power, there were times when I felt captive under TAC's bureaucratic thumb. With its century-old amateur tradition, TAC saw its survival as dependent upon athletes' meekness. We were still not free to publicly earn a living for our work. Officials attempted to keep the amateur reins tight, and we were made to feel as if earning money for running was a crime. It was humiliating.

Road racers the year before had openly accepted payments at a 15-kilometer event in Portland, Oregon. This act was intended as a direct challenge to TAC, and after a number of athletes initially had their amateur status (and Olympic eligibility) taken away, TAC gave in and came up with a scheme that put a happy face on a sleight of hand. Officials created a new trust fund system that allowed payments to athletes to be placed in bank accounts for "training" purposes. Naturally, TAC controlled the accounts, but everyone knew you could draw funds at will and continue to pocket cash at meets without being challenged. It was a farce, but it served its purpose as a temporary solution, and one that could pacify the IAAF as well.

I never put a dime of my track winnings into the account. I didn't know any athlete who did. The only time I can remember earnings funneled into the trust was at the Fifth Avenue Mile, which had an announced prize structure and a close association with TAC leadership.

Clearly, TAC did not attempt to enforce its own rules. But the appearance of a crackdown and the resulting compromise—a get-tough, save-face front—won favor with the highly political IAAF. The IAAF could now follow TAC's lead and implement the same concept worldwide.

The atmosphere of scraping for a buck like some kid stealing a smoke in the school bathroom distorted my sense of proportion. Because I had a family to provide for, I ran some races solely for the money. After the Bislett Games, instead of relaxing for a week before the lead-in to my world record attempt at the second Oslo meet, I traveled to Budapest for a 1,500.

Over the summer of '82, I was getting an average of $2,000 per race. I figured that if I ran 15 races, I'd come home with $30,000. I should have realized that if I ran only 10 races but broke the world record my fee would jump to $10,000 a race and I'd never have to run in Budapest.

The trip to Budapest took all day. Four days after my 3:48 mile, I ran tired, but still won the 1,500 over Walker, Flynn, and Boit, and left a little richer for Byrkjelo, on the west coast of Norway for a tuneup 800. We connected to Byrkjelo on a six-seater that took us over the fjords. It was a luscious setting in the recesses of Norway with a state-of-the-art track amid the cliffs. The small-town meet, held on the American Independence Day, capitalized on the availability of athletes running again in Oslo three days later.

The setting inspired me to win the 800 in 1:45.05, cutting my fastest time by a healthy .86. For my showing, I earned all of $500. Observing my performance, Walker's coach, Arch Jelley, gave me some ammunition for the Oslo Games. He told John that no one could run a world record for the mile (Coe's 3:47.33) unless he was capable of a 1:45 800. I felt like this was it. I was winning every race, even 800s, and was in magnificent shape. And it was Oslo. I thought nothing could steal my thunder.

At the Oslo Games, I went out and won, broke my American record again, ran the second fastest mile in history, and came within a tick of Coe's world record, 3:47.69.

Nobody cared.

Instead, this night of July 7 belonged to David Moorcroft of Great Britain, who set a world record in the 5,000 meters. He defeated the previous world recordholder, Henry Rono, and demolished Rono's record, running 13:00.42: within a whisker of the 13-minute barrier. Moorcroft's pursuit of the record brought the 6,758 Oslo fans to a frenzy. And afterward, when Moorcroft told how he'd listened to the sound track from *Chariots of Fire* for inspiration and used the performances of Coe and Ovett for motivation, the European press was driven to new, frenzied heights of journalistic worship.

Moorcroft was a fine fellow who deserved his due. I just picked the wrong night to run 3:47.69.

I'd gone after Coe's 3:47.33 under the same conditions that existed at the Bislett Games eleven days before: cool, calm, seductive. I conspired with John Walker and Ray Flynn. We were a threesome on the circuit and were all ready to run fast.

This was a different kind of race for me, because I was pursuing a time, and in my heart I didn't like it. The only strategy was to follow the rabbit, then go for it. After Mark Fricker led the first half in 1:52.7, Walker generously took the lead. He knew he probably couldn't win but wanted to keep the record pace alive. The three-quarter split was 2:51.4.

Seeing John ahead fueled my competitive instincts. It became a race again. I had not heard the splits and did not have an sense of how close we were to the world record. I waited just a little too long to make my move. I should have passed Walker immediately on the final lap, but I held off until the first turn with about 350 meters to go. This hesitancy cost me the record.

I pushed the last lap hard but it was not a gasping effort. As I crossed the line and saw the clock flash 3:47.69, I felt the dull ache of a missed opportunity. I was off Coe's world record by .36 seconds, one stride-length. The crowd heaved with disappointment. The world record would have changed my life. Coe's standard was safe for now and all of Britain sighed with relief.

———————

It was my nature to be hopeful, and I felt sooner or later the record would be mine. And if I didn't set it, I felt another American would. It never occurred to me that the standard I set that day in

Oslo in 1982 would still be the American record going into the 1998 season. Behind me, Walker (3:49.08) and Flynn (3:49.77) had run their fastest miles. We had plenty of racing left that summer, and we had each other for solace on days when life on the road could be empty.

Like me, Ray had initially considered himself an apprentice to Walker, who was older, wiser, and an Olympic champion. John, Ray, and I felt like pioneers—the first of a new breed of touring mile performers. We put up with brutal travel to pick up a few thousand here and a few thousand there, racing the track and the emerging circus-like road miles on six continents. Sharing room and board, pizza and beer, nightlife and boredom—not to mention victory, defeat, and the mile itself—we made "life on the run" a way of life.

In Europe, we spent hours killing time in hotels waiting for the moment to suit up for our race and head for the stadium. We played cards or sat over coffee talking track. With a race to run, I did not want to be on my feet all day. International track was not the glamorous life people thought. I did not spend my days visiting the great cathedrals of Europe. I needed to rest.

With the anxiety of waiting all day to compete, I always looked for a way to get a laugh. Before one meet that summer, I decided to break the tension at the expense of Bill McChesney, who was trying to break the American record in the 5,000 meters. In my best Scandinavian accent, I called Bill's hotel room, said I was the meet promoter and told Bill to forget the record because he was needed to be the rabbit. My ruse went undetected and Bill vehemently refused. Then I told him he'd get $5,000 for his trouble and Bill had a change of heart. I played this dialogue for all it was worth. When I finally came clean, Bill was a good sport and we roared with laughter.

Moments like that were rare. It was often lonely on the circuit and I never liked being alone. Though surrounded by athletes and meet people, I could still feel isolated and longing. The tension of racing and turning out my best stuff two or three times a week was hard to shoulder. Sometimes, I just needed someone to lean on other than one of the guys.

Other athletes needed pure sex, and that was not hard to find. There were track groupies everywhere, and the prominent black sprinters had to fight them off. In largely white European nations, a mystique surrounded the American black athletes. Most of these guys were young and single, and some were happy to oblige the ladies.

White middle-distance runners like myself did not have the same appeal. If we wanted action, we had to go looking for it. One world-class miler, engaged to be married at the time, was as reputed for his pickup success as his racing performances. He was like a vampire searching for blood and whenever he thirsted for companionship, he put on this one particular sweater, which we dubbed his "pickup sweater."

He would go to a bar, approach the most attractive woman, and make his move. If he was spurned, he'd go for the second most attractive woman. But he was not often spurned. He was a closer.

I was the closer that summer, too—but on the track. Two days after the Oslo Games, I won another 800, in Paris, over six-time American champion James Robinson. With me in the 800, Ovett felt secure enough to try the 1,500, and that was big news even though he failed to finish. On the last lap, badly beaten in fourth place, Ovett fell to the ground writhing with what the media referred to as "stomach spasms." He was carried out on a stretcher, taken to the hospital, and released without explanation from doctors. The British press later identified Ovett's ailment as "colic."

I took exception to the attitudes I saw in the European press. British writers seemed to believe every race was run for the lasting honor of the Mother Country. And then *L'Equipe,* the respected

French sports daily, got it wrong when I raced a 1,500 in Lausanne against Sydney Maree.

I told *L'Equipe* I didn't care to chase records that evening, but if Maree was fresh the rivalry between us could produce a fast race. In its meet preview, however, the paper stated I would go for Ovett's world record, 3:31.36. I proceeded to win in 3:32.33. This was the fastest time in the world thus far that season, but it was met with disappointment from the expectant Swiss fans.

After going home for the mid-summer hiatus, I deposited Corey with my in-laws so Kim could accompany me back to Europe for seven races in eighteen days beginning with a 2,000 in Nice. Kim and Corey had been with me in Europe in July but had to leave early when Corey got sick.

I continued to remain close to my track buddies, male and female, even while Kim was around. Since we were all merely friends, I didn't see the problem. But Kim, observing the bonds among us, let her imagination run wild and suspected the worst. When Kim voiced her objections, I dismissed them and soon resentment built up between us.

Late that summer, after eight months of racing, I was starting to run out of gas. I denied it. I was supposed to be impregnable. I told myself I had plenty of racing left. I also had a financial quota to meet.

Though I twice broke the American record for 2,000 meters and was able to run a winning 3:49.72 mile even on my last legs, the race that would count the most was the 1,500 at the Weltklasse meet in Zurich. The Zurich meeting, growing richer by the year, had become the highlight of the second season. Even Coe was there, but not in the 1,500. He won the 800, all the more "notable," according to the press, because Coe had been in some kind of scuffle at a Swiss resort three days earlier. But a new British miler had emerged, 21-year-old Steve Cram. I didn't know the young

Cram; he'd raced little and was invited to Zurich after capturing the British 1,500 title.

In Zurich, I lacked confidence. Days earlier, I'd pulled a muscle in my rib cage, which made breathing difficult, so I had to take a muscle relaxant. With a lap to go, positioned within striking distance of the leaders, I lapsed into feelings of doom. I kept waiting to die, kept waiting for the field to leave me. I could not explain it. By the time I woke up and gathered my resources, we were nearing the finish, Cram was winning, and Todd Harbour, one of Joe Douglas' journeymen, was sneaking past me for second. I placed third, about a half-second behind Cram.

The repercussions of my poor showing were startling. Despite a year in which I'd won both Oslo miles, come close to the world record, run three sub–3:50 miles, and raced undefeated in the mile and 1,500 except for Zurich, I was ranked second behind Cram in the 1982 world 1,500 rankings by *Track & Field News* magazine. Zurich was Cram's only invitation race at the 1,500 or mile the entire season.

I could only guess that the magazine's rankings panel, heavily European, could not accept an American as the world's number-one miler. The slight reaffirmed my goal for 1983, which was to win the 1,500 at the inaugural World Track and Field Championships in Helsinki, Finland. There, the atmosphere would be as heady as in Oslo.

CHAPTER SIX

Living and Dying by the Sprint: 1983

I ran 48 races in 1983. That must be some kind of record for a miler at the peak of his career. I ran indoor track, outdoor track, flying all over the world. I ran 30 races at the 1,500 meters or mile, six 800s or 1,000s, one 3,000. I even ran eleven road races, and I didn't get paid for those. All the while, I continued to train over 90 miles a week with a steady diet of hard interval work on the track. I never got injured and was having too much fun to realize this approach might not be the best way to win a world title or set a world record.

Encouraged by John Walker, I returned to New Zealand and Australia in January for their summer season. Running Down Under had given my '82 season a perfect liftoff. John urged me to come down again, to do the groundwork that would enable me to break the world record in the mile and capture the 1,500-meter title at the first World Championships of track and field in Helsinki later that year. It would prove to be a costly trip.

By passing up several key American indoor meets, I took a pay cut to leave the States for most of that winter. I traveled with Kim, our son Corey, then a year and a half, and Kim's grandmother as babysitter. We purchased all the airline tickets up front, planning on a reimbursement from the meet organizers.

I ran in Christchurch, Auckland, Melbourne, and Sydney, winning all four of my 1,500 and mile races. I also won two 1,000s but lost an 800 to Peter Elliot of Great Britain. My earnings for the seven races totaled only about $12,000. With travel remittance, I had about $20,000 in cash in my pocket when we departed Sydney for the return trip home in early February. Only it wasn't actually in my pocket; I had the money buried in my luggage, which was sitting in the hotel room as we waited by the pool for the ride to the airport.

When it came time to leave, we went to get our bags, and the money was gone. Every cent of it. Traveling with us was Gary Wilicki, a discus thrower from Arizona, and we'd been playing practical jokes on one another. I thought this was his prank; no such luck. Someone had broken into our room.

As shocked as we all were, Kim and I were thankful that it was only money we'd lost. During our stay, we'd left Corey alone in the room a few times so he could sleep and we could get something to eat. We shuddered at the thought that we had naively risked our child's well-being.

Still, it was hard for me to feel relief when we'd blown 20,000 bucks! I'd been given most of the money in the last day or so and hadn't had a chance to convert it to paper or wire it home, so we had nothing. We called the police, but what could they do? It was cash. We didn't even have money to pay the export tax, $20 per person, that was required on departure at the airport. The bureaucrats gave us a hard time. They even wanted us to sign a document assuring that we'd forward the tax after we got home.

Track at that time was still a cash-and-carry operation. To collect your fees, you had to wait on a long line outside the meet promoter's room at the hotel. One by one, you were called into the "office," where the promoter dug into a petty cash box and counted out your award. I'd heard of other athletes who'd been robbed of money they'd left in their rooms. But I think my 20 grand was a record.

Despite that devastating loss, I still felt invincible every time I stepped to the line. Once home, I resumed my indoor matchups with Eamonn Coghlan, who also felt unbeatable that season. Our shared readiness made for pure, passionate racing, the kind I liked. What I didn't like was that no matter what strategy I used on the boards, Eamonn almost always nailed me.

After I won miles at the *L.A. Times* and Foot Locker meets, Coghlan used a 53.9 last quarter to beat me at the Michelob meet in San Diego. Eamonn had twice set the world record on this track. I hated losing in my own backyard in San Diego. A big local Irish contingent turned out wearing kelly green T-shirts lettered with: "Flamin' Eamonn's Track Club, San Diego-Dublin."

It seemed wherever I ran I always competed against the Irish: Ray Flynn, Marcus O'Sullivan, Frank O'Mara, Niall O'Shaughnessy, and, of course, Coghlan. One year at the press conference before the Fifth Avenue Mile, I remarked that the winner would definitely be Irish because, as I thought I'd been told by my family, "I'm part Irish." That quip made the papers and my mom, whose ancestry was German, called me to disavow that claim. She said I was wrong; in fact, I had no Irish blood in me.

I sure could have used some that indoor season. My rivalry with Coghlan had piqued the interest of International Management Group, Mark McCormick's powerful sports conglomerate. IMG saw potential in track, which was becoming more professional—a little bit pregnant, you could say. Earlier, IMG had tried hard to recruit me as a client, but I was suspicious of IMG's hardball approach. Besides, I felt I was doing fine negotiating my own race fees and shoe contracts. I worked out a loose arrangement with IMG to see if the company could bring me a sponsorship deal I might not get on my own. Nothing materialized and after a year we parted company.

The day after the San Diego meet, the annual Knights of Columbus meet was held in Cleveland, where IMG was based. IMG put together a deal for Eamonn and me to run an indoor "dream mile," to be televised by ABC. There was a $5,000 winner-take-all purse. Some reporters were led to believe it was more like $25,000.

I welcomed the match. On a weekend with back-to-back miles on Friday and Saturday nights, Eamonn had trouble sustaining the strength to be equally effective in the second race. I had found I had the stamina to handle a weekend double and actually seemed to get stronger. This was my chance to finally get the measure of Eamonn in a high-profile indoor race. Because the meet in San Diego was at night and Cleveland was in the afternoon, Eamonn and I had to take a red-eye east and ended up sleeping for a few hours in the Chicago airport waiting for a connection. Eamonn was not comfortable roughing it like that. Perfect, or so I thought.

In the San Diego Sports Arena, Coghlan had sat behind and kicked me down. He had explosive speed on short indoor tracks and wily instincts put to effective use in tight quarters. In Cleveland, where the track at Ohio Coliseum was even tighter than the one in San Diego, 9,783 fans showed up. I planned to make my move early and take the steam out of a tired Coghlan. With a lap to go, I was ahead and had Eamonn on the ropes. I could sense he was tired.

On the next turn, in desperation, Coghlan charged nominally ahead, darted to the inside and cut me off. I was forced to come to a dead stop. Had I let my momentum carry me, I would have collided with Coghlan and the two of us would have gone sprawling onto the track. Stunned, I had to restart, feeling like dead weight. Coghlan won in 3:57.23. Jose Abascal of Spain passed me for second (3:58.22) and I took third (3:58.42). I should have shoved Eamonn, but it had happened too quickly and I lacked his physical racing style.

Coghlan had pulled the same move on me in 1981 on the last turn of the mile at the indoor stop in Ottawa. With less than 100 meters to go on the 13-lap-to-the-mile bandbox track, he cut me off and I cursed him out.

Eamonn's tactic in Cleveland was grounds for disqualification—and he knew it. He also knew he could get away with it. No indoor meet promoter would disqualify Eamonn Coghlan, especially with IMG engineering the deal. The respected track official Bob Hersh, on hand for the meet, agreed that a foul should have been called. But Eamonn had the victory on national television, the $5,000 prize, and the media swooning all over him.

I wanted to strangle him. On the ABC interview with Coghlan, my voice could be heard in the background muttering, "Cheap victory." I told Eamonn so. Angrily, I went up to him and said, "Next time you pull something like that, I'm going to knock you out of the arena."

The brawling between us stayed on the track. Eamonn and I liked and respected one another. He was superior indoors, I was the better runner outdoors; we nipped at each other in our respective domains. But I was surprised to learn that Eamonn's fear of me contributed to his world indoor record the week after Cleveland at the Meadowlands Arena in New Jersey.

A two-foot blizzard in the New York area had canceled the Vitalis/Olympic Invitational earlier in the month. As an Irishman from Villanova, Coghlan was so deep in the New York indoor scene that he had been asked to help design the Meadowlands

10-lap-to-the-mile track. It was fast. Still, I did not take the hype over the record attempt seriously. Every indoor meet promoter, including Vitalis' Ray Lumpp, liked to predict records. I'd heard it all. Besides, I was not kept in the loop. The pace and the rabbit, everything about the race, was set up for Eamonn. It was his party.

All winter, Eamonn had sat on me, then kicked. At the Meadowlands, he sat on the rabbit, Ross Donaghue. Now I could sit on Eamonn and I liked that. God, we were flying. At the half-mile, Donaghue stepped away, giving Eamonn a clear path. The three-quarter mile split was 2:54.8. I was right there.

I still thought I could run Eamonn down. But the pace caught up with me and Ray Flynn moved into second to vainly pursue Eamonn. Later, Eamonn said he thought I was still chasing him: His fear of my threat pushed him to a new world mark of 3:49.78, the first sub–3:50 indoors. Flynn held second in 3:51.80. I held off Abascal to take third in 3:52.28.

I felt I had blown it. I had lacked focus and lost the chance to shoot Eamonn down in his own playpen. That race raised Coghlan to God-like status on the boards. He could do no wrong. He was unimpeachable. He was the best forever. I had to settle for supporting player, a role that had pained me all too often throughout my career.

After 15 races that winter of '83, seven Down Under and eight indoors, it was the perfect time for a break. The first World Championships in Helsinki were five months away. With boycotts at both the 1976 and 1980 Olympics, the event in Helsinki would be the first full-fledged world track gathering in eleven years. Track leaders were talking it up, and the U.S. team would be selected at our national meet in June in Indianapolis.

Instead of cooling my heels in early spring, I made another trip to New Zealand for a three-race series of oddball miles organized by John Walker. I could never say no to John. The first race was run on a horse track, the second on a beach. The finale was the Queens Street Mile, the notorious downhill race in Auckland that I'd won before. Mike Boit of Kenya swept all three. His Queens Street time was 3:28, a new record. I ran 3:29.

The trip satisfied my need to extend childhood as long as possible. Ray Flynn was with me and we would sneak into other athletes' rooms and drag their beds into the shower. We put shaving cream in Boit's toothpaste. We had water fights. We bandaged our legs and told the race promoter we were injured and couldn't run.

Boit almost couldn't run the Queens Street race. At a pool party beforehand, we were tossing people into the water. It was good-natured, but when we grabbed Mike by his spaghetti-like arms and legs he fought us off and landed on the pool's concrete edge, hurting his hip. Nothing could keep Boit down. A decade later he was winning masters mile races on little more than jogging for fitness.

I returned home with 18 races under my belt and the outdoor track season had not even started. That kind of schedule was unheard of, but I was propelled by emotion, not intellect. I was on a perpetual high, held aloft by the transcendent powers of conditioning and wanting to challenge everyone, everywhere, at any time: C'mon, let's go, let's you and me line up side-by-side . . . and race. I just kept going.

For me, the game of life was the game of racing.

I was addicted to the track circuit. I got paid to indulge my zest for play on and off the track and hang out with my track buddies all over the earth. I loved rubbing shoulders with Walker, Flynn, Coghlan. It was like being in the marines. We milers were at war. These guys were my unit. When you went home, you wished you were back at war.

You can't share that experience with anyone else. Who would understand what it's like to base your life on running four laps around the track? Who would understand the training, the travel, the hotel life? At home, I found it a stretch to relate to the normal people, the "civilians." On a break from the circuit, I'd find myself calling Europe, tracking down some of the guys and saying, "Hey, how's it going?"

Kim did not appreciate my longing for the battle front. It was hard enough on her when I was away and she remained at home. When I was around but wondering about the 1,500 at LaCoruna, or who was sitting on the beach at Nice between workouts, I was not an ideal soulmate either.

The track scene was like a mistress. I won most of the races I cared about, got to show off before appreciative crowds, and did not have to put on a shirt and tie. Amid the euphoria, I never stepped back to consider the long view. I missed what Deep Throat told Robert Redford he was missing in *All The President's Men:* the overall.

Coe and Ovett and Cram—they were not missing the overall. They did not race a lot or travel much. They did some cross-country running, maintained stability at a sedate training camp, say, in the south of Spain, hardly ever ran indoors, and picked their summer events in Europe like every race was a mutual fund.

I won my next meeting with Eamonn Coghlan, at the Bruce Jenner/Michelob Light Classic in San Jose, California, but when he beat me two weeks later at the Kinney Invitational, it was another freaky situation. I had not lost to Eamonn outdoors since '79 and did not consider him a threat. The meet was televised and because of camera positioning, the finish line was placed in the middle of the home straight as opposed to its customary spot up near the turn. I led Eamonn down the stretch. He inched ahead, sprinted for all he had and leaned at the finish. Not expecting the line that soon, I held back a touch and did not lean. Eamonn won in 3:52.52. I ran 3:52.53. Ouch!

Around this time, we learned Kim was pregnant with our second child. With the experience of Corey's birth in '81 and an Olympic year coming up in 1984, we'd tried to eliminate any potential conflict between the due date and the track circuit. Kim was due in February of '84. I was safe.

After routinely winning the 1983 U.S. Nationals 1,500, I ran the United States' dual meet against East Germany at the Los Angeles Coliseum prior to the European season. American athletes were given the option of taking part. I wanted to get the feeling of the stadium where the Olympics would be held the next year. My 1,500 was a bland sit-and-kick race, which I won. In combined men's and women's scoring, the Germans, on the strength of their dominant women (suspicions of drug use later proved true), outscored our squad, 197-181.

The exercise of going through the pre-race procedures was comforting. Officials conducted the event as though it were an Olympic dress rehearsal. The athletes were collected in a small stable, held for a short time, then formally marched out onto the track. That ritual was repeated six weeks later in Helsinki, when I felt I was in the best shape of my life.

I left for Europe to defend my "Dream Mile" title in Oslo as a stepping stone to the World Championships. Initially, I used Oslo as my base, living out of a hotel for a month instead of traveling from city to city. I could train in the forest, on lakeside trails, and do my track work at Bislett Stadium. Kim would join me later, then my coach, Len Miller, and his wife would also come over. It was beautiful. Everything was perfect.

I felt inner strength and contentment. My body emitted rays of confidence. I had my own space, like territory ceded me. Every other miler was set back. They could sense my aura. Every day, I could not wait to train and draw in the pure Oslo air. I could not wait to race and show I could win at will. Coe? Coghlan? It didn't matter. This was my time. This is what Len told me would one day happen. This is what I had imagined track could be like.

I tried to separate myself from the athletic persona. In a race, like the 1,000 meters at nearby Byrkjelo. I felt like a performer for the crowd of 3,000 that packed the small stadium in the midst of the fjords. It seemed every Norwegian within a hundred miles of Byrkjelo had come out for the meet. After the race, I felt an obligation to sign every autograph. I was usually the last athlete to leave a meet. I had seen other athletes snub the public and found that embarrassing.

I won the Byrkjelo 1,000 in 2:16.4 and that evening, well past midnight, some athletes were invited to fish for salmon in the fjords. The river was clear and twilight draped the valley. Supposedly, the salmon were practically jumping into your pocket at this hour, but we didn't catch a thing.

Soothed, I returned to Oslo for the "Dream Mile" at the Oslo Games without a care in the world. I didn't even let a little rough-housing by Coghlan affect me. This time it was seemingly inadvertent. In the opening strides, our 13-man Bislett Stadium field got knocked around like bumper cars. To hold his balance, Coghlan straightarmed me. I gave him one back. As we all found our rhythm, I fell toward the back, happy to operate in my own zone.

At the bell, Coghlan led with a three-quarter split of 2:55.9. He was a different miler outdoors. With about a half lap to go, I took off from behind feeling fresh, buried the field, and won in 3:49.49. My last quarter was 53.4, the fastest last lap in a sub–3:50 mile at the time. It felt like a walk in the park.

One writer described my countenance during the last 200 as "berserker's rage." That was my zone at work. I tuned everything out, shrunk my world, and stared through a small hole in my consciousness to a greater mission. Like a quarterback fading into the pocket, ignoring 300-pound linemen and pinpointing his receiver, I cut my life in those spare moments to the essentials: beating the British.

Neither Coe nor Cram ran Bislett. Ovett had been scheduled in the 800 but withdrew earlier in the week. Joachim Cruz, the young Brazilian out of the University of Oregon, must have scared him off.

Would I scare off Coe or Cram? Soon, after winning a mile in Cork, Ireland, in 3:50.99, I got my answer. A special invitation mile was added to the British Championships in London two weeks later. It was another TV package. We'd run at night, but with the time difference ABC would telecast the race live during Saturday afternoon's prime-time sports window. Though Cram stuck with the 1,500, Coe agreed to meet me in the mile. It would be his first major international mile since setting the world record (3:47.33) in Brussels in 1981.

It was a chilly evening at London's Crystal Palace. I had never beaten Sebastian Coe. A month earlier in Paris, after his first 1,500 loss in seven years, Coe said, "The old snap wasn't there." Fleet Street headlines crucified him.

The pace was slow. Bob Benn, Ovett's prize rabbit, and Craig Masback (who would become track's leading TV commentator in the United States), had been enlisted to set the pace. After a 1:57.08 half, I pulled behind the two leaders. Benn soon stepped away and Masback and I ran shoulder to shoulder at the front. Heading down the home straight for the bell lap, another Briton, Graham Williamson, went for the lead. He did it in typical European style—by barreling between Masback and me and knocking us off stride.

Fine. I whipped ahead of Williamson on the backstretch and, passing the crowd, Coe followed me around the bend in close touch. Coe needed a victory, and where better than in Crystal Palace. But our roles were now reversed. I was in command and powered home the winner in 3:51.56. The crowd fell silent. Coe held second in 3:52.93.

Afterward, the word went around that Coe had been under the weather because how could he lose—in London no less—if he wasn't? But I knew Coe would never race me, in London no less, if he were not in tip-top form and confident of winning.

But this was no time for carping. Coe and I generously praised one another before the media. I gave Coe the benefit of the doubt. In turn, he said no one could have beaten me this night. Len Miller told anyone who would listen that maybe I'd finally get some recognition, and that it was a crying shame I had not even been named athlete of the year in Arizona where I lived.

Arizona would have been nice, but now I faced a much larger arena.

———————

When the 1983 World Championships began in Helsinki, Kim and I were across the Baltic sea in Stockholm, taking it easy. Len and his wife were with us. We shopped, went sight-seeing, and visited islands in the Swedish archipelago. I didn't want to be in the midst of the meet environment until it was necessary. The 1,500 rounds would not begin until the end of the week-long program.

In Stockholm, once rated the world's number one city for running, I trained in the parks and in Olympic Stadium, an arena with warmth as well as a touch of class. Sweden was my favorite nation in Europe. The Swedes seemed open and friendly.

Stockholm balanced its modern sector with a charming old quarter, and with kids cruising around in their dated cars the city had the innocence of an America long gone.

Len and I barely talked about my race. I felt I could win off a slow pace or a fast pace, whatever kind of race developed. In my last bit of training, I ran my 200s as fast as 23 seconds. It felt easy. I ran my 400s in 49 seconds. That felt easy, too. One of my workouts consisted of a 300 meters and three 200s. I ran the 300 in 36 seconds. The 200s were 24, 24, 23. What could go wrong?

Because the Olympics were the overwhelming signature event in track and field, it was hard to predict how the inaugural World meet would come off. Our sport was still not fully professionalized, and the event offered no prize money.

Track had been desperate for a world championship. All the other major Olympic sports, like swimming and gymnastics, had one. The meet was created as a quadrennial event, just like the Olympics, with much the same week-plus, day-by-day schedule as the Games. Previous attempts at broad multination events, like track's World Cup or Pan American Games, had been weak. Since many of the best track and field athletes competed against one another through the summer in Europe, would this championship be little more than a dressed-up version of any big meet on the circuit?

Most of the athletes, including myself, underestimated the weight of the Worlds. But the buzz around town was stirring. Legions of Finnish track fans, all looking fit and eager, filed past a statue of Olympic legend Paavo Nurmi to fill the stadium constructed for the 1952 Olympics. Angelic Finnish girls hawked track paraphernalia and the Opening Ceremonies had beauty and grandeur. Every race received headline treatment in Europe, NBC coverage generated good ratings back home and I started to think, hey, maybe this is a big deal, did I have every single thing covered?

I thought I'd better check out the dungeon-like call room in the bowels of the stadium where the athletes are summoned to wait moments before their race. I simply wanted to see what it looked like. The room was small and unremarkable except for a black bra hanging by its strap from a light fixture. Before an important race, I liked to know what to expect—on raceday, the flash of recognition gave me a sense of security.

A *Track & Field News* panel of experts declared me the favorite and that's how I felt. I breezed through the 1,500 heats and semis and felt no residual fatigue on the day of the final. I tried not to think about the race; I didn't want to work myself up. Len was laid back. He could see how confident I was. We saw no reason to sit down and analyze the field.

I jogged a relaxing two miles that morning before heading for the stadium. Once in the call room, I sat on a wooden bench trying not to make eye contact with my opponents. (The bra, by the way, was gone.) I tried to direct all my energies inward. I wanted to strike a combative posture. Eye contact compromises strength. It takes you outward. Even a momentary glance into the eyes of an opponent can suggest weakness or unlock negative thoughts. You want to step onto the track with your mind clean.

Physically, I felt light and easy. I tuned in to my body: Achilles tendons? Check. Hamstrings? Check. Quads? Check. Perfect. On the TV monitor, I watched Eamonn Coghlan win the 5,000. Now it was my turn.

Like caged lions, we were led out of the call room and into the light of the arena. It was an intensely competitive field. John Walker was always tough, intimidating. Said Aouita of Morocco, later the world recordholder, was a brash upstart. Ovett was aloof. Others down the line, from East Germany and Yugoslavia, would think nothing of cutting you off, snapping at your heels, clipping your shoulders. Hostility smoldered. I did not focus on beating any one athlete, just winning.

When the gun went off, it was like waking up from a dream into another realm. We were crawling. It was a joke. The crowd whistled its disapproval. This was the World Championship and our opening 400 was 65.0, slow even for a high school race. The crawl continued; the 800 was 2:07.8.

No one would take the pace. No one spoke or gestured. We were one big blob. I positioned myself on the outside near the front of the 12-man field. The pace was about as fast as I'd done my warmup. Everyone waited. The crowd grew more and more impatient.

Later, I was criticized for not taking the pace. I still felt I should have had the speed to run with anyone. My kick was my weapon. All year, I'd won from behind, and was not practiced or comfortable leading. I had to remain faithful to my instincts.

With 500 meters to go, Aouita split from the pack with the force of a billiard ball on a break. I went with him; so did Steve Cram. On the backstretch, it was Aouita, Cram, and me, one-two-three, single file, in a mad sprint. With about 250 to go, Cram passed Aouita and opened daylight around the final turn. That should have been my move. I should have initiated the attack instead of having to respond to it. Instead, I was forced to run wide around Aouita on the turn to have a shot at Cram. I had underestimated Cram's kick.

On the homestretch, I pulled abreast of Aouita as he went after Cram. Cram was on my left. I couldn't catch him. I was beginning to tie up and realized it was over. It took all I had to hold off Aouita, who cut to the inside lane. Cram won in 3:41.59. I was second and Aouita third.

I was disgusted with myself. This had been the time and place to stake my claim as the world's best. The opportunity might not come again. This was a race to define a career, to catapult me to the apex of my sport, to make me financially secure. The "best miler in the world" is like being "the world's fastest human" for sprinters. People come to you.

If only I'd made my move a moment earlier, I kept telling myself. Cram defeated me by 26 hundredths of a second. Aouita was .15 behind me in third. Ovett was .32 back in fourth. I came across the line behind the exultant Cram in an aching, desperate lunge.

I took the disappointment hard. I had a difficult time accepting the way the race had transpired: that a glacially slow pace had made me vulnerable to tactical error. It was my second lost opportunity in two years. It gnawed at me that in 1982 I'd missed the world mile record by .33 seconds.

Faced with another three weeks of racing in Europe, I needed comforting. It was hard for me to shoulder disappointment and feel alone. Kim was going home the next day. In the course of the season, mutual friends would remark to Kim that they'd see me hanging around with a few of the female runners, one in particular, and Kim was still convinced, wrongly, that I had not been faithful to her. It was all very innocent.

I think what hurt Kim more than anything was the impression that I had feelings for another woman and that there was an emotional connection between us. That was true. Unfortunately, Kim and I rarely talked out the problem. The issue of "another woman" usually just sat there, building and building. Kim did not want to disturb the momentum of my running, which was finally at the level I'd worked so hard for and, after all, was also my job and the source of our family income.

I considered John Walker and Ray Flynn intimate friends, too. We were all milers in the trenches of the track circuit—training our guts out, racing under impossible pressure, existing in a fantasy world in which the boundaries of "real life" and "play time" blurred.

In reality, I was two different people. I was the husband and provider at home in Arizona, helping care for Corey, going out to punch a timeclock at the track, relaxing in the backyard Jacuzzi. And I was the miler in the swirl of the track circuit, a kind of circus performer on the high wire, relying on another "family" for comfort, support, survival. After the track season, we all went back home to our real homes and real lives. The war, and the party, were over.

Feeling cast aside by my allegiance to my track buddies, Kim shunned me in Helsinki, and I felt a void. This magnified my own insecurities, and soon I became more than just friends with this other woman, a competitor from another country. At great peril to my marriage, she and I were companions for the rest of the summer season.

From every standpoint, the 1983 World Championships were a smashing success, giving track and field a terrific boost leading into the Los Angeles Olympics. It was the first big show for Carl Lewis, the sprinter and long jumper out of the University of Houston who won three gold medals and would become, in the minds of many, the greatest track and field athlete ever. A lot of people didn't care for Carl's showboating style. At the '83 U.S. national meet that spring in Indianapolis, Carl glanced back at his opposition several times in the closing strides of his victorious 200 meters. Some said it looked like he was mocking his competition. Carl said he was expressing jubilance over his triumph.

Personally, Carl's flamboyance didn't bother me. I considered myself a performer, too. Everyone had his or her own style. But Carl could have been more careful in crafting his image. In dealing with the media, he might have learned a lesson from Sebastian Coe, who managed to ingratiate himself with everyone and still create the aura he wanted.

Three days after my loss to Cram at Helsinki, I won the mile at West Berlin in mid-August. Though I was emotionally flat, I ran 3:49.21, the fastest mile of the year, a testament to my reservoir of training. Walker was second in 3:49.73. The first two laps went in 56.38 and 1:54.50. That's what we should have had in Helsinki. I told Walker we should have made a pact, a "Helsinki Accord," to keep the World Championship pace honest.

I wanted another shot at Cram. However, Cram, basking in his world title, avoided me. He'd passed up West Berlin and then Zurich, too, where I won the 1,500 in 3:32.71. Two days later, I could have met Cram in the Brussels 1,500. He would have liked that. While I'd run two exhausting marquee miles against world-class opposition within one week, he was coasting through star turns at an obscure Finnish meet in Kokkola and the pedestrian European Cup in London.

I said no to the 1,500 in Brussels. Instead, I ran the 3,000 and got buried in eighth place. But at least the money was decent—my fee had risen to $4,000 per race and I was now making a six-figure annual income.

Next it was Ovett who avoided me. In Koblenz, the promoter had to set up both a 1,500 and mile. Andy Norman, the British agent who also managed Ovett, had his hands on almost every big meet in Europe. Ovett ran the 1,500 and won. I ran the mile and won.

Ovett had been dodging me for three years. There was nothing I could do about it. If a European reporter brought it up, I expressed my displeasure. Inevitably, the stories portrayed me as the brash American and Ovett as the mature professional. There were virtually no American reporters to come to my defense. After

Helsinki, they went home. It seemed even *Track & Field News* was washing its hands of the Brits' dodging tactics. In its Koblenz story, it wrote, "A fabulous collection of milers ended up split into two groups" without further comment.

Ovett's specialty was the world record attempt. With the season just about over, Ovett went to Rieti, Italy, and regained the world 1,500 record from Sydney Maree against a weak field. The race was essentially a time trial.

I felt capable of a world record myself—I was certain I was in better shape than when I ran my 3:47.69 mile the previous year—but was unable to effectively respond to the demands of running for time. It just didn't work in my circuitry. I needed to see myself beating another man. I could spread out the options in my mind and envision a wide berth into which different tactical scenarios could unfold. The concept of winning, though based on complex strategies and versatile running talent, gave me room to roam.

But running for time was always too narrow an idea to inspire me. It was filled with unnecessary pressure, with fear of failure; to "win" you had to hit the bull's-eye. How likely was that? It also seemed beside the point. I took up running to pit myself against other people, not the stopwatch. If you won, did your time really matter?

Probably the best way for me to run a 3:46 mile that summer was for my coach to have enlisted Flynn and Walker as pacesetters without telling me. Seeing them ahead would have fired me to race my heart out, perhaps enabling me to run my fastest time in the process. But that didn't happen.

Meanwhile, Sydney Maree was running against me in New York's Fifth Avenue Mile, which I won in 3:49.77. The road event was of no consequence on the track circuit, but it was good to win a big media event as the summer season ended.

In a final 1983 World Championships assessment that fall, the *Track & Field News* editor, Bert Nelson, added to the consensus that my fatal flaw was in allowing the 1,500 to become, in effect, an 800:

> *Scott had to be ahead when the real running started and he could match his strength against Cram's speed. . . . If you live by the sprint, you eventually die by the sprint.*

I had lived by the sprint, but in mile races that were fast and honest. In those races, it was my strength, borne from thousands of miles of unrelenting training, that had given me the power to uncork the last lap with life in my legs while others fizzled. If the pace was unbearably slow, as in Helsinki, my closing power was rendered less effective. My opponents, barely breathing from the coasting, would have all their speed left. One-on-one, I would not quite prevail in a flying dash for the finish.

I vowed not to let that happen again. Next year, at the 1984 Olympics in Los Angeles, I would make sure the 1,500 meters would be different.

CHAPTER SEVEN

Running Into the Abyss: The 1984 Olympics

In 1984, lacking the experience of the 1980 Games, I was unsettled by the Olympics. Not only were the Games being held in the United States for the first time in 52 years, but they would be run in Los Angeles, in southern California where I'd grown up, made my reputation, and was considered a favorite son.

The pressure was enormous. I'd never felt anything like it. In the past, if I missed a day of training to go hunting, it was no big deal. Now I thought, I can't do anything but train for the Olympics. When I picked up a little hamstring injury and had to lay off for a few days, I panicked. Oh my God! I missed three days of training! Where had the fun gone?

I had certainly always taken my running seriously. Who else but a serious runner would pace around the house all day until 8 o'clock at night, then run five miles to a steep hill, sprint the hill 30 or 40 times until his legs turned to mush, run the five miles back home, and collapse on the sofa with a beer?

I put myself through workouts like these because I had so much fun running the mile. Even though track was my livelihood,

I had learned to mediate the pressures with spontaneity and impulsiveness. Race in New Zealand? Put me on the first flight to Auckland. Go for the run/golf "record"? Gimme my clubs. Run a meaningless road race? Sure. Unlike other athletes, my training was not determined weeks in advance. And I raced everywhere, drawing youthful joy from competition and being careful not to deny the whimsy I brought to the arena.

This was my way of being free. I would try to be the best miler in the world, but I would do it on my own terms. I was not going to map out my life stride by stride, minute by minute, heartbeat by heartbeat, even for something as tantalizing as Olympic glory.

Don't get me wrong: I craved that glory like any other athlete. But now, 28 years old and at the peak of my career, I did not want to feel like a puppet at the mercy of some fire-breathing Olympic beast.

But in 1984, it seemed as if the fun was being crushed by a spirit that distorted the very nature of competition. Now I'm not that naive. I know the Olympics have more to do with corporate largesse than with what Roger Bannister called "the sweat of honest toil." But there was something about the atmosphere in L.A., a kind of rank stupidity, that, for example, made it easy for people to find fault with Carl Lewis after he won four gold medals.

It was common knowledge that many of the people watching us perform in Los Angeles Coliseum were seeing the first track and field competition of their lives. They were not interested in track and field. They were interested in three things: the cachet of attending the Games; American gold medals; and Carl Lewis, by now an icon. The Angelenos did not care about the dynamics of racing or level of performance. They cared about Americans taking victory laps with the flag and standing atop the medal podium as "The Star Spangled Banner" played. Anything else was a waste of their time.

That's why Lewis practically got lynched by reporters (just as sadly ignorant as their readers) when he passed up a few of his long jump attempts to conserve energy for the 200 meters. The folks sitting in the sun with their official Olympic hats and official Olympic pins had no clue that if Lewis pushed too hard in the jump he might not be fresh enough to win the 200, and then wouldn't that be a bad hair day in L.A.?

But this was the American Way. For three and a half years, the masses and most media ignored and even dismissed "Olympic sports" such as track and field. Then, with the quadrennial Games approaching, people woke up and felt it was the duty of athletes lucky enough to make the U.S. team to win big.

At times, the public's ignorance or misconception about track and field reached the absurd. Word spread about spectators who didn't know where races started, which direction athletes ran on the track, what the hurdles were. Anything mildly technical, such as wind readings in the sprints, might as well have been spoken in another tongue.

In just about any other country, with less national arrogance and a more supportive tradition of sports appreciation, track athletes would have been hailed in the proper light. There would have been many gradations of success, not just the gold medal. Simply being an Olympic qualifier would have been worthy of honor.

Oh, how we lacked the Finnish graciousness from the previous summer's world championship meet in Helsinki. The Finns may have booed the slow pace of our 1,500 final in Helsinki, but that was to their credit. They knew we were dogging it.

I was committed to upholding a properly-paced 1,500 in L.A. But I found my path obstructed by the sense that I was no longer running for myself but for a misguided national interest. Every facet of the Los Angeles Games was fed, piece by piece, into some mammoth public relations machine designed to show the might and superiority of America.

The city of Los Angeles, the Los Angeles Olympic Organizing Committee, ABC TV, sports fans picking up on Olympic fever—every source of Games interest delivered the message that victory and nothing less was the American mandate. The Olympics were a convenient political vehicle, and after the U.S. boycott of the 1980 Moscow Games it was time for us to kick some ass. The Soviet bloc retaliated by boycotting L.A.? Screw 'em.

It was muted public interest in the faraway Iron Curtain Moscow Games that had enabled the Carter Administration Olympic boycott to take hold. Now in L.A., people felt a proprietary interest in the swelling us-versus-them ardor, and athletes were treated like one more Olympic trinket to be showcased and then disposed of.

Everything was out of whack. It was like a high school basketball tournament, blown up a billion times, in which the locals who really didn't understand the game were mobilized to feel that their pride, their values, and their way of life was somehow wrapped up in the final score.

I don't know how many times that 1984 season some sportswriter from the football beat or some blow-dried TV interviewer asked me whether I was going to "win the Olympics." I could tell these characters didn't even know basic things—for example, that instead of a mile in the Olympics there was a 1,500 meters, the "metric mile."

The confluence of these forces changed me. A stronger man might have coped better and shucked the pressure off. But I felt I had to win the 1,500 in Los Angeles. Otherwise, I felt I'd be dog poop.

After placing second in the 1983 World Championships—a failure I attributed to the warped, slow pace that obviously benefited the winner, Steve Cram, more than it had benefited me—I sat down with Len Miller and devised a new strategy for 1984. We figured that in the tradition of recent Olympic 1,500 finals, the pace would be slow. Every contender, Cram included, would prefer strolling along, conserving energy, measuring the field, and sprinting the last lap rather than fooling with any tactic perceived as risky. Taking the lead and pushing the pace was considered the riskiest way to run. You were a sitting duck waiting to be swallowed whole.

Even John Walker, my early mentor and no slacker when it came to asserting himself on the track, had used a slow pace to his advantage in his 1976 Olympic 1,500 victory. Though he'd become the first sub–3:50 miler in '75, Walker followed the Olympic field in Montreal through a 3:01.2 split for three-quarters, then sprinted to victory. He covered his last 200 meters in 25.4 seconds. Eamonn Coghlan, with less native sprint capacity, ended up fourth, missing a medal by inches. He was devastated.

I knew that could happen to me. Len and I decided early in the season that I could not let a slow pace dictate the final result. Off a slow pace, my talents would be compromised. I wanted to make an honest race of the Olympic final. It deserved that. And I needed to win.

Our plan called for me to do the one thing no other contender would dare do: take the lead early and push the pace. No Olympic 1,500 finalist had done that since Kip Keino ran away from Jim Ryun in 1968.

If the prospect of me walking out of Los Angeles Coliseum with a silver or bronze medal had been deemed acceptable to the masses, I would not have changed my running style. I would have been free to go with my instincts—instincts that had served me well for years. I would have trained with anticipation, raced with gusto. Maybe I would have won; maybe I would have run second or third as in Helsinki. If the audience at the Games had understood the dynamics of Olympic racing as well as they did a World Series pitchers' duel, I would not have felt compelled to think of the Olympic final as an all-or-nothing crucible in my life.

But I had to lead, and everything I did and felt in '84 grew out of that rather shaky commitment. My training was based on learning to sustain concentration for longer distances at the front of the field. Two minutes out front in a three-and-a-half-minute race could be an eternity. In L.A., I would have to make every second count.

As the season went on, the plan didn't seem right. I grew uncomfortable with changing my basic nature, my proven running style. I was edgy. I kept checking the papers for track results from Europe. Every time I felt a little ache, I ran to the doctor. That wasn't me. Once, when I couldn't finish a workout, I rushed to get a blood test.

I was so sensitive to Olympic pressure, real or imagined, that I played a cruel joke on my mother when the blood test results came back. Her habit of calling to ask how my training was going seemed like just one more person—my mom yet—telling me it was my job to win. So when the blood workup came in I made up numbers that led Mom, a nurse, to think I was really sick. It was thoughtless and a couple of days later I stopped my scam. But with all the pressure, I had needed to pick on someone, and Mom happened to be in my radar.

There was certainly nothing wrong with me—at least not physically. I was actually in great shape as the Olympics approached. A month before the Games, I did probably the best training session of my life. I ran two sets of a 200, 700, 800, 400, 500, 600, 400. I tried to run every repetition at 55- or 56-second

400 pace, and I did. My 800s were done in 1:52. I pushed my last 400 down to 51.8. As in '82 and '83, I felt capable of a world record.

But I didn't trust the American media to comprehend an athlete's capabilities and the pulse of a championship final. Few reporters covered track as a beat. Most covered track as an Olympic happening, boiling it down to the gold medal and some cute asides. The British press had its faults, but at least they treated track as a major sport.

My race plan, created out of desperation, was not the only issue that had me off-balance that season. My training partner was Tom Byers, also an Olympic 1,500 contender. Tom had the physical ability of a Cram or Coe but was not known for his acuity on the track. With his erratic racing style and fragile self-image, Tom was like a gifted child incapable of managing his talent. I was still living in Scottsdale and, late in '83, at my urging, Byers had moved nearby. Len welcomed him. He saw Tom's fatal flaws as a coaching challenge.

Tom was a friend and we got along fine, but from a running standpoint our union turned out to be a mistake. I always preferred training partners of lesser ability so that I could dictate the pace. The worst thing I could do in training was compete against another runner. I found that Tom liked to train himself to death. He had no patience. He did not take easy days. He competed, and since we were both in the same event, I was drawn into his intemperate ways. We hammered each other.

I should have known better than to let myself get hooked up with Tom. No runner was flakier or less stable. One year at the Pepsi meet at UCLA, Tom was in great shape but finished last in the mile in 4:12. Right after the meet, to prove to himself he was still good, he ran himself dizzy with a complete speed workout of ten 400s.

Another hallmark of the Byers legend came during one Christmas when he was visiting his folks in Ohio. Tom's dad happened to mention that he'd never seen his son run a sub–4:00 mile. No miler is in any shape to speak of in late December, but Tom went out to the track in wintry conditions and, with his dad watching, broke 4:00.

Tom couldn't stand being away from the track. During periods when I would normally stay off the track for more sedate road work, we trained on the track. Len wanted to kill me. But I was so off balance, I began to think maybe crazy Tom was right: Maybe I should do more intervals, faster intervals; the L.A. Olympics are coming up, right?

———————————

At least one of my plans that year turned out right. In February, before Olympic madness reached a pitch, our second child, Megan, was born. After Corey, now 2½, I had hoped for a girl and felt particularly blessed because this time I did get to assist Kim in the delivery. I may be the only person in my family who's not a doctor or nurse, but, sure enough, I delivered my daughter.

This time, Kim had a routine labor. Since I'd taken Lamaze classes and gone through pre-birth prep for Corey, I needed no additional schooling for Megan. Again in the Alternative Birthing Unit of Upland's San Antonio Community Hospital, with the doctor and many family members in my shadow, I performed the entire delivery and cut the umbilical cord. The experience was meant to strengthen the parent/child bond and I feel it did.

Unfortunately, the birth did not have the same bonding effect between Kim and me. Tensions continued to simmer over my affair, and my marital conflicts had taken on a new dimension. I was no longer being truthful with Kim. If she asked if I was sleeping with another woman, I squirmed out of it and said no.

While insisting that I end the suspected affair, Kim did not want to impair my Olympic preparations. She saw how the pressures were getting to me and waited until after the Games to really corner me with an ultimatum.

Proud of my sense of loyalty and basic good nature, I felt enormous guilt over my affair but couldn't stop it. Fearing emptiness on the road, I could not let go of the other woman. Our relationship was not based on sex. We'd been comrades for three years before sleeping together and still enjoyed each other's company purely as friends. Sitting over a beer at each city on the European circuit, or gabbing about track and kidding around, was new and exciting. It got me through tough times. The woman didn't ask about Kim and I didn't ask about her husband. We never spoke about leaving our spouses for one another. There were no strings attached, no responsibility. After a few races, we'd go our separate ways.

I was left to bottle up the guilt, one more burden to carry during the Olympic season. At one point, I became so distressed that I got an unlisted phone number so I would not have to speak to reporters. I kept thinking about the risky race strategy Len and I had come up with for the Olympic final.

Because of the Olympics, I cut back my '84 racing schedule. In the winter, I remained home rather than make another trip Down Under, especially with Megan on the way. I wish I could have allowed the happiness of Megan's birth to offset my Olympic obsessions. But soon after Megan was born, I was irritable with worry that her late-night crying would disturb my sleep and have a detrimental effect on my training.

A few days before the birth, I'd won the Wanamaker Mile at the Millrose Games. Eamonn Coghlan was injured and did not run. Indoors, I also won the Sunkist mile and the mile at the U.S. Nationals. In all three races, Byers ran second. Great titles, but it was a tepid season.

Byers was my shadow. I opened my spring campaign with a 5,000 at the Sun Angel meet in Arizona, winning in 13:48.66. Byers was inches behind in 13:48.72. Every race was a tuneup for the Olympic Trials, which was a tuneup for the Games. Only one race really counted: the Olympic final.

I showed my fitness was coming along with a victory over a newcomer, Joachim Cruz, in the Pepsi meet at UCLA in mid-May. An 800-meter runner who would win the Olympic gold medal in L.A., Cruz, a Brazilian attending the University of Oregon, chased me down the homestretch in his mile debut. I held him off in 3:52.99. Cruz ran 3:53.00. A tall, strapping (6'2", 170 pounds) 21-year-old, Cruz was considered an excellent candidate for an 800-1,500 double at the Games. In fact, he would attempt the Olympic 1,500, winning his heat but then withdrawing with an illness.

Even in my victories, I felt an undercurrent of anxiety. Though I was an experienced athlete, I had never experienced the impact of an Olympics. The 1980 boycott took that opportunity away, and as I confronted the pressures of '84 I was like a high school novice running his first conference meet. I had no combat tools. I didn't know how to relax, how to tune out the tumult. In my last race before the Olympic Trials, I ran a miserable sixth in an 800 at the Prefontaine meet in Eugene. That was not a good sign; the Haywood Field track in Eugene had always been a favorite of mine.

Was I the only athlete who'd let a big race get to him? One day at a meet I was sitting around with Jackie Joyner-Kersee, the future heptathlon champion. I asked her how she prepared mentally for the competition. She looked at me blankly and said she did nothing. Her attitude seemed to be: "Don't worry. Be happy." It made a lot of sense. That was the old me.

By late spring, I was training in southern California. I was now sponsored by Nike in addition to Sub–4, and with race earnings my income had grown to around $200,000 a year. The previous fall, we'd purchased a second home a block from the Pacific in Leucadia, California, about an hour's drive from where Kim and I had grown up. We called it our "beach house." Kim loved the beach and with me away for much of the summers, the house gave her an outlet and a place for the kids to run around as they got older.

Megan turned into a mellow baby, the opposite of cranky Corey. I held her and played with her, and if she did cry my embrace seemed to quiet her. Being with Megan was a welcome respite from the track.

I trained without a break at San Diego State for the Olympic Trials, held, like the Games, in Los Angeles Coliseum. Though considered a lock for the Olympic team, I still felt nervous. That one weak 800 in Eugene had rattled me.

I wondered whether I should have taken some rest. Doubts piled up. Where was my confidence? My bulletproof nature? Olympic strategy, race selection, travel plans, training schedule, running partners, body signals . . . nothing was tidy. I had no sense of contentment. The Olympic monster was everywhere.

The other favorites for the U.S. 1,500 team were Jim Spivey, improving fast since winning the 1982 NCAA 1,500 at Indiana, and Sydney Maree, who briefly held the world 1,500 record in 1983. Spivey was funny. He was the most meticulous runner I'd come across. In his training log, which he proudly showed me, Jim would record every run—including his rest periods—in painstaking detail.

Though it was prestigious to win at the Trials, the victory had no consequence and, indeed, Spivey beat me. He ran smartly, timed his kick beautifully, and nailed me on the home straight. The third Olympic berth went to Maree by a hair over Chuck Aragon, who'd taken a year off from medical school to train. Byers, now injured, finished twelfth and last. Afterward, Spivey's assessment was right on the money. He told the reporters, "Steve was training for the Games and I was training for today."

After the Trials, I stayed home instead of going to Europe to compete as I had done every July for seven years. I wanted to keep my travel to a minimum. Another mistake. Racing on the circuit would have sharpened my form, given me back some confidence, kept me away from the Olympic kaleidoscope in California. But I was too uptight to see that. Again I told myself: It's the Olympics, lay low.

I ran some local races, including an 800 in a poor 1:50. In contrast, before the '83 Worlds, I'd run 1:45. Desperate to prove to myself that I still had it, I continued the tin-pot racing, as the British call it, without success.

Through all the anxiety and doubt, I should have leaned more on Len, who was good at keeping an athlete at ease. All summer, Len was holed up in a condo he'd rented in nearby La Costa to work closely with me. I guess I was confused by all these new and troubling feelings and ill-equipped to bring them out in the open. Len was not the type of coach to smother an athlete with his concern, and maybe I took the freedom he gave me as an excuse to hide my weaknesses.

Probably out of embarrassment, I never brought up my affair with Len. When I began competing abroad, Len had no experience guiding an international athlete and never counseled me on the temptations I might face while away from home. I never talked about family matters with John Walker, either. Though John and I were close, he was still a rival of mine and in 1984 he might be running against me in the Olympics. I didn't want him to think I was going through any marital trouble that might affect my running.

Once the Games began, I became a hermit. Instead of mixing with other athletes and getting out and seeing things, I avoided people, closed myself in, and put more weight on my shoulders. I didn't march in the Opening Ceremonies for fear of expending energy. And the first round of the 1,500 was almost two weeks away.

Two days before the 1,500 started, we dropped the kids at my mother-in-law's and Kim and I sequestered ourselves at a downtown hotel. Len was at the same hotel. I wanted to avoid the Village housing at USC. We killed time trying not to talk about my racing. Instead of looking forward to my Olympic assignment, I shrunk from it.

The hotel turned out to be a terrible location. There was nowhere in the immediate area to run, adding to my skittishness. At least at USC I would have had soft footing to do my casual daily jogging. And I probably would have bumped into Walker and Flynn.

I made it through my qualifying heat and semi-final into the final. The three races were run on consecutive days. I wasn't worried about qualifying. But in my semi, crossing the line out front with Jose Abascal of Spain, I felt a bite of tension. A switch clicked in my body and I finished a little short of breath. Our times were 3:35 and change, quick for a semi, but I should have coasted through it.

Suddenly, with the final around the corner, I met with Len to discuss the final, and for the first time I told him I wasn't sure about the race plan. His reaction was not so much to reinforce the plan but to boost my confidence. We agreed as before: I would feel out the pace and if it wasn't to my liking, I would take off.

I remembered that the only time I had done that was one year against Steve Ovett at the Bislett Games in Oslo. The pace was slow so I took off. I ended up eighth.

All three Britons, Ovett included, made the Olympic 1,500 final. Ovett was shaky. He'd finished last in the 800 final, collapsed, and was hospitalized with a respiratory disorder. Considering

Ovett's history of suspicious ailments, it was hard to grant him much pity. Still, Ovett ran the 1,500 rounds and took the line for the final. Give him credit for that.

Ovett probably felt the British press would butcher him if he didn't start. They had already pummeled Coe, the defending Olympic 1,500 champion, whose selection to the British team was hotly debated. Coe had not run well in a long while and placed second to Peter Elliot in the British championships. For once I agreed with the British press. I did not consider Coe my competition. In L.A., he first ran the 800, taking the silver medal behind Joachim Cruz. That was nothing to be ashamed of, but it seemed Coe's best form was behind him.

Cram—he was my competition. Cram was stuck in my mind from Helsinki. There were rumors that he'd had some minor injuries, but there was no way to really know. He had not run any big races before the Games. Despite his '83 world title, he expressed concern about meeting me in L.A. Discussing the Games, Cram was quoted as saying, "Steve's going to be on his home patch . . . which is going to make it more difficult for us." Little did he know.

I imagined myself leading the final. I also imagined myself losing. To ease the burden, I tried to come up with a worst-case scenario that would not ruin me. I figured if I died out front, I could still hang on for the silver or, all right, if I really died . . . I would still get a medal, wouldn't I?

A *Track & Field News* preview named me the consensus favorite with Ovett second, Cram third, and Coe fifth. Certainly the thousands of people seated in the Los Angeles Coliseum had me as their favorite. I was the American from southern California. That's all they needed to know.

I did my warmup, sat in the call room, and waited. Would I be able to hold the lead if I took it? Why was it taking so long for us to be called onto the track? Finally an official escorted us out in the sunlight and we were led single file to our lanes. I wanted to jog a few laps and shake out my legs as always. But I couldn't. Olympic procedures confined us to our lane markers. In my fragile state of mind, every bit of pre-race loosening up that was denied me hurt.

Spectators called to me, but I ignored them. I deposited my sweats in the basket provided the athletes and stared blankly down the track. It was time to run the Olympic 1,500 final before 92,000 people in the Los Angeles Coliseum, in southern California, where I'd grown up, run in high school and college, and instead I wished right then I was in Byrkjelo in the fjords with the salmon running upsteam at 3 o'clock on a Scandinavian morning.

The gun popped and Coe, carried by momentum, glided ahead in the opening meters before braking and settling in. There were 12 men in the field. Omar Khalifa of Sudan and Joseph Chesire of Kenya went for the lead. Coe slipped into third on the outside. I was back in the middle hugging the inside. It felt like a walk. The 400 split was 58.9—not fast, but not a walk. But I had so much emotion driving me I felt I would explode if I didn't run faster.

In a championship 1,500, after the opening 400, there can be a momentary lull when the field slows a touch while assessing the first lap. The first 400 is nothing more than a prelude. Then, for a few seconds, there's a pullback. In those seconds, you can accomplish a lot. I could not wait.

In one move, just past the 400, I swept brazenly from eighth into the lead. We had two and three-quarter laps left, two and a half minutes of running. My cheeks puffed like bellows. I carried my arms high. My eyes blinked in distress. Coe stuck behind me in second. Abascal was third.

Once you're in the lead, you have to direct your energies down the track in front of you. You can't worry about the action behind: where a certain contender is, who's making moves, what trouble lay in waiting. You must be able to divorce yourself from the field. It doesn't matter if the field is breathing down your neck. You have to be able to make that emotional break. Few men can do it. Could I?

Holding the lead around the second lap, I thought, Okay guys, I'm going, you'll have to catch me. Cram, Coe, Ovett . . . see ya later. . . . But too much of my energy was channeled behind me. I kept listening for footsteps. Where was everybody? My senses were acute. I could feel Coe and the others on my shoulder. My 800 split was 1:56.9 and in desperation I pushed even harder on the ensuing backstretch. But as I willed my body to accelerate, my mind was beginning to lose control.

It's been said that running is 50 percent physical—and 90 percent mental. I buy that. I could never accomplish anything my mind did not embrace. From my first four-minute mile on, I had never doubted myself.

Until now.

Abascal and Coe rushed by me on the far turn with 600 to go. I tried to steady myself, thinking I was finally where I wanted to be: behind, in my comfort zone. Now I would sit behind them and kick them down.

But I had little fight left and one by one virtually everyone else poured ahead. Everyone but Ovett, who dropped out with 400 to go and was taken to the hospital. I ran as hard as I could in a numb state of survival. It was the longest lap of my life. In the biggest race of my career, I faded farther and farther behind, deeper and deeper into the abyss.

Coe outsprinted Cram for the gold medal, and Abascal took third. I finished tenth in 3:39.86. Coe's was a brilliant run, making him the first man to repeat as Olympic 1,500 champion, and his 3:32.53 established an Olympic record. Though I could not focus on the aftermath, I was pleased to learn later that Coe had made a point of rebuffing the British reporters who'd knocked him. "Perhaps you'll believe me now!" he called from trackside.

After the race, I was dazed. Everything was black. It was like wandering around in a dark castle. People tried to make me feel better. They told me I had run courageously, that I ran with honor, but I would have none of it. My competitors gave me credit for, as Coe put it, "taking this by the scruff of the neck." All I felt was total failure.

The linchpin to success in running is emotional control. Up to this time, I had been able to detach myself from the hubbub and psych myself down rather than getting too keyed up. I liked to live below the surface of the hype. That way, at some level deep within me, each race was the same: talent vs. talent. Each race counted the same. That is to say, each race didn't count at all. What counted was not the decoration but the feeling: winning or coming close. And the feeling of training, the adventure of being in shape to win.

At my core, I had managed to keep running as my little secret: a joyful childlike game I was good at, a place in which I could exist that was mine alone for its bliss and purity. Now, at the conclusion of the Olympic 1,500, I was cut open, naked, my little secret undermined by a new and terrible reality.

———————

I lapsed into depression. After several years as the equal, more or less, of Coe and company, I now felt inferior. My entire outlook changed. I followed the track circuit to Europe for the remainder of the season, but my heart wasn't in it. Len came with me for support. He said he'd give me one day to straighten myself out.

After winning three races in Germany, I went to Zurich for the 1,500 against Coe. I hoped to get my little piece of flesh, but once in Zurich, I realized I couldn't make up for the Olympics. When you are called to your marks for the Olympic final, the results stand for all time. In Zurich, everyone was cordial to me, but I walked around with the feeling that I'd choked and that all the respect I had earned over the years was gone. Ultimately, I would be judged by my performance at the '84 Olympic final.

In Europe, I commiserated with Walker and Flynn, both of whom ran the 5,000 in L.A. They'd placed 8th and 11th, respectively, and we cried in our beer together. Many of the Olympic champions, including Carl Lewis and Evelyn Ashford, were featured at Zurich. Ashford set a women's world record in the 100. Coe beat me, 3:32.39 to 3:33.46. I ran a decent race, but that was all the energy I could muster. Going through the motions, I went on to run 7th and last at Koblenz, and 5th at Rieti. It was time to put the track season to bed.

Once home, I got sick but still went to New York in September for the Fifth Avenue Mile. It was easy money that I could not afford to pass up. Nike and Sub–4, my two sponsors, had dropped me after the Games. Nike cut back on track and field promotions, ultimately broadening its marketing strategy to make a global statement. I was no longer considered one of the elite. Sub–4, in a financial crisis, cut endorsements.

I had one remaining source of income: race fees, and with my Olympics showing I commanded less. So I came to New York, collected a few thousand dollars, ran with walking pneumonia, and placed 11th.

Money contributed to the pressure I felt in L.A. As an Olympic winner, I could have tripled my annual income. For someone like me, with a growing family and an insecure line of work, there was a lot at stake. I think I was the only man in the 1,500 final with a wife and kids.

The difficulties in keeping my marriage intact while racing the track circuit reached a boiling point at the Fifth Avenue race. My illness in New York seemed to reflect the entire year's failures. During the race I felt like I had a bowling ball in my chest and was being knocked to pieces.

When I returned to Europe following the Olympics, I was more vulnerable than ever. Despite Kim's protest that I stop seeing the other woman, and my promise that I would end it, I'd resumed the relationship in my swing through Germany, Switzerland, and Italy.

Kim had come with me to Fifth Avenue and was seething. She'd already heard through the grapevine of my continuing transgressions in Europe. Then, to top it off, the woman, as usual, was at Fifth Avenue, too. Even with Kim along for the weekend, I chose not to ignore her.

I don't know what possessed me to be so insensitive. All along our problem was that old marital standby: lack of communication. Fixated on my running, I shelved the issue of my marriage and it was never properly aired. It was only a year or so after Kim and I were married that the other woman first came into the picture. Kim and I were young and not very good at understanding each other's feelings. Our frequent separations pulled us apart emotionally and, like a runner drifting farther and farther behind, it was hard to catch up.

When Kim and I returned to Scottsdale, she threw me out of the house. But first she lashed into me with the full force of her anger. She told me how hurt and frustrated she was. She was relentless and I had it coming. She forced me to admit everything and to give her the details of my liaison. I was still in love with Kim and told her so. But it was too late for that.

This went on for a couple of weeks until finally Kim demanded that I call the woman and end the relationship for good. So I did the only thing I could do: make the call. That was a tough call, but not unexpected. We cared for each other, but all along we both knew this thing could not go on forever. We agreed not to see each other anymore at meets, not even to say hello.

Even after the call, Kim told me to get lost for a while. I grabbed my toothbrush and running stuff and, in the first of a number of separations like that, went to the beach house in Leucadia.

I feared my marriage was over, but after a week Kim said she wanted to come join me to make amends, and she did. But we didn't patch things up in the best way. We should have worked through the many issues generated by my affair, and found some middle ground over differences in our needs and expectations for a permanent reconciliation. Instead, we quickly said, okay, let's put everything behind us, kiss and make up, and move on. That was easier than really facing up to our problems.

For the time being, Kim and I went down to Mexico for a couple of days to reclaim our relationship. We succeeded in keeping our marriage together, but inevitably the wounds remained open. As 1984 ended, I had damage to repair, both on and off the track.

CHAPTER EIGHT

Flashes of Brilliance: 1985–1991

I t was during the 1984 Olympic year that I realized my collection of sub–4 minute miles was growing and that I would soon run my 100th. After my failure in Los Angeles, I latched onto this approaching milestone. Even though the first sub–4:00 (3:59.4) was run by Roger Bannister in 1954—and hundreds of athletes had done it since—the 4-minute mile still had prestige and I needed a goal. This was perfect. Other than evidence of my durability—and of my proclivity for racing a lot—running 100 sub–4:00s was not terribly important in the big picture. The chase had no risk. There was no question I would achieve it. There was only one way I could "lose"—if someone beat me to it.

I finished 1984 with 89 and that did not count the additional 100 or so 1,500-meter races run at 3:42.2 or better, the metric equivalent of sub–4:00. There was only one other runner in the world who could match my total: John Walker, my idol, mentor, confidant on the track circuit, former world recordholder, and 1976 Olympic champion from New Zealand. At the end of the '84 season, Walker had 88. The race was on. Who would reach 100 first?

I found out that, despite his exalted place in the annals of track (he was the first one to run sub–3:50, for crying out loud), Walker really cared about being the first one to run his 100th sub–4:00, and hoped to cash in on it. I spoke to John early in 1985 and proposed that we reach No. 99 at about the same time and go after the 100th in the same race. I would come down to New Zealand to meet him on his turf. It would not be an exhibition. We would race. He said no.

Walker, at 33, was four years older than me and looking at the end of his career. He needed a boost. He also needed to consider his earning power. He wanted to capitalize on the opportunity with sponsorship deals. If he lost to me in New Zealand, John felt he'd blow everything.

Approaching the age of 29, I still felt at the peak of my powers and was firmly implanted in Peter Pan Land. I thought my career would never end; I'd be cruising down Main Street on a Friday night forever. With the traumatic '84 Olympics hopefully behind me, I began to feel like my old racing self and competed like crazy. I wasn't winning much, but I was having fun adding to my sub–4:00 collection, and that was the point.

From mid-January to mid-February, 1985, I ran eight indoor races, all but one under 4:00. Eamonn Coghlan was winning everything, beating me left and right. At the Millrose Games, Coghlan ran 3:53.82 to win his sixth Wanamaker Mile, tying Glenn Cunningham's record, while I took fifth in 3:56.61. That was typical. My only indoor victory came a week later at the *Dallas Times-Herald* meet, where I defeated Ray Flynn (Coghlan had chosen to run the two-mile). That was my 94th sub–4:00 and I'd hoped to line up additional outdoor races for easy pickings.

Walker was pursuing the chase even more aggressively than I was. Taking advantage of the summer season Down Under, Walker ran five sub–4:00s in New Zealand in December and early January, giving him 93 when he came to the United States for the indoor circuit. Competing side by side with me in Los Angeles, Johnson City (Tennessee), New York, and Chicago, Walker brought his total to 97.

We kidded each other and fought hard in competition. Though it didn't really matter who beat whom as long as we broke 4:00, oneupmanship between us was unavoidable. I had not given up on convincing John to race me for the 100th and kept needling him. He wouldn't budge. I told him he and I could generate the appeal of a Coe-and-Ovett type of showdown; maybe that was an exaggeration, but it did seem to me that we could break the spell of top milers going to great lengths to avoid one another.

The media picked up on our dual mission as a minor curiosity. With Coghlan the darling of the circuit and stars Carl Lewis and Mary Decker Slaney breaking records, a couple of '84 Olympic also-rans running sub–4:00s while eating Coghlan's dust didn't make for good copy.

I'd come closest to beating Coghlan that winter in Chicago, at the Bally Invitational. Two days after Millrose, we drew even onto the homestretch of the Rosemont Arena and kicked fiercely to the tape. He defeated me, 3:57.25 to 3:57.33. Walker sneaked under 4:00 with a fourth-place 3:59.39, but the next weekend in Toronto, Walker's luck ran out. Coghlan edged me again, 3:59.05 to 3:59.66, and Walker was fourth again but ran only 4:01.52. In early February, Walker returned to New Zealand for his final push.

I had 96 on February 17 when Walker went for number 100 on his home track in Auckland. Ours was a friendly rivalry tinged with just a touch of envy. Before the race, I casually proclaimed, "I think John is a little more interested in this than I am. It's a big deal in New Zealand." Walker ran 3:54.57 to "win" our duel, then said on TV: "Eat your heart out, Steve Scott."

Two weeks later, with nothing at stake, Walker agreed to race me in Auckland. It was a good promotion. I won big in 3:53.7 for No. 97. Then I made my own push in May on three consecutive weekends in California. First, I won a 3:58.60 mile at Modesto. After that, in Los Angeles, I took second by inches to '84 Olympic 800 champion Joachim Cruz at the Pepsi/UCLA meet. He ran 3:53.19. I ran 3:53.20. Ninety-nine down, one to go.

There was little drama to my 100th as I took the line at the Bruce Jenner Bud Light Classic in San Jose. Naturally, I wanted to win. Facing Ray Flynn, Mike Boit, and Sydney Maree, I felt in close to 3:50 shape again.

The Jenner meet was historic for another reason. This was the first year of the IAAF/Mobil Outdoor Grand Prix, the international track series that awarded prize money to athletes as the hypocrisies of amateurism were finally being put to rest. By placing in various meets, most held in Europe where track is a marquee sport, you would score points toward a final standing and be eligible for cash awards. These awards served as bonuses since they came in addition to the appearance fees and prize money paid to athletes by the individual meets.

Few American meets have been solid enough to earn Grand Prix status. The Jenner event, a circuit mainstay, kicked off the 1985 series with a national television deal. A sold-out crowd of 9,000 filled the San Jose City College stadium to see '84 Olympic gold medalists Valerie Brisco-Hooks (400 meters) and Roger Kingdom (110 hurdles) and the muscular Czech, Jarmila Kratochvilova, the women's world recordholder in the 800 denied the '84 Games because of the Soviet-led boycott.

Competing as a sideshow with number 100 on my chest, I reeled off a 55.2 last lap to clock 3:56.5 for a stride-length win over Flynn. Whoopee! Number 100! Afterward, I told the press. "I wish John Walker had waited to become the first with 100 so we could have raced for the honor." Now, that really would have been significant. "But when I retire," I added, "I'm going to have more career sub–4:00s than him." It would be a total nobody would challenge for a long time.

After all of my near-misses on a world scale, I needed some distinction of historical permanence. Trying hard was my talent and I set out to make good on my promise.

I also made good on my promise to Kim. Whenever I saw my woman friend at meets, I ignored her. She made it easy because she was standoffish toward me.

Without her company, running seemed more like a job to me. I still socialized and hung out with the Walkers and Flynns, but I guarded any inclination of mine to be a little flirty. At times when some of the guys would go to a bar to pick up women, I wouldn't go with them. I felt contained by boundaries.

But not athletically. With the tight reins I put on competition in the '84 Olympics year, I saw '85 as a time to spread my wings again and see the world. I didn't like everything I saw. My first outdoor track race was a 1,500 in March in Kobe, Japan. I found the city stifling. There was nowhere to run, everything cost too much, and there was nothing in English. I guess I was the ugly American. I defeated a weak Japanese field, collected my money, and promptly left.

My last track race of the season, six months later, was in Nairobi, in my only trip to Kenya, nowadays the cradle of distance running. It was stunning. I competed in a 1,500 held in honor of Mike Boit, the great Kenyan who was retiring. Though Mike's birthdate was listed as January 1, 1949, he was not sure of his age, which was thought to be a lot older than his passport indicated. When in 1989 he came out of retirement to run some masters mile races in the U.S., he ran 4:15 and set a masters indoor record on pure memory. In all likelihood, Mike was over 40 when he was still breaking 4:00, but there was no way to prove it.

After winning the 1,500, I went on a three-day safari. Trying to forge a renewal, Kim was traveling with me that summer and we stayed in a grass hut near Mombasa on Kenya's east coast. There was no gate that could prevent animals, even lions, from dropping by. Sitting at the swimming pool in our complex, we could see giraffes, zebras, wildebeest within close range. We did the tourist number, snapping pictures from a van that took us through a game preserve.

Between Kobe and Nairobi, I ran a dozen races in Europe. I was earning from $4,000 to $5,000 per race and was in the first year of a three-year contract with the Asics shoe company. Whatever I did in 1985 countered the experience of '84. I avoided pressure and had no focus. I didn't want to train very hard. All I wanted was to go from race to race in a kind of brain-dead state and let the wounds heal.

While my season was unremarkable—my only victories were a 1,500 at Stockholm and 3,000 in London—I did break 3:50 with a 3:49.93 fourth-place in the "Dream Mile" at Oslo and also came close to the American record in the 1,500 with a fourth-place 3:31.76 at Nice. Steve Cram won both races.

While regaining some lost status that season, I was no longer the top-rated American. After eight straight years of number-one ranking, I was now surpassed by Sydney Maree, who'd broken my U.S. 1,500 record and this season further improved it to 3:29.77, just off the world mark. Maree, the South African émigré, had drawn enormous support for his anti-apartheid stand. How could anyone not root for the guy? On the top of that, he was a Villanova graduate.

Villanova was to milers what Notre Dame was to quarterbacks. Villanova had the glamour guys, the whiff of legend from Ron Delany and coach "Jumbo" Elliott up through Marty Liquori, Eamonn Coghlan, and beyond. I was a doctor's son from California, not the all-American boy by any means, but no one who could engender much sympathy. You needed a reason to root for me, and if you didn't live in southern California, you probably didn't have one.

I'm sure it was tough being in Maree's position. As a man who'd fled his native land, he may have felt out of place in America. Conditioned by a lifetime of apartheid, Maree seemed to view track through the prism of race. He was standoffish toward his mostly white opposition. At one meet in Germany, where Maree was racing Ray Flynn in the 3,000, Walker and I were on the sidelines cheering for Ray, our buddy. I sensed that Maree may have taken this as an insult since later at the hotel he chastised Walker and me.

In the mid-eighties, Maree was the only black man among the ranks of America's top milers. While African nations like Kenya produced a surplus of extraordinary middle-distance runners, U.S. men's running was still divided among racial lines. Blacks continued to dominate the sprints; white athletes took the distances. This pattern had nothing to do with aptitude. It began at the school level and involved coaching bias and ignorance. A black kid came out for track. Typically, the coach put him in the 100. A white kid came out for track. The coach made him a miler.

During 1985, I moved back to California from Scottsdale. We bought a house on two acres at a good price in Fallbrook, a conservative community in northeast San Diego County known for its avocado groves. We wanted to get out of Scottsdale, especially since my frequent training partner, Pete Heesen, had left.

Like other women, Kim needed to seek her own identity and get out of the house. Corey, now 4, was now old enough to enter the community soccer program, and Kim got involved, not only as a "soccer mom," but eventually as a coach, referee, administrator, and player. As an excellent athlete who'd kept in shape over the years, Kim did not miss a beat even as the oldest player in a women's league populated by college-age athletes. I played soccer with Corey in our backyard. I also pitched baseball to him, hundreds and hundreds of balls, as my father had done with me.

Kim returned to work with a series of part-time jobs. At one point, she sold water filters at an air-conditioning company. For a while, she worked in event management for Elite Racing, a firm that organizes road races that I've done work for over the years. Later on, Kim took a position as a headhunter in a company serving the health-care industry. At home, I did my share of child care but, framed by old-fashioned chauvinism, had to get used to the idea of Kim leaving her role as full-time homemaker for a life outside the family.

Change was everywhere. After 12 years, I was about to lose my coach, Len Miller. He was given the ax by Arizona State and returning to California to go into another line of work. Inadvertently, I had played a role in Len's dismissal.

Two years before, I had done Len a favor by visiting two nationally-ranked high school distance runners from Shawnee Mission, Kansas, that he was trying to recruit. During my visit, I stayed at the home of one of the boys, and the parents couldn't get enough of me. Though Len could be strict in coaching attitude, he was not a stickler for regulations. He neglected to give me any instructions for my visit. Len had no ulterior motive; he just forgot.

Later it came out that, as a representative of Arizona State, I'd broken every NCAA rule in the book. I stayed too long with the boys. I ran with them. I drove around with them in my car. Since there were track fans in the area who were keen on seeing the boys attend Kansas University, and since NCAA headquarters were right there in Shawnee Mission, my innocent transgressions were hardly a secret.

This stuff hit the papers in Kansas, giving Len a black eye in Tempe. It was his second black eye. What really brought him down occurred in 1984. Len's assistant coach had turned him in to the school for giving money to an athlete. Though the athlete, a sprinter/hurdler, was on scholarship, he did not have enough money to pay his tuition one month. Purely out of generosity, Len gave him the money so the athlete could stay in school and get his degree.

After Arizona State gave Len his walking papers, he gave up coaching and opened up a card parlor in Oceanside, California, where such gambling was legal. In addition to his disillusionment over the college situation, Len was worn out from my instability in '84. I think he also felt I held him responsible for my Olympic failure, which was not the case at all. It was probably the right time for Len to move on to something else, and he proceeded to put 18 hours a day into his gambling establishment. We would continue to see one another on occasion and remain good friends to this day.

———————

After my respectable transition through the post-Olympic season, I felt my status boosted in 1986 with some of my best racing ever. It almost felt like '82 and '83 again. The morning after winning the Jenner Classic mile in San Jose, I set a world record (13:33) for a 5-kilometer road race in Carlsbad, on a course routed close to my home. This was the inaugural Carlsbad 5K, an innovative short-distance road event. Most road races were at least five miles or 10K (6.2 miles); the Carlsbad event was part of a movement to create more 5Ks and make road racing more accessible to the masses. The previous record of 13:52 was soft, but I defeated some good runners like Michael Musyoki of Kenya, the '84 Olympic bronze medalist in the 10,000, who would set a world half-marathon record the week after Carlsbad.

From there, I regained the U.S. national championship in the 1,500, winning my seventh title. My time was slow, but I sprung myself out of a box off the last turn to edge Jim Spivey. Subsequently, both Spivey and me were named to the U.S. team for the inaugural Goodwill Games in Moscow, but first we ran the Bislett Games "Dream Mile" in Oslo against Steve Cram. With Spivey and me charging hard on the last lap, Cram held us off to win in 3:48.31. I was second in 3:48.73 with Spivey third in a personal best 3:49.80, making him one of three Americans under 3:50.

As a reaction to the last two Olympic boycotts, the Goodwill Games—alternating sites in the United States and the Soviet Union—were created by Ted Turner, who saw marketing potential in a mini-Olympics that could bring the two superpowers together. The first meet was an administrative fiasco. It took us all day reach Moscow and once we arrived at the airport we were left helpless. U.S. team managers were nowhere to be found. We didn't know where to go to get organized and pick up our uniforms. The hotel was a drab box with no air-conditioning, and this was July in Moscow. The food was inedible. Fortunately, I roomed with Spivey, who'd been through several Eastern bloc trips and came prepared with a cache of peanut butter and jelly sandwiches. We lived on that for our stay.

At this time—1986—the Cold War still defined U.S./Soviet relations, and from our hotel window we could see a guard patrolling the courtyard. We wondered how closely we were being watched, whether our room was bugged. At night, it was stifling. No air circulated. We lay in bed unable to sleep. One night it was late and I got up to check on the guard. I had some crummy apricots I'd gathered as contraband for a snack. I grabbed the apricots and started chucking them at the guard to see if I could hit him. Yep, the old pitching arm was still there. Spivey was hiding under the covers, pleading with me to knock it off.

The next morning there were apricot pits in a pile outside our door.

Despite rampant disorganization, the Goodwill Games was a good meet for the U.S., for it was here that Jackie Joyner-Kersee set her first world record in the heptathlon. I was second in the 1,500 with Spivey right behind me in third. The Soviet who won acted suspiciously after he crossed the finish. He rushed to a nurse who started drawing blood from him. While some thought the blood was taken as a fitness measurement, others, including myself, disagreed.

The track circuit has always been rife with paranoia about drug use. It's part of the track culture to be suspicious of anyone performing especially well, anyone new who rises quickly to the top, anyone whose physical appearance (for example, women taking on male characteristics) changes in ways that seem to reflect drug use. I accepted as fact, for example, that just about any athlete from East Germany was on the sauce. Once the Iron Curtain came down, and revelations came out of Germany, our suspicions were proved accurate. No athlete from any country was beyond suspicion. There were also people who pointed fingers at me. I laughed it off.

Typical of the circumstantial evidence I'd hear about was the story about Romanian middle-distance runner, Paula Ivan, who won the 1988 Olympic 1,500 in Seoul. Lynn Williams of Canada was also in the 1,500 final and her husband, Paul, a top runner himself, was closely observing Ivan prior to the race. According to Williams, Ivan spent an inordinately long time in the bathroom with her belongings while the finalists were doing their last warmups. Ivan went out and won by 40 meters in the second fastest time in history. She tested negative in the Olympic drug testing.

After Moscow, I barnstormed through Western Europe winning miles or 1,500s in Nice, Koblenz, London, and Zurich, where

I defeated Sebastian Coe. I sprinted the last lap of the 1,500 in 53.1 to edge Coe, 3:35.14 to 3:35.22. Too bad I was two years late. The Zurich excitement revolved around Said Aouita of Morocco, the world recordholder in the 1,500 and 5,000 who attempted to add the 3,000 record to his collection. He fell just short. I would see more of Aouita in the years to come.

I concluded the '86 track campaign in Rome in September at the Grand Prix final, which awarded double points in the yearly standings. A pair of Spaniards, Jose Abascal and Jose-Luis Gonzalez, double-teamed me with their aggressive tactics. I was still able to hold off Abascal, 3:50.28 to 3:50.54. John Walker was third and Spivey sixth. I was proud of running a fast time so late in the season. The victory gave me the Grand Prix title in the 1,500 and a $10,000 prize. I earned another $10,000 by placing third in the overall standings combining all 17 events and ended up being ranked number three in the world for the year. With the next World Championships coming up in 1987, not to mention the Seoul Olympics in 1988, my career was definitely on the upswing.

Once the track season was over, it was time for dessert on the road mile circuit. No pressure, no consequences, great crowds. Road miles are like tennis exhibitions or state fairs. The money is good and you don't have to try very hard. I competed in Spain, Germany, and back in the United States. One event I missed was in Rio, where the promoters used the lure of female companionship, at a price of $100 for the weekend, to line up the field.

By 1987, with Len out of the picture, I'd been coaching myself for over a year and starting to toy with switching my event from the mile to the 5,000. I mistakenly believed I didn't need a coach at this point in my career. Left to my own devices, I overdid it in training and came down with the first significant injury of my career.

After winning nine straight races—in the 1,500, mile, 5K, and 10K, including two races in Israel—I developed a hamstring injury in June. It flared up at a road mile in Albuquerque, where I finished far back in 4:10. I had no appreciation of the need for rest. Len would always tell me when to back off. By myself, if I did a set of five 800s in a workout the year before, this year I'd do seven.

Even though the high mileage and distance runs I did were already geared to the 5,000, I felt I had to shoulder more long intervals—fast, repeated runs of 800 and longer. I strained a muscle in the area where the hamstring attaches to the buttocks. Physical therapy helped, but the pain nagged, on and off, for the entire year. It hurt most when I had to open full stride and sprint. From the bolstered workouts, I was going into every race tired.

Spivey beat me at the U.S. Nationals, then I placed fifth in each of my first three races in Europe before returning home for the Carlsbad 5K, which I won again. I could handle a 5K on the roads like Carlsbad, where marshaling late-race speed was more gradual than on the track, in which a sudden, jolting kick was required. At the Pan American Games in Indianapolis, Spivey again outran me, for second, as the win went to Brazil's Joachim Cruz. Back in Europe for the Zurich meet, I placed eighth in the 1,500; things were not looking up for the World Championships, due to start at the end of August in Rome.

The overtraining had poisoned my system. My training with Len all through the years always had me on the edge of the envelope. It was right; I could nudge up to the limit. But now I was over the limit, and the worse I ran, the harder I trained. It was killing me.

I could do no better than fifth in an 800 at a rinky-dink meet in Nykoping, an hour out of Stockholm. It was like a high school track with a grandstand on one side. We had dorm-style rooms. The promoter dispensed funds from a trackside trailer. White guys won the sprints. If you didn't grab the institutional meal dished out at the meet, dinner was boiled hotdogs at a truck stop at midnight.

In track, you could be high one day and low the next. My running was sour and my platoon was breaking up. Walker and Flynn were not around as much. Jim Spivey was a formidable athlete and a good guy, but we were not on the same social wavelength. Jim was mature.

At the World Championships in Rome, I looked at the heat sheets in the 1,500 and got nervous. Could I make it through the heats? Could I make the final? The only championship in which I hadn't made the final was my first NCAA as a college sophomore eleven years before. In Rome, I ran fourth in my heat to make the semi; but, then, my semi had most of the favorites: Abdi Bile of Somalia and George Mason University, defender and favorite Steve Cram, Gonzalez of Spain. . . . I ran fifth to squeeze into the final.

The final was slow, almost as slow as the embarrassing pace at the '83 world meet in Helsinki. The field hovered around 2:04 at the 800. Bile, who'd been injured all winter and had not resumed training till late April, moved up from dead last midway with a sweeping 52.64 last lap for the 3:36.60 victory. Talk about the value of time off. Gonzalez got second and Spivey, in a rare medal-winning performance for an American distance runner, placed third for the bronze. I was never in it. I finished 12th and last. Even the runner who fell—Kenya's Kip Cheruiyot—beat me.

It was a dismal year and I was tumbling into obscurity. Injury, fatigue, last place in the world meet . . . no coach to set me right. . . . You're only as good as your last race and European meet promoters never let you forget that. They want who's hot; everyone else can go suck an egg.

ABOVE
Steve addressing the San Antonio Community Hospital Health Forum,
May 1980.

ABOVE

Olympic Trials, Eugene, Oregon, 1980. Steve won the trials but the U.S. boycotted the Games so he could not participate. (Photo by Paul J. Sutton/Duomo)

ABOVE
1981 Millrose Games, Steve center, Eamonn Coghlan at left. (Photo by Steven E. Sutton/ Duomo)

LEFT
Competing in Brussels, 1982. Steve front, John Walker behind. (Photo by Steven E. Sutton/ Duomo)

TOP *Life on the international circuit: Swiss alps, the Eiger Sanction, 1982. Steve and Kim taking a break between races with runner Steve Lacy and his wife Kathy.*

BOTTOM *1983, Steve and Eamonn Coghlan. (Photo by David Madison)*

ABOVE
1984, Pepsi Invitational, UCLA, Joachim Cruz at left.

ABOVE
1984, Kinney meet in Berkeley, California. John Walker at left, #349.
(Photo by David Madison)

RIGHT

1984 Olympics,
Sebastian Coe at left.
Steve took the lead and
set the pace, but Coe
won. (Photo by Paul J.
Sutton/ Duomo)

RIGHT
1988 Olympics, Steve
took 5th. (Photo by
David Madison)

ABOVE
1984, at the Olympics.

TOP

*1988 5K road race, Carlsbad, California. Steve set the world record for the second
time with a time of 13:30.*

ABOVE LEFT

*Steve and Megan on their way to a father-daughter dance sponsored by
Megan's Brownie troop, Leucadia,1989.*

ABOVE RIGHT

Halloween antics 1989: Steve, center, Kim, right, and friends.

Family portrait: Kim, Corey, Steve, Megan, their dog, Tubbs, and their cat, Blue.

RIGHT

On a family vacation in Yosemite, 1991, a perfect place to keep in shape.

RIGHT

1992 Olympic Trials in New Orleans, 1500 meters, Steve going around fallen Joe Falcon. (Photo by David Madison)

TOP 1993 *National Cross-Country Championships, Missoula, Montana. Steve raced uphill in 6 degree weather. He placed 10th at 30:32, one of his last races before the cancer diagnosis.*

BOTTOM 1993 *National Cross-Country Championships, Missoula, Montana, with teammates, left to right: Justin Snook, Tony Bergman, Steve, Scott Wilson, Kevin Burko.*

TOP
At home in Leucadia, Dad Steve and new baby Shawn, 1992.

ABOVE LEFT
Press conference for Millrose Games, February 1993.

ABOVE RIGHT
*Steve's parents, Mary and Gordon, at Steve's induction ceremony to Orange
County Sports Hall of Fame, Anaheim Stadium, December 1994.*

ASICS

STEVE SCOTT

American Record Holder
Mile — 3:47.69

A B O V E
Steve Scott promotional piece for Asics.

ABOVE

Legends of Running: Eamonn Coghlan, Sir Roger Bannister, and Steve Scott
at the Discover Card Fifth Avenue Mile, New York City, September 28, 1996.
Frank Litsky of the New York Times reported:

"So the hero of the day's mile races turned out to be an old hero resurrected
– Steve Scott, who has run 136 sub-four-minute miles on the track, more than
anyone in history. Here, Scott won two one-mile races 40 minutes apart, an
achievement for any 40-year-old, let alone one who found out in May 1994 that
he had testicular cancer.

"First, Scott, as a guest runner in the masters race for men 40 and older,
won by 140 yards in 4 minutes 6.57 seconds. After a short rest, he ran a relaxed
two-man legends race against 43-year-old Eamonn Coghlan, the only master to
have bettered four minutes for the mile (3:58.15 two years ago indoors). With a
sly burst in the last 20 meters, Scott beat Coghlan in 4:37.02."
(Photo by Brian Myers, courtesy of New York Road Runners Club)

Once again, I feared for my future earnings power. Whenever my running was sharp, I didn't fret over whether a promoter was paying me what I was worth. My mindset was, "Sure, that's fine, I'll run for that." I felt the well would never run dry. When my running was in the pits, I would start to feel desperate.

After competing without sparks at Rieti and Brussels, I agreed to be the rabbit in the 2,000 at Lausanne to conclude the season. The promoter would not give me a spot as a regular competitor. I had to be the rabbit, the role played by an understudy hungry for exposure and a few dollars. Me: the rabbit? They offered a thousand bucks and I took it. I did my job, taking the pace through the mile in 3:54, then stepping off the track with a lap to go. Spivey won in 4:52.44, an American record.

At the '87 world meet, drug suspicions were hard to suppress after a bulked-up Ben Johnson of Canada ran an incredible 9.83 100 meters to set a world record and leave Carl Lewis a long stride behind. That fall, I considered taking drugs myself to boost my sagging performances. A coach from the Santa Monica area, Chuck Debus, a controversial figure who coached a lot of top young female runners approached me. He offered to work with me and serve as my manager. I said okay. We got together once a week. He took me through his plyometric drills to build leg power and had a physical therapist available for rubdowns.

One day, Debus asked me to meet him at his apartment in Santa Monica. He told me the plyometric drills—bounding exercises like hopping in the style of a triple jumper—would help me break the world record in the mile. He also said if I really wanted to be the world record holder, I should be taking anabolic steroids. He told me everyone was doing it, including all of my leading competition.

I was down and out and vulnerable. I told Debus I was against taking steroids, but he kindled my interest in blood doping. I was not philosophically against blood doping—withdrawing blood, storing it, and putting it back at an opportune time for an oxygen boost—even though, like drug use, it was against the rules. I likened the advantage to that of someone who strengthened by growing up at high altitude. In blood doping, I rationalized, you did not put any foreign substance into your body.

Debus pushed the blood doping and I agreed to look into it. I found a doctor friend who said he would supervise the procedure. But before it went any further Debus returned to his argument for drugs. He emphasized how steroids would help me train harder with less recovery. Debus knew which buttons to push. But I got fed up and ended the relationship. Deep down, I knew I couldn't go through with it.

Three years later, Debus was banned for life from sanctioned track and field in the United States by The Athletics Congress. TAC had convened a special investigative panel to look into "allegations of impropriety" associated with Debus.

In 1988, with the Seoul Olympics coming up, drugs dominated the track landscape. I was determined to get to Seoul through natural means and I needed a legitimate coach. I arranged to work with John Walker's coach, Arch Jellie, of New Zealand. We got together briefly in California. I showed Arch my workouts and he saw what was wrong. I'd been doing mile and 5,000 training all at once. I was putting my system under far too much stress. Jellie slowed me down.

First, he had me do long runs, for as much as two hours, but at almost a jogger's pace. He emphasized that I did not have do every distance run at a less than 6-minute-mile pace. If I covered

15 miles in two hours, that was fine. After three years of coaching myself, I was prepared to accept any new idea. Jellie was relaxed, flexible, much like my high school coach. There was only one problem: He was in New Zealand.

We'd confer weekly. He warned me that I would have one peaking period, for the Olympics, and that I could not expect to be in shape early in the year. Arch knew I had to make a living off the track circuit, but I had to accept that gratification would be delayed until the summer. The ground rules were laid, and I placed fifth, fourth, and eighth in my only three indoor miles of 1988. I didn't break four minutes once. In training, I was building strength, not speed, and when I moved up to race a 3,000 I won. Arch's coaching made sense.

It felt good having a coach again. Another new wrinkle from Arch were time trials in which I'd run very hard but with ample rest. I'd run a mile twice but take ten minutes to rest between each run. He also cut my racing schedule pretty much in half. Many of his ideas were fundamental. Having someone to answer to made all the difference to me.

Soon enough, the new system began to pay off. After winning three road races to open my '88 outdoor season, I continued my streak with three straight track victories at the Jenner, Pepsi, and Michelob meets. Then, I was off to Europe for an abbreviated schedule: three races in six days, prior to the Olympic Trials. I ran well in Europe. Though fifth at Bislett, my time was 3:50.09 as Cram triumphed in 3:48.85. I won a mile in Cork, Ireland, in 3:55.4 and finished with a close second to Aouita in the London 1,500 in 3:36.76.

I'd only raced 15 times that year prior to the Olympic Trials, held in late July in Indianapolis. I'd sacrificed income to try and run better at the Games. I made up a little of that by starting the sport sunglasses craze. Earlier that year, Smith, the company known for its ski goggles, approached me with a possible sponsorship. That didn't materialize but then I connected with Oakley, which gave me a sponsorship contract and made its first venture into track and field. I wore the sleek, pricey glasses in races and gave them terrific visibility at the Olympic Trials. In a relationship that would last six years, I continued wearing the glasses at the Olympics, where I personally handed out pairs to all the U.S. distance runners. Before long, running magazines were publishing photo spreads on the glasses, and they took off.

For me, the '88 Trials were similar to '84 in that I was thinking two months ahead, this time to Seoul. Again I ran the 1,500 meters, but the complexion of the race differed. The pace was exceedingly slow. Runners threw plenty of elbows. It was hot and humid. In the scratch-and-kick scramble for the three Olympic berths, everyone got shoved. Spivey stumbled and finished fourth behind unheralded Mark Deady and I got second behind Jeff Atkinson. Jeff was a colorful character, a free spirit always ready with a quip. He was very tough mentally and surprised a lot of people when he went on to make the Olympic final.

After the Trials, rather than go to Europe I stayed in California to work with Arch, who came to join me from New Zealand. While training for the Games, I was also house-hunting. Kim was bored in Fallbrook, and over the summer we were looking to move to Leucadia, where we already had the beach house. We didn't want to move permanently to the beach house because we sometimes rented it out; and since the neighborhood near the beach was seedy, with drug deals out in the open and shady characters milling about, it was not a good family atmosphere on a year-round basis. So we went about selling our Fallbrook home and buying a second dwelling in another section of Leucadia.

Kim was happier with our decision to move closer to the beach house, which she counted on as a place to unwind. We were still having our marital bumps and bruises. I never felt Kim gave herself enough of a grieving period after my affair before attempting to put her feelings behind her. She stored up too much resentment and, in the aftermath, could not let go of it. I had come to terms with assuming the role of the guilty party with ground to make up. Too often we were still not on the same page.

Kim saw my running as a symbol of what had gone wrong with us. It was in the track world that I had strayed. In late summer, I left for the U.S. pre-Olympic training camp in Chiba, Japan, while Kim remained at home to engineer our move from Fallbrook by herself. Things like that, which Kim saw as negligence on my part, would add up.

This time, in contrast to '84, I wanted to immerse myself in the Olympic culture and do everything with the U.S. team. The week-long training camp, a good bonding opportunity, was part of that. Our itinerary included an excursion to Disneyland of Japan. In '84, I would have avoided that like the plague. But now, I wanted to connect with the athletes, be part of the flow, benefit from group support. It was also my way of saying, whatever happens in the stadium is fine, I just don't give a damn. I could not allow any notion of desperation to enter my system. I even marched in the Opening Ceremonies.

Once our move to Leucadia was complete, Kim, Corey (age seven), and my parents made the trip to Seoul in late September for the Games. There was separate housing for family and friends. I stayed with my family and also at my assigned room at the Olympic Village. My roommate was Pat Porter, a 10,000 runner who'd won eight straight U.S. national cross-country titles but had not distinguished himself on the track. I ended up rooming with Pat because none of the other distance guys wanted to. I think they felt he tooted his own horn a little too much. I didn't have any problem with Pat: He made for an easy mark. We also roomed together in Chiba, where there were huge praying mantises. I caught one and put it in Pat's bed. A bunch of us were sitting around playing cards when Pat came in. He was always the first guy to get into bed for the night. We held our cards and waited. *Argggggh!* Pat let out a scream and we doubled over in laughter.

In Seoul, I was relaxed and ready to run. My workouts were sharp. I'd run a 1,200-meter time trial in 2:50. All the ingredients for success were there, including my sophomoric tendencies. I instigated water balloon tossing from high up in our Village apartment. That was a good sign.

My relaxed mood was not entirely appreciated by the regimented Korean mindset. At Disneyland, a few us picked up Mickey Mouse ears as souvenirs and we decided to wear them during the Opening Ceremonies. Every nation filed into Olympic Stadium with appropriate patriotic reverence. Then came the Americans, a loose, out-of-sync blob as usual and, worst of all, three guys in particular showing criminal disrespect. Doug Padilla, Henry Marsh, and I wore our Mickey Mouse ears. Padilla and Marsh were not even cutups like me. They were Mormons.

The Koreans did not turn the other cheek. As a result of our antic, they withheld perks—such as extra Olympic tickets for family members. The Korean Olympic Organizing Committee sent a letter of reprimand to American team officials. The letter talked about the disarray of the Americans and specifically referred to the Mickey Mouse ears. To prevent an international incident, my cohorts and I had to personally apologize to the Korean officials.

We suited up in our Olympic dress attire and marched over to see the Koreans. These were the same uniforms we had to wear in the Opening Ceremonies, and as we entered the Koreans' offices someone in the U.S. delegation noticed I still had the Mickey Mouse ears sticking out from a pocket. American officials pleaded with me to get rid of it. Other athletes dared me to wear it as I greeted the Korean bigshots.

I couldn't. We had to go on. I was only thankful the Koreans had not traced the path of the water balloons back to my window. Who knows what the punishment would have been for that offense.

Going into the Games, the 1,500 favorites were Said Aouita and Steve Cram, who'd switched off breaking the records and, like Coe and Ovett, tried to avoid racing one another. The '87 world champion Abdi Bile also figured to be in the mix along with Britain's Peter Elliot, second to Cram at Bislett. I was rated seventh by *Track & Field News,* which called me "less consistent than five years ago" when I achieved my best championship result of second in the inaugural world meet. Fair enough.

On the day of the first round of the 1,500, I woke up with a touch of the flu. All that bureaucratic stress must have gotten to me. Thankfully, it did not affect my running. I made it through in perfunctory fashion. The next day, I won my semi in 3:38.20 with Kenyan Peter Rono stuck to my heels. I'd been at such peace with myself I stayed with my family even as I competed. But the semi was not a walk, and with the final early in the afternoon the next day, I decided to return to the Village that night. For the final, I could get the Village shuttle to the stadium and avoid the traffic from Kim's hotel. Who needed to be stuck in traffic on the way to the Olympic final?

My decision proved to be a fatal mistake. I was alone that night. Everybody in my complex at the Village had already finished competing and they were out on the town. Porter had taken up with a high jumper, Trish King (whom he would eventually marry), and they were out. Spending the evenings with my family, my mind was occupied and not at all focused on my races. Now, by myself, I had nothing to do but think about my race.

The Olympic final. Arch Jellie was in Seoul and after my semi he'd told me I could win the gold.

I spent the entire night visualizing about winning; how I would handle the victory, what I would do with the gold medal, what I would say at the press conference. With every thought, my heart raced, adrenaline pumped and energy was spent. It was like running the race itself. I ran the final over and over again.

As things developed, Aouita had aggravated an injury placing third in the 800 and would not run the 1,500. Bile was also hurt and not competing. Cram, among the walking wounded, had also run the 800 and didn't make it past the prelims. He'd made it to the 1,500 final but was obviously not in good form. I didn't even have Jim Spivey to deal with since he'd failed to make the U.S. team. Who was left?

My pre-Games number seven rating was suddenly irrelevant. I was fit and confident. I had no injury. It was anybody's race. The only problem was that I could not get my mind off it. On the eve of the final, the race possessed me. My cool detachment had been rattled.

The next day, lining up for the start of the 1988 Olympic 1,500 final, I considered Peter Elliot and even a sub-par Cram my main opposition. Marcus O'Sullivan of Ireland led the first 400 in 59.7. Peter Rono nudged up to the front at the 800 in 2:00.3. It was predictably slow but at least not embarrassingly so.

O'Sullivan, an indoor specialist in the Coghlan mold, and Rono, a 21-year-old sophomore at Mt. St. Mary's University in Maryland, were not runners to worry about. There was no evidence that either man could kick here when it counted.

As I moved on the outside to get into position on the third lap, Omar Khalifa of Sudan, known for his sudden bursts, cut me off and threw me to the inside. I stayed put, waiting to mobilize my kick. I felt safe. There was room to breathe.

Rono, still ahead, charged the third lap in 56.4 for a 2:56.7 1,200 split. Now we were running. There were 300 meters to go. I was fifth. Rono, Cram, Elliot, and Jens-Peter Herold of Germany were ahead of me. All of us began to sprint, but no one could muster the speed to catch Peter Rono, all 5' 3¾" and 119 pounds of him.

I gave it everything I had, but it was not nearly enough. It was bewildering. How had Rono gotten away like that? Not one of us—four contenders with proven records—could nail Rono? He held on to win the gold in 3:35.96, close to his personal best. Elliot, Herold, and Cram placed second, third, and fourth, respectively. I was fifth in 3:36.99.

Rono's victory was the upset of the Games. Just five months before, he couldn't even win the 1,500 at the Penn Relays. In Oslo, less than three months before, he was denied a spot in the "Dream Mile" and instead ran a secondary 1,500, which he won over a field of no-names.

What we should have paid more attention to was his triumph at the Kenyan Olympic Trials, which can be vicious. In fact, Rono talked about that event after his Olympic victory: "It was tougher to win the Kenyan Trials. We have many young talents back home and it is not easy to make the Olympic team." The Kenyan Trials are held at high altitude, and, amid the reservoir of Kenyan distance runners, anyone who can win a Trials race is evidently prepared to fight for the Olympic gold medal.

Rono's win added to Kenya's powerful Olympic comeback. Four years before in 1984, beset by a period of mismanagement, Kenya had come up with only one Olympic victory (steeplechase) and two men's track medals overall. That hardly lived up to the legacy left by Olympic legend Kip Keino and company. At Seoul, Kenya took gold in the men's 800, 1,500, steeplechase, and 5,000 meters and added a bronze in the 10,000 plus silvers in the steeple and marathon. That was more like it.

Fifth place seemed to be the American theme in the men's distances. In addition to my showing, the United States got fifth in the 800 (Johnny Gray) and 5,000 (Sydney Maree). Only one other American (Marsh in the steeple) made the top eight.

The sprints were something else, of course. Canadian sprinter Ben Johnson tested positive for drug use after his ridiculous 9.79 victory in the 100 and made headlines in every newspaper worldwide. Hysterical commentators said the Games were scarred beyond repair. Once again, track was lambasted for something for which other sports—baseball and basketball, for example—routinely get a slap on the wrist.

If anything did scar track, I don't think it was Johnson's actions alone but the feeling among both athletes and the press that drug tests caught some cheaters while failing to catch others.

After the 1,500, I walked off the track with my head high. I missed a medal by .78 seconds. This Olympics I accepted my performance and felt I had given some closure to the crushing experience four years before in the L.A. Coliseum. Even without a medal in my pocket, I felt good.

The only blemish to the entire '88 year had come earlier in the season on that very Coliseum track. I ran a mile staged as an added feature to a 10K road race that finished on the track. The infield had been reseeded and fencing had been installed to prevent runners from straying onto the grass.

As I led the field down the homestretch for the bell lap, a wind came up and blew a piece of fence onto the track and into my path. I jumped to avoid it and caught my foot in the fence twine. As the field raced by, I could only watch from the ground as I tried to free my tangled foot. By the time I got up, I was 100 meters behind. I resumed running just to finish but recorded the race in my diary as a "dnf"—did not finish. That Coliseum track was murder.

I thought then that my Olympic career was over in the 1,500. I would be 36 by the next Olympics—too old, I felt, to make the U.S. team, let alone make the Olympic final or be a medal contender. From what I observed, as milers aged we lost some of our natural speed, just enough of a deficit to make a difference. Studies of muscle fiber and other components of speed corroborated this. But we did not necessarily lose strength, which is tied more to consistent training than to young legs. In order to sustain world-class running, I felt I needed to finally make a commitment to the 5,000, which required more strength but less speed than the mile.

To reach my goal, I got rid of my coach. Makes sense, right? I decided that even though Arch Jellie was a fine coach it was impractical to work with someone in New Zealand most of the time. Back on my own and wedded to the longer distance, I would intensify my training but not until the following spring.

I carried my Olympic-year strength into 1989 and went up against Said Aouita in probably the most memorable indoor race of my life. Aouita, the Moroccan who'd won the 1984 Olympic 5,000, was back in peak form after his disappointing showing in Seoul. Aouita mopped up on his first American tour. He hung me out to dry in his U.S. indoor debut in the Millrose 3,000. I pushed the pace but to no avail. Though new to the indoor board track, Aouita triumphed as I placed fifth.

Indoor track was alive with excitement. Aouita was something of a mysterious figure—a breakthrough athlete from Moslem North Africa, brash, with rock-star aura, always accompanied by an entourage. He could hold impromptu press conferences, gesticulating in French, Arabic, or broken English in hotel lobbies, or he could surround himself diffidently with bodyguards in leather jackets. He'd predicted he would hold every world outdoor record from the 1,500 through the 10,000 and he was well on his way. By February '89, he held the marks in the 1,500, mile, and 5,000. Competing in the United States for the winter, he tried for the indoor records.

Two days after Millrose, Aouita won the 5,000 at the Mobil One meet in Fairfax, Virginia. With a large Moroccan flag waving from the small grandstand, Aouita went after the world indoor record of 13:20.40. He missed by two seconds and complained that he was confused by the intermediate times given—in English, of course—by the announcer.

The next week, at the Vitalis/Meadowlands meet in New Jersey, where six years earlier I'd chased Eamonn Coghlan to the world indoor mile record, I was set to race Aouita in the 3,000. In the style of a Coghlan setup, the entire event revolved around Aouita. I was little more than window dressing but that was okay. He was the star and 19 laps was a long way for me.

Still thought of as a miler, I was not even considered a long-shot. The *New York Times* said Aouita's "opponents in the 3,000 will include Doug Padilla and Brian Abshire, the best Americans." Padilla and Abshire were solid distancemen who knew how to handle the tricky indoor tracks.

Aouita was a sly one all right. Leading into the Meadowlands meet, he was initially cast as the spoiler in a "Dream Mile" matchup with Marcus O'Sullivan, clearly the best indoor miler now that Coghlan had retired. When Aouita was switched to the 3,000 field, some people said he was afraid of O'Sullivan; Aouita said that was ridiculous and that he'd wanted to run the 3,000 all along. For his part, Coghlan said Aouita was "definitely" ducking Marcus.

All of this jockeying only added to Aouita's aura of intimidation. He then announced in no uncertain terms that he was going after the world indoor record again. The Meadowlands meet would be Aouita's last record attempt of the winter. The 3,000 record, 7:39.2, had stood since 1973 and was one of the oldest on the books. The New York papers built up the record attempt, especially with Aouita's confusion over the intermediate times at Fairfax. This time, however, things would be different. Meadowlands' officials decided that the splits would be called out in French. That wouldn't help me or the other Americans but what the hell. This was Aouita's curtain call.

The pace was hot and I sat back waiting to die. As the laps went by, I managed to stay alive. We were cooking. Just by holding on, I kept passing people. Coming up on a lap to go, everyone had fallen back but me. I was on Aouita's shoulder. I didn't know what I was doing there, but I figured I may as well make the most of it. Suddenly, I felt invigorated.

At the bell lap, I brought the crowd of more than 11,000 to its feet. As though attempting a coup to overthrow a head of state, I tried to pass Aouita. He was a very proud, very gutsy runner. He gritted his teeth and protected his lane. I tried to go around him. The crowd roared, and it felt wonderful to be given such cascading support.

The arena rocked. And why shouldn't it? This was track and field at its best, one runner versus another, head-to-head, no funny business, with a fast pace and a world record on the line. Aouita pressed the envelope, just as he'd promised. But me? With about 150 meters to go, I imagine a good many fans were wondering: "Steve Scott? The miler? Where did he come from?"

I must admit I was wondering the same thing myself. I'd had no inkling that I could run with Aouita to the last step of a razor-sharp indoor 3,000. But without a coach, I had no one to judge my training, interpret my responses, and tell me what I was prepared for.

Now I drove elbow-to-elbow with the wiry Aouita. Drawing on every ounce of energy, I fought to a half-step advantage, but it was not quite enough to cut him off. In that position, I should have cut him off anyway, throwing Aouita off-stride; moves like that were almost expected indoors. Maybe I was foolish, but I preferred to race cleanly. I ran out of track and Aouita won.

He just missed the world record in 7:39.71. I set an American indoor record of 7:39.94 that still stands. *Track & Field News* hailed the race as "A 3,000 for the Ages." It proved to me once again how well I could run when relaxed. The race also affirmed my decision to put more energy into the 5,000. I felt I could run as fast as 13:10 and be a contender in the next world outdoor championship, at Tokyo in 1991.

The hopes were false. Without a coach, I could not resist the temptation to overtrain that spring of '89. Thinking I needed even more strength if I was going to dabble in the 5,000, I added another repetition workout of 800s, 1200s, or miles to my weekly regimen. I pushed these laps on the track with little rest and at 85 to 90 percent of maximum capacity. It was harder than racing. I'd already been doing this session weekly and needed as much as seven days' recovery. Doing it twice a week wiped me out.

I developed "heavy leg syndrome" and my '89 outdoor season fizzled. I was up and down. I could chase Marcus O'Sullivan with a 3:53.83 runnerup mile at the New York Games, then run eleventh in the 1,500 at Zurich and 13th in the 5,000 at Oslo. There was no stopping Aouita. After winning the 5,000 at Zurich, he became the first man to break 7:30 in the 3,000 at Cologne with a 7:29.45 world record. I had no delusions of challenging Aouita, but as the 1980s ended, so did my residency among the world class.

In 1990, I could not make the longer races work for me. Although I won three indoor miles, including my sixth national indoor title in an estimable 3:57.35 (tying with Marcus O'Sullivan) on the slow Madison Square Garden track, I only ran sixth in the Millrose 3,000, eighth in the Meadowlands 3,000, and tenth in the Carlsbad 5,000. I got buried at Carlsbad, but my kids had a ball. Corey, almost 9, and Megan, 6, ran the Carlsbad junior races just for fun. The distances began with a quarter-mile for the youngest children and went up to a mile for pre-teens. Scores of parents brought their youngsters, some suited up like little stars. I was careful to avoid pressuring my kids. If they wanted to run, great. It was up to them.

But I pressured myself. I thought, "You're getting older and need to train harder to make up for age." It was so hard for me to accept the idea of cutting back when I believed all my opponents, young and older, were going to the limit. I was 34 years old; how much time did I have left? How much longer could I run for my life? Decline in the mid-30s was common to middle-distance runners. Coghlan hung up his spikes at age 37.

I could not dig out of that harder-is-better mindset and my racing continued to suffer. That spring, I placed an abysmal ninth in the 1990 national outdoor 1,500, my worst showing ever. For the first time, I skipped the European track circuit where I earned my bread-and-butter, making only a token appearance at the end of the summer. At the Grand Prix Final in Athens, where I was given a spot out of pity, I ran eighth in 3:56.34. The winner was Noureddine Morceli of Algeria, a young Algerian who has dominated the mile since. I could no longer compete well on short recovery. Two days after Athens, when I would normally be strong, I ran 13th in a 1,500 at Rieti. I believe my imprudent work ethic caused me damage at the cellular level, and the only way out was a four-letter word: rest.

Over the summer, not being in Europe, I'd taken a brief respite to see what would happen. Apparently, it wasn't enough to make a difference. But during a period of minimal running, I picked up swimming and bicycling for cross-training and on a whim entered a triathlon held nearby at Solana Beach.

Talk about a fish out of water. I noodled around on my bike and swam laps with some good swimmers and thought I was pretty good in the water. How tough could a little triathlon be for a 3:47 miler? I knew I was in trouble when just about everyone showed up on the beach in wetsuits. I was the one wearing nose-plugs. You may as well have thrown me water wings. Make that water wings with Mickey Mouse ears.

I didn't wait very long to make my next big mistake. When the gun went off, I raced into the water because, hey, I'm the 3:47 miler. I'm sprinting. I'm thinking, this is cool, I'm first into the ocean. I proceeded to get the shit kicked out of me by all the better swimmers who trampled me to get ahead. I swallowed more water than I'd ever drunk. The distance was supposed to be a quarter-mile. As I got tossed around in the surf, I glanced at the buoys marking the course and thought, "That's no quarter-mile."

It had to be a half, but it was too late too turn around and go back. I pulled myself through the swim, through the 13-mile bike ride, thinking, "Now it's time to kick ass on the run." Except that I'd swallowed so much water I could barely move. The water kept sloshing around in my stomach. It gave me a terrible side stitch and I thought I was going to burst. I don't think I passed anyone on the 5K run and when it was all over I felt I still needed to prove something.

So I proceeded to run home from the race. It was eight miles. For some reason, I needed an extra eight miles under my belt. But I couldn't make it. I hit the wall. I was beaten and hungry. I stopped after three miles and called Kim to give me a ride home. When Kim saw me, she gave me one of those I-told-you-so looks. I had it coming.

Kim was used to shuttling family members to sports events. We both put a lot of energy into the kids' teams. Kim continued coaching soccer in the fall, and I coached baseball in the spring. Weekends revolved around one game or another. I changed my training schedule to be available for Corey's late-afternoon practices. Before long, Megan would also play sports.

As the kids got older, we went on family camping trips, sometimes venturing as far as Arizona for the fishing. We had a favorite spot there at a campground near Alamo Lake, situated about 40 miles from anywhere. We'd pitch a tent, and the four of us would pile into a motorboat and fish for bass. In the evenings, we'd get a fire going and horse around. I didn't miss the track circuit at those times.

———————

The next year, 1991, was a world championship year and I felt this could be my last opportunity to compete in a world or Olympic event. Every day, however, as I drove from home to the track, I thought, "Well, what's the workout today?" I'd start warming up and still be thinking, "What's the workout? What's the plan?"

I trained on my own at either the University of California at San Diego, Point Loma Nazarene College, or Balboa Stadium near the San Diego Zoo. I felt rootless. I needed a coach. I needed a coach for security, confidence, wisdom. There were coaches in the area, but no one I could trust, no one I could put my faith into as I had with Len Miller. With every coaching experience, I appreciated Len more. Len and I were perfectly compatible. Arch Jellie was a master but probably too low-key for me as a 30-something athlete needing a jolt. Working with a coach by phone or fax didn't make sense. I needed the human touch on a daily basis.

I always saw the coach/athlete relationship as a dependent one. I did not want to design my training, analyze my needs, or have the responsibility for determining the correct plan. I wanted a coach to do that. I wanted a coach to do everything including pat me on the rear and tell me I did a good workout and everything was okay. Maybe it was irresponsible of me, but I just wanted to show up and run.

I knew that other runners, like the marathoner Frank Shorter, took pride in coaching themselves after college. Shorter praised his coach at Yale, Bob Geigengack, saying that Geig's gift was teaching Frank and others how to coach themselves. I'm different from Frank in that way. Frank thrived on independence. I needed a shoulder.

In my mid-30s, I was still like a child who could not fend for himself. I envied other runners like Jim Spivey, who went to Indiana University, remained in the Bloomington area, and had access to the great I.U. coach, Sam Bell, for as long as he needed. Carl Lewis, a 1996 Olympian at age 35, admits the key to his success has been his longstanding relationship with his coach, Tom Tellez.

As Carl got older, Tellez helped him refocus and make adjustments. He built strength and fitness, cut back on competition, took the long view. Carl could not continue to sprint and long jump with abandon. He was 35, not 25. We have learned, and Lewis is excellent testimony, that athletes can sustain peak form into their 30s. But you have to make changes and you need guidance. Lynn Jennings was 36 and Mary Slaney 37 when they made the 1996 Olympic team. Each woman revamped her training with the continuing benefit of a close coaching relationship.

Now 35, I ran 80 to 90 miles a week, all of it intense. Most of my average runs were faster than 6-minute-per-mile pace. Once a week, I did a two-hour run. I did hill repeats, sprinting up a 200-meter hill until my legs turned to rubber. On the track, I would run ten 800s in 2:05, or five times a mile in 4:20 to 4:30. I'd abandoned the idea of running the 5,000 and concentrated only on the

1,500 and mile. Taken by themselves, none of these workouts was wrong, but doing them everyday without easing up and without a concrete strategy ruined me.

My performances were only half-bad. I would show flashes of brilliance, shades of my old self. That reinforced the problem, because I'd forget the lousy races and think, "Okay, I'm back. The training is working."

Athletes have terribly selective memories. Every good race, like a 3:37.3 1,500 win that spring at a meet in Santa Monica, distorted reality. The next poor performance was just around the corner. It always seemed that when my running was weak I had the worst luck. I placed second in the 1991 Nationals 1,500 in New York to earn a berth on the world team for Tokyo. But times were uncharacteristically slow, and going into the summer I was just a fraction off the world championship qualifying time of 3:37.00. Without that time, I could not compete in Tokyo.

The initial 3:37.3 at Santa Monica so excited me that I had a reaction worthy of Tom Byers. After the race, barely catching my breath, I went out into the street in Santa Monica and stepped off a rough 200 meters. I proceeded to run six fast 200s as though doing speedwork on the track.

Running a qualifier became my project as I left for Europe. Meet promoters were no longer interested in me. They fawned over young talent and would have preferred putting me out to pasture. At 35, I was in the twilight zone of track existence. I was too young for real midlife but smack in the throes of track midlife. My clock was ticking.

I missed the qualifier in Berlin and again in Helsinki, where the rhythm of the race was ideal for me, but I ran 12th in 3:40.4. At Lille, France, in the mile I showed one of those semi-brilliant flashes with a 3:54.13 for third, outrunning '88 Olympic champion Peter Rono. But five days later in Oslo, I sputtered in 13th and last in the mile in 3:58.00. I still needed a 1,500-meter qualifying time for the world meet. In a final stab, I went to a meet outside of Helsinki, but managed only 3:45.4, not even close. It was time to go home.

Before getting my feet on the ground, I was already thinking about trying for the 1992 Olympic team. I was optimistic to a fault, and that 3:54 from Lille stuck in my mind. As I surveyed my competition, I saw few Americans running that well. Maybe I *could* make the Olympic team at 36. I still felt I could lick my training problems.

My marital problems were something else. I grew tired of being the guilty party over issues that should have been put to rest. Kim just wouldn't forgive or forget. I felt I'd taken enough hammering and at the end of the year I walked out of the house and moved in with a friend. Kim and I finally went for counseling to try and work things out.

Through every hurdle, on and off the track, I never let go of my running goals. I'd come too far to give up without a fight. I suppose if excellence in running were easy, being a miler would not be nearly as rewarding. However, my ability to persevere was soon put to the most formidable test yet.

CHAPTER NINE

Cancer Strikes: Healing Body and Soul

The 1992 Olympic Trials were held in New Orleans in late June, and the steamy weather was the talk of the meet. Temperatures were over 100 degrees with humidity to match. Conditions were deadly—far worse than what was anticipated at the Games in Barcelona that summer. Many athletes at the Trials suffered from dehydration and heat-related ailments such as muscle cramping. During the decathlon, the most grueling competition of all, athletes were offered intravenous solutions to maintain healthy fluid and electrolyte levels.

The heat didn't phase me a bit. As a California boy who'd trained for years in the Arizona desert, I was a happy camper. At 36, most milers were considered washed up and I ran with no pressure on my shoulders. Based on age alone, I was counted out by just about everyone, and, in addition, my '92 performances did not entitle me to contender status. In the spring I'd picked up an Achilles tendon injury, which I abused. Coaching myself, I would run hard on the foot as soon as it felt a little better; then, of course, it would hurt again.

I came into the Trials with only a handful of races under my belt and having barely broken 4 minutes in the mile that season. Still, I felt I had a chance. Jim Spivey, now America's best miler, was the only true favorite for an Olympic 1,500 berth. The other two spots on the U.S. team were up for grabs. I saw no reason why I couldn't make a serious bid for one of them.

Spivey, a classy athlete, showed maturity at 32. Our careers had overlapped and a few years before Jim and I had been linked as "Scott-and-Spivey" in references to American mile hopes world-wide. The other two leading contenders according to the statistics were Steve Holman and Joe Falcon. Holman showed potential as an NCAA champion at Georgetown. Falcon, 26, had become only the fourth U.S. miler under 3:50 when, two years before, he'd won the "Dream Mile" in Oslo.

Falcon, however, was very insecure. There were two types of milers: those who talked about their training, and those who did not. Some, like Falcon and Tom Byers, liked to boast of their workouts, typically inflating their times. They were always mining the grapevine for news of their opponents' training techniques. The more stable athletes were above that.

In New Orleans, I ran smoothly in my heat and semi-final round of the 1,500. In the semi, I swung wide on the homestretch and ran down the field. That was my statement: You guys aren't rid of me yet! But in the final, Falcon showed instability under pressure, and it cost me dearly. On the opening lap, barely 200 meters into the race, Falcon got too anxious. In traffic, he cut from the inside for breathing room on the outside, took a bad fall, splattered to the track and was out of it. In the domino effect, I was forced to a dead stop and in an instant, I, too, was out of it. I would finish 13th, next to last. Falcon, jogging in, was last. Spivey won.

That was my '92 season and, as it turned out, my last Olympic Trials. Pretty soon, I had a new goal in mind: running a sub–4:00 mile at age 40. A masters mile circuit for top runners 40 years old and up had generated a lot of excitement with races at the Millrose Games, Penn Relays, and other major meets. At Millrose, the masters event, which had featured stars like Mike Boit, Wilson Waigwa, and Byron Dyce, had earned almost the same billing as the Wanamaker Mile. No masters runner had broken 4:05 outdoors or 4:14 indoors, and Eamonn Coghlan was thinking about coming out of retirement to go for sub–4:00 when he turned 40 in 1993. I would watch those developments closely.

For the first time, in 1992, I had not been ranked among the top ten American milers for the year. I was making little money from the track circuit and needed a job to support our growing family. Counseling had been helpful and I was back home. Kim was pregnant with our third child and in September our second son, Shawn, was born.

Continuing the Scott tradition, we used alternative birthing methods at San Antonio hospital in Upland, and this time the doctor encouraged Kim and me to have Corey and Megan participate in the delivery. The doctor felt this role would give the kids an immediate attachment to the baby and be an important bonding experience for the whole family.

Together we put on our scrubs, masks, and gloves. Each of us had a responsibility. I paced Kim with her breathing exercises, Corey delivered Shawn, and Megan cut the umbilical cord as a roomful of family members looked on. But at the moment Shawn came into this world, instead of bawling he was limp. The doctor grabbed him and, as everyone's heart skipped a beat, got him howling in seconds. Shawn had had fluid in his chest, and once the doctor took care of that, the kids beamed with pride and we had a healthy family of five.

With dwindling income from running, I found work as an hourly, part-time employee of Elite Racing, a firm headed by a friend, Tim Murphy, that organized road races. I still had time to train and race as I wished. For Elite, I did TV commentary, which I liked, and solicited sponsorships, which I didn't like. I had a hard time selling.

I had a hard time selling myself, too. I don't doubt that meet promoters and sponsors took advantage of me in negotiations over the years. At the end of 1992, I struck up a relationship with Irv Ray, who coached track and cross-country at nearby Azusa Pacific University. I'd known Irv for a long time, and took him on as my coach and agent. Finally, I had someone I could trust again. Irv knew his stuff, was a good runner himself and an upstanding guy. He took my haphazard training and gave it structure.

I got pretty strong in the winter of 1993 and without any speedwork to speak of ran a 3:59.8 mile for third at the Sunkist indoor meet in Los Angeles in February. I lost a fight with Joe Falcon and Greg Whitely on the last turn when Whitely threw me off pace with an elbow to the ribs. If that had been Falcon's elbow, I would have returned the favor and then some. But I had a connection to Whitely. His father had been a professor at Cal-Irvine when I was there and I'd followed Greg's running in high school and then at Brown. If he could run against with me with aggressive tactics, good for him.

That was my 136th sub–4-minute mile.

The same month, Coghlan, looking like his old self, began his assault on sub–4:00 at 40. His midlife comeback was the talk of track, and I took note. Eamonn ran 4:05.95 at Millrose, a masters indoor record. Then, he made a terrific bid at the USA Indoor Nationals, running 4:01.39 to bring down the house. I was inspired that sub–4:00 seemed possible for a 40-year-old, but relieved that Eamonn hadn't succeeded. That meant the possibility was still open for me to do it. Eamonn vowed to return the next year.

That spring of '93, at age 37, my season sputtered along. I didn't always listen to Irv's admonition not to train myself into ground. Fatigued, I didn't run a single track race the rest of the year. But I had more time to put into family activities. With the arrival of infant Shawn, we became a typical 1990s family, juggling a million activities. Kim's soccer playing was a critical outlet for her and at times she took Shawn out to the field in his baby carriage during her practices.

I coached both Corey's Little League team and Megan's softball team. With all that activity, plus soccer, Corey, then 12, and Megan, 9, were always in good shape, and both ran the Carlsbad junior division. For their age groups, the distance was only a mile, but there were times when Megan would trip and fall, finish in tears, and swear she'd never do that again. It was a wonderful surprise when she later took to running as a teenager. As for Corey, he's not been too excited about running but I'm still working on him.

With our various coaching assignments and our own workouts, Kim and I were oftentimes ships passing in the night. The marital counseling we'd undergone did not have a lasting effect. The kids' sports and our camping trips were still the best common ground for us and we managed to co-exist through the ups and downs for the benefit of the family.

The break from racing that spring gave me a new breath of life and by the fall I was rolling again as the USA National Cross Country Championship came around in late November. When Irv analyzed my workouts, he told me I was headed for a 3:54 mile the next spring at age 38 and that the cross-country meet would be a good barometer of my strength.

The meet was held in Missoula, Montana, and it was 4 degrees and snowy, hardly my kind of weather. But my experience paid off. I started out conservatively, passed droves of people in the last couple of miles, and wound up a very respectable tenth. I was only 20-odd seconds behind winner Todd Williams, America's best

10,000 man, and other Olympic distancemen such as Pat Porter, Ed Eyestone, and Mark Coogan. As a younger man, I had rarely run that well in the nationals.

In the warming hut after the race, I was standing around and overheard a conversation between a couple of younger competitors. One of them said to the other, "Did you hear Steve Scott got tenth? I thought he was retired." To which the other replied, "I thought he was dead."

———————

A month later, around Christmas time of 1993, I felt a little swelling in my testicle. If I crossed my legs, it hurt. Eventually, I had my father take a look at it and he thought I should have it checked out. I was planning to go to my urologist anyway, because after Shawn was born Kim thought it was time for me to take some responsibility for birth control. She insisted I see about having a vasectomy.

Some time later, in May of '94, I saw my local doctor. He was not sure what to make of the swelling. A testicle can get twisted and go dead from lack of blood supply. It sometimes happens to cyclists. The doctor sent me to a specialist, Kevin O'Brien, a urologist at San Diego Medical Center who treats a lot of cancer patients.

O'Brien, a former college lacrosse player, knew about my running background. We talked sports and he examined me. Then he ordered a blood test, X ray, and sonogram. He told me I could have a dead testicle. He also told me I could have cancer.

A sonogram uses ultrasound to produce a picture. Since most sonograms are done on pregnant women, the technician was a woman, and she happened to be quite attractive at that. As I sat there naked in a hospital gown, she proceeded to administer the test in a way that made me worry about embarrassing myself. Fortunately, I held control.

After the sonogram, I could tell I was in trouble. Instead of letting me leave, the technician told me to wait and called in O'Brien. They lined up the pictures of my testicle and said I had a tumor. When the woman asked me how I had discovered the swelling, I joked about playing with myself. She was surprised at my cavalier manner. But that was how I would handle the entire ordeal. Kidding around was my style of crisis management.

Other tests confirmed the tumor and O'Brien then told me he had to surgically remove the testicle. A biopsy would thereafter be done on the testicle to determine the type of cancer and best course of treatment. Removing the testicle would also halt the spread of the disease.

Testicular cancer is rare, affecting one in 100,000 American men aged 15 to 45. It has a very high cure rate, over 90 percent, but the cancer moves fast. There was no time to waste. The surgery was scheduled for two days later.

When I called Kim after my consultation with O'Brien, I told her there was good news and bad news. She asked to hear the good news first. I said, "The good news is I don't need a vasectomy. The bad news is I have to have my nut taken off."

Kim proceeded to call my dad and my brother, also a physician, to investigate my disease. She had a hundred questions. She wanted to know as much as she could. I had barely asked O'Brien anything. I tend to be trusting, even in a situation as serious as this. If a doctor gives me a diagnosis, I say "Okay," ask little, and move on.

That was the first time I'd ever had surgery. It went fine and a few days later they took the sutures out. I only missed a couple of days of running. Less than a week after the operation, I wanted to make sure all my plumbing was working normally. Kim and I got together one night and right about when the earth began to move I felt an odd, scraping sensation. I darted to the bathroom and saw that our groping had opened the incision exposing some organs. "So that's what my bladder looks like," I thought. I rushed to the hospital for a patch job. After that, it took longer for the incision to heal.

Within days the biopsy results came in, and Kim and I went to O'Brien together. He explained that there were two categories of testicular cancer: seminoma and non-seminoma. Seminoma was effectively treated with radiation therapy. That was the form of the disease contracted by baseball's John Kruk, diagnosed just a couple of months earlier. My cancer was non-seminoma, which O'Brien referred to as a "mixed germ cell" tumor. My running would have to be put on hold for a while, he explained.

I had two options. I could do nothing, hope the cancer had not spread, and take a periodic CT scan to check on the condition. This was like waiting for bad news. If untreated, the cancer cells could divide and spread, eventually taking root in the liver and brain. Then I'd need chemotherapy, which would likely damage lung tissue and compromise my running goals. This wait-and-see scenario had a cure rate around 80 percent, but I wanted to do everything possible to avoid chemo.

The other option was immediate surgery. That was the wiser choice, according to O'Brien. Since this cancer was known to head from the scrotum up through the lymph nodes, the surgery would be intended to remove 39 lymph nodes from my body. If doctors found the cancer had not spread, I'd be in the clear. O'Brien told me I wouldn't have to worry about carrying on without the lymph nodes, which seek and destroy cancerous cells. Beyond the 39 I was to have removed, the body has many more lymph nodes to take up that surveillance.

I knew I had to take a proactive approach. I'm an athlete. I wanted to resume running and competition and try to run a sub–4-minute mile in two years when I turned 40. I discussed all of this with O'Brien. He supported me all the way. He told me that physically active people like me could overcome this cancer and regain their athletic powers. In fact, he had operated on a sprinter who was over 40 and had fully recovered, going on to excel in the masters division.

I also had heard of the case of Kevin Hall, a world-class sailor and contender for the 1996 Olympic team, having had a far worse case of testicular cancer than mine. Hall's cancer was found in both testicles and he had to have both removed. In all, he had to undergo three major operations, including the very same operation I would have to remove lymph nodes.

Hall's fight continued beyond the operating room. He had to take testosterone injections for survival. However, since testosterone is a banned substance in Olympic sports, Hall had to petition the authorities to grant him a waiver to compete in the Olympic Trials. Finally he got the waiver and competed, but he did not make the U.S. team for Atlanta. I felt for Hall. I had one testicle left and was healthy by comparison.

Though I knew I'd choose surgery, I deliberated on the options using techniques I'd learned as an athlete. I was inherently optimistic, feeling things would turn out okay. In a lifetime of running, I had learned to face pain—the benign, fleeting, and even welcome pain of racing—but pain nonetheless. I got ready to face the pain of cancer. I visualized the outcome of surgery and of chemotherapy as well. I ran through the whole picture in my mind. Whatever my thoughts, running sub–4:00 at 40 always popped up as well. I would not let go of my running goals. My life depended on that, too.

In a family of doctors and nurses, I did not concern myself with the medical intricacies of my disease. My parents and brother, Kendall, were checking with Dr. O'Brien and speaking to their medical colleagues, and I felt I was in the best of hands. I tried to think ahead, to my running, as though the surgery were already done and I had a training schedule to meet.

A positive outlook is apparently common to athletes confronting cancer. A survey of 261 members of the American College of Sports Medicine, commissioned for the 1993 book *Edge Against Cancer* by Robert Brody, suggests that athletes do indeed have an "edge" in confronting disease. For example, 67 percent of respondents said athletes have more focus, discipline, willpower, and stamina than non-athletes in dealing with the anxiety, depression, and despair that often strike cancer patients.

Champion marathoner Mark Conover was an excellent example of this strength in crisis. Winner of the 1988 U.S. Olympic Marathon Trial in 2:12:26, Conover was diagnosed with Hodgkin's disease, a form of lymphatic cancer, in the fall of 1993. He went through chemotherapy and endured a devastating ordeal with great courage and heroism. In mid-1995, he was able to run a 2:20:35 to qualify for the 1996 Olympic Trial, held in Charlotte, North Carolina. There, Mark placed 71 out of 90 finishers in 2:31:01, but to my mind he was the star of the show. "I think I'll be a healthy person exercising for the rest of my life," Conover would say later.

I confidently told O'Brien I'd have the surgery. Because the doctors would work close to the spine and major arteries, I had to give three units of blood as a precaution. In addition to facing the risks of any surgery, I was told I could end up with some sexual dysfunction or loss of bladder control. But even if surgery posed immediate risks, I felt it was better than doing nothing. As far as I was concerned, the payoff was greater.

I could not imagine life away from the track. My identity, pride, and self-image all came from running. No other kind of work appealed to me. I had not prepared for a future beyond running. We had our two homes, huge bills, a lot of debt, and I still saw running as the best way for me to earn a good living. My only remaining sponsorship was with Asics shoes. It was obvious that financial pressures had contributed to the tensions in my marriage. I needed running both as a job and way of life.

I also relied on an increasing faith in God to fortify me. For years, I'd been a "closet Christian." We never went to church as a family or paid much attention to religious ritual other than saying our nightly prayers. A year earlier, when I had begun training under Irv Ray, he had seen it as part of his mission to give me more of a spiritual foundation and strengthen my commitment to God. Irv was a deeply religious man and recognized that, as I neared the age of 40, faith would be a valuable resource. As a result of Irv's influence, even before the cancer struck, I had started praying more and reading the Bible. I needed the strength to face marital issues and the fact that, sooner or later, my career as a miler would be over. When I began searching for answers in the liturgy, I had no idea I would soon need this same spiritual guidance to help me through a life-threatening disease.

Once word of my condition got out, I also had help from other fronts. Shortly before the surgery, I got a call from a young triathlete in Las Vegas who'd gone through the same cancer successfully and was competing again. He described the surgery step by step and told me I could expect to be running within a month following the operation. That call had a calming effect on me. Prior to the surgery, I was relaxed. I slept well the night before. I thought that everything I would go through would be worth the end result.

Dr. O'Brien headed a three-man medical "Dream Team." In surgery, he was joined by another prominent urologist, Jon Kaswick, of Los Angeles Medical Center, and a third doctor, the oncologist on my case, Jonathan Poliakoff of San Diego Medical

Center. Dr. Kaswick was renowned for his testes cancer surgery, having performed over 500 successful operations of this kind. The chemistry of this team—and I include myself—was ideal. Kaswick was a big basketball fan and Poliakoff was a runner. We talked sports, and all three men were extremely sensitive to my needs as an athlete.

O'Brien said he saw his relationship with patients as that of a coach or mentor. He pointed out that many cancer patients fought with their doctors over issues of "control," but that athletes were inclined to accept their doctors' coaching. We are accustomed to being trusting and following orders. It was not a stretch for me to consider O'Brien as my coach.

The surgery was performed on May 24, 1994, about two weeks after the initial operation that removed the testicle. My whole family came to the hospital: Mom and Dad, my sister and brother, Kim of course, plus Len Miller and his wife. The turnout gave me a sense of the gravity of the situation. It was like the time a couple of years before when everybody had shown up for my father's quintuple bypass operation. Though a doctor, my father smoked, drank, ate poorly, and did not exercise. He came out of the operation all right but with a patchwork quilt of scars.

Mom, on the other hand, had kept up her running all through the years. By this time, at 65, she'd begun to replace some of her running with walking (up to five miles a day). She followed my track exploits, keeping thick scrapbooks of meet clippings. She'd watch races like Oslo's "Dream Mile" on TV, and I know she was tickled that her son who once had balked at running had made a decent career out of it.

It's interesting how being an athlete—being different from the typical patient—can affect medical procedures. As a runner, I had a low resting pulse of around 40 beats per minute, and I told the anesthesiologist this. She had to take that into account in determining the drugs to use.

Right before sliding off into la-la land, I told O'Brien, "Make sure you put everything back where you found it." He laughed; O'Brien had a real good sense of humor.

The surgery took five hours. O'Brien and his team cut a 24-inch incision in my abdomen and removed the 39 lymph nodes. To expose the lymph nodes, which track up along the aorta, the doctors had to move several organs out of the way, being careful not to nick the aorta. O'Brien referred to the task as a "high-wire act."

The surgery would have been even more difficult had I been out of shape and overweight. Low body fat, I was told, enabled the doctors to work more "cleanly." What impressed O'Brien most was the integrity of my psoas muscle, which runs from the spine down to the pelvis. It is an important lever in running. O'Brien said that in size and shape I had "the most incredible psoas muscle that he had ever seen on a human." I guess that's what 100,000 miles of running can do for you.

Most importantly, my lymph nodes were clean. As O'Brien explained it, the nodes function as a tollbooth for the cancer cells. The cells collect at the nodes and multiply into clusters. Doctors found no such clusters, and I was pretty much home free. Though I was probably "cured" and the cancer was not likely to recur, I would have to take a blood test every three months and chest X rays every six months as monitors. O'Brien and Co. had done their good work. Now it was up to me to recover.

———————

I remained in the hospital for five days, about half the normal stay for a patient in my situation. The first night after surgery, Kim spent the night in my room. The second night, my mom stayed. Megan came to visit. Corey, however, didn't want to come. He found the ordeal hard to take and dealt with it on his own.

I got many calls and letters, from people I knew and many I did not. There was a steady stream of visitors. One of my former college teammates, Ralph Serna, brought a collage he had made of old photos from our days at Cal-Irvine. Another friend, Gordon McMitchell, son of 1940s mile champion Leslie McMitchell, brought a six-foot basketball hoop so I could shoot from bed. He also brought in a blowup doll from a sex shop and sat it down next to me. We joked endlessly with the nurses.

After a few days, with the I.V. and other gadgetry taken away, I could walk around. Merely going to the bathroom, however, shot my pulse to 150. That was my first reality check. I thought, man, this was going to be a long haul. I was weak not only from the surgery but from the three pints of blood I'd given. (If I had ever wanted to do any blood doping, this was going to be my chance— and legally.) I was supposed to receive the blood back, bolstering recovery. But there was a mix-up in the storage of my blood. I never found out exactly what happened, but they simply could not be sure which blood was mine. So I got none back.

Before long, I felt a little like my old self again. The first indication was when the nurse gave me a sponge bath and I started getting horny. My sexual desire and capacity were unaffected by the surgery, but I was no longer able to ejaculate. This result is common. Removing lymph nodes shuts the valve that facilitates ejaculation.

Once home, I had a fever and digestive problems, but medication soon fixed that and I was on my way. Healing from this surgery normally took months; for me, it took a few weeks. Kim and Megan took care of me, preparing meals, keeping me company, boosting my confidence.

The ordeal was hard on the kids. Corey couldn't deal with his emotions. He said little to Kim or me and finally broke down to a school counselor. Megan, who's very loving and my kindred spirit, wanted to be in on everything and had even wanted to see me immediately after the surgery. Kim didn't think it was a good idea for Megan to see her dad in that weakened and unfamiliar state, and Megan was terribly upset at being left out at that moment. As usual, Kim was a rock and had everything under control. As a result of her research and questioning, she knew a lot more about the cancer than I did.

I was anxious to resume running, but Dr. O'Brien told me not to run for two months so I didn't. By mid-summer the two months were up, and I did my first jog at 8,000-foot altitude at a running camp in the Sierras. I had not run since early May, the longest layoff of my career. I started with a few miles and worked up to five miles in the morning and another five in the evening on luscious mountain trails.

After two weeks of that, I fell apart in exhaustion. I'd committed the quintessential novice mistake: too much too soon. I should have stuck with no more than two or three miles a day. A blood test showed I was anemic, with low levels of testosterone. Again, the pre-surgical blood store—that I never regained—was the culprit.

I had to stop running until my condition normalized. I received a testosterone injection, took monthly blood tests, and waited. This was a demoralizing time, and I began to lose confidence in my body and question the timetable I had set for myself.

I wanted to just barrel ahead as though nothing had happened. I wanted to make myself whole in a snap. O'Brien had spoken about cancer victims who were ready to fold up their tent and others who could put cancer behind them and live out their passion. He even had a friend with cancer who played ball and coached a team. O'Brien said his friend had a zest for life. I seized that idea as my model.

More and more since the running movement began in the seventies, people with cancer were fighting back with exercise.

They improved the quality of their lives and perhaps their longevity as well. Robert Fisher, a runner who'd trained eight miles a day, exemplified this approach. At age 45, in 1975, he was diagnosed with incurable leukemia. Despite nine major operations, at age 49 he bicycled 3,700 miles across the country from Los Angeles to New York.

Exemplifying this new approach, a Runners With Cancer group sprang up from the New York City Road Runners Club. The members ran, walked, did whatever they could. They met regularly and supported one another, and a few even participated in the New York City Marathon. I was so glad when the group's organizers contacted me. To a cancer survivor like me, hearing from other victims who were refusing to give up their active lifestyles gave me greater hope in achieving my own goals.

The group's hero—the hero of so many cancer victims—was of course Fred Lebow, the club president, the Marathon's director, and running's most dynamic impresario. Fred was diagnosed with brain cancer early in 1990 but continued to go about his business without complaint. He underwent brain surgery but would not fold his tent. Treated with chemotherapy and radiation, Fred ran or walked the hospital corridors or roof for exercise. He calculated the number of "laps" per mile, telling other runners, "I learned that even if you are sick with a life-threatening illness, you can still move." I had visited Fred in the hospital during his illness and thought of him as an inspiration in my own recovery.

Once Fred's cancer went into remission, in 1992, he resumed his world travels and an ambitious running program. "I know of no fuller way to live than to run," he said. Incredibly, Fred vowed to run later that year in the race he had inaugurated, the New York City Marathon. Grete Waitz, the nine-time champion, would accompany him.

The day of the '92 event, emotions were overwhelming. A million-plus New Yorkers turned out on the streets, on rooftops and balconies and fire escapes—from Hasidic Jews calling out in Yiddish to chic Manhattanites coming out of East Side bars with their Bloody Marys—to rally behind Fred.

A Holocaust survivor from Transylvania who'd fled Nazi Europe as a teenager, Fred had helped create the running boom, not only in the United States but worldwide, fueling it with his energy, passion, and imagination. The New York City Marathon, first held in 1970, was his baby. Now, as he literally ran for his life, Fred was embraced by every citizen, runner and non-runner alike, the fit and the stout. Who could not marvel at this humble man who'd lived by his wits, gone against the grain, and brought a generation to its feet? The filmmaker Spike Lee was waiting along the course to greet Fred. Mayor David Dinkins stood at the finish line.

With Grete jogging at his side like a tugboat, Fred's mission attracted interest that overwhelmed the attention paid to all others, even the Marathon's winning runners from South Africa (Willie Mtolo) and Australia (Lisa Ondieki). When all of the elite athletes, male and female, were done after two and a half hours, Fred was still poking along near the halfway point in Queens. He would take another three hours to complete his journey, and the city waited. Once at the finish line in Central Park, in 5:32:35, he knelt and kissed the ground. Then, he and Grete embraced in tears. There was not a dry eye in town.

In meetings with the press, Fred spoke of running's profound impact on body and soul and its central position in his life. "The real change is inside me, a change I understand best through my running," he would later write. "I'm glad to be alive, and I live with that feeling every day. It's like being a beginner again, in love with the idea of my body moving along. . . ."

Unfortunately, Fred's cancer returned and he died in October of 1994, a month before the 25th running of the Marathon. But his legacy lives on. Among the numerous tributes to Fred is a statue at the Marathon finish in Central Park. A runner from San Diego,

Dan Mitchavitch, was involved in commissioning the work from a sculptor in California. When it came time for the unveiling, Dan contacted me to appear at press events announcing the work, which I was honored to do. When people asked me how I was doing, I told them how moved I'd been by Fred's courage.

That fall, following Dr. O'Brien's decree, I was impatient to resume running. I wanted to be like Fred. If he could run the marathon, I could run the mile. Since my illness, I had begun to look at time differently, seeing it in finite terms. Finally, O'Brien gave me the signal, and in December, after a three-month layoff, I forged ahead.

I started with a couple of miles and continued jogging for a month. This time I made incremental increases. I still had doubts, though. It was hard to summon confidence when 5 miles at an 8-minute pace took some getting used to. My longest run was an hour. Would I ever be able to sustain 2-hour runs at sub–6:00 pace again?

After six weeks, in January 1995, I ran my first race in a year—like Fred, my own race. Each January, I conduct a Steve Scott Festival of Miles, a road event, in Santee, California. Tim Murphy of Elite Racing came up with the idea and we've worked on it together since the first event in 1994. We have a slate of eight 1-mile races, in age groups from children's up through the masters, plus invitational divisions, and a separate 5K run/walk. We boast several sponsors and $30,000 in prize money. My role is mainly as goodwill ambassador, but what I enjoy most, of course, is racing myself.

I amazed myself by running 4:24 and showing some competitive instincts. Considering how little I'd trained, all I'd expected was something closer to 5:24. It was as though I had some degree of mile memory in my legs. Len Miller always said my long years of training were like money in the bank and that I could run off the interest. It seemed he was right.

As the saying goes, that 4:24 on January 8, 1995, was the first day of the rest of my life. A sub–4:00 at 40 still seemed possible. I was almost 39. I had a year and a half to lose 24 seconds. Even though by now Eamonn Coghlan had achieved sub–4:00 at 40, the goal was still critical to me as a factor in my recovery.

At Irv's urging, I trained with a heart-rate monitor to better gauge my running intensity and prevent myself from overdoing it. The computer-like device is strapped to your chest while running and programmed to monitor your pulse and yield other information. Not being computer-minded at the time, and an old dog who prefers the "run how you feel" approach, I ignored the gadget's messages at first and probably did overtrain on occasion because of that. Finally, like a resistant student pulled by his ear, I capitulated and then everything sailed along.

Initially, Irv asked me to keep the intensity at no higher than 70 percent of maximum. Before long, he and I decided it was time to step up the workouts; that spring of '95, I began doing a weekly 10-mile run at 85 percent of max, a gauge I would use for a year. The first time out I broke an hour and within a couple of months I was down to 50 minutes. I was a real runner again. I ventured into the Carlsbad 5K, in which I'd set a world record in 13:33. I live only a mile from Carlsbad and had always been the hometown boy of the event. This time out I ran 14:20, another encouraging sign.

I ran another 5K in San Francisco, where I saw Mark Conover, the marathoner, who at the time was still fighting Hodgkin's disease. The worst of Mark's illness was behind him and he spoke confidently about making the '96 Olympic Trial. And of course, we compared war stories. The knowledge that other athletes fought serious illness while continuing toward their goals was always encouraging. We were fellow warriors.

I considered this period Phase One of my comeback. It was time to step back. I didn't want to run too fast too soon in the mile—I wanted my progress to be gradual. There was no point in running a fast mile at age 39. From a financial standpoint, I could lose money if it looked as if I was "certain" to break four minutes at 40. When Eamonn Coghlan went after the mark, meet promoters offered him a bonus of $50,000 and hedged their award with insurance policies that carried a premium of around $5,000. That way, a meet would have the bonus covered through insurance and only have to pay the premium on the policy. I thought that if I looked like a cinch, the premiums would be high—perhaps beyond a meet's budget—and I might not have a chance for a bonus myself.

I knew only too well that as my world-class years waned, I had to take advantage of fleeting opportunities for big paydays. Building up my body that spring of '95, I still faced financial uncertainty. How would I earn a living, and would my work fit in with my running? I could not see myself in the corporate world. What could I do? I imagined myself as a firefighter or paramedic, but that wasn't practical.

Finally, out of desperation, I started a car wash in Fountain Valley with a partner, Bob Davis. We'd been talking about it and planning it for a year, but it wasn't until I had proven to myself that I could train at a high level that I felt I could stop running for six weeks and devote myself day and night to a new business. I figured once the car wash hit its stride, I could resume running, but with some peace of mind.

I handled the day-to-day management of the business while Bob handled the finances. Money was tight, and I missed running but focused on getting the business going. It didn't help that Kim and I didn't always see eye-to-eye on money matters. I wanted to sell our second home to give us a little cushion, but Kim felt we needed to hang on to it and we argued over that.

It's commonly said that the three greatest stresses occur in the marital, financial, and professional realms. I was facing all three at once—not to mention the cancer. The disease had made me especially attuned to the mind-body dynamic and the effects of emotions on physical health.

I could see as never before how intertwined all facets of my life were, how emotional stresses could affect my overall health. While not all physicians give much credence to the mind's effect on the body, I know Dr. O'Brien would agree that stress can depress the immune system—though he would not go so far as to say that stress can cause cancer.

In the case of my particular cancer—testes cancer—he did say that one possible cause is trauma. He didn't mean the blunt trauma that might come from an accident, but rather the trauma of having your scrotum continually bounce off your leg during 20 years of running. But this was speculation.

Looking back over the years leading up to my illness, my instincts told me that stress had made me vulnerable to disease. In the early nineties I had been in a constant gloom-and-doom mindset. My optimism as an athlete had gone out the window. I was doing what psychologists call "catastrophizing." Constantly coursing through my mind were thoughts like: How are we going to pay for this or that? How are we going to survive? What are we going to do? Why is my running going bad?

No matter how bad things got, if my running was good, then everything else did not seem so bad. But whenever my running went sour, every other problem seemed worse. As the ups and downs became a vicious cycle, I became more and more anxious and depressed, until I felt I had nowhere to turn.

I even developed a callus on one side of my tongue. I'd wake up in the middle of the night and my tongue would be sore. Finally I realized I was chewing on my tongue all the time as a nervous habit. And, eventually, the cancer hit: the culmination of all the stresses and strains on my psyche and on my physical system.

But good things came out of my illness: The crisis brought Kim and me closer together, at least for a while, and her care was critical in nursing me back to health. Being ill also put me in a position to experience the outpouring of concern from the running community: It was overwhelming. In fact I was a little embarrassed by the attention, as well as deeply touched by it. Most cancer victims suffer a far worse fate than I had and all along I felt I didn't deserve the fuss—but I am incredibly grateful for it. Since that time, I have tried to not wear the illness on my sleeve, but I have spoken frankly about it.

As a result, I've wanted to convey to others the message that a cancer victim can live an active life. In an article about my experience that appeared in a 1995 issue of *Runner's World,* I described how my strength as a runner and my faith in God had helped get me through the surgery and back on my feet as an athlete. A number of cancer victims told me they were helped by this article and my expression of faith, and one urologist told me that after reading the article, three of his patients had discovered their own testicular cancer through self-examination.

It is rewarding to know that my experience can somehow help others. Ironic as it may sound, the entire cancer episode also helped me: I learned to handle stress differently and to get a better grip on my emotions. I learned that I could not afford to let stress dictate to me; I would dictate to it.

How am I different? Now, if something bugs me, I don't internalize it and allow it to fester inside like some poison. I become aware of the incipient stress and defuse it, not allowing it to burden my system with fear. Continuing to hold the American record in the mile still did not pay the bills, but I made a pact with myself not to worry about that. Instead, I now lay plans for positive action and set meaningful goals.

Thus, however passionate I may be about both running and career-related goals, as a result of the cancer I've got my running in better perspective. In a sense, I have brought running full circle, back to innocence. Running, while my job, had been pure fun for me—until the 1984 Olympics. Then, when I failed to win a medal at the Games, I was left not only unable to reap the spoils of success but also with two mortgages, three kids, and a dog— and the need for peace of mind. Running almost lost its purity for me and took on a different flavor; it became my livelihood, not my passion.

Cancer had shown me the need for balance. That stressful dark time behind me, I felt like shouting through a megaphone: It's all over, folks—bring back the fun!

After my self-imposed six-week break from running in mid-1995, I resumed training and felt good. It was as if I had never stopped. Sad to say, the car wash never took off and we had to get rid of it, but I didn't let that get the best of me.

Fall arrived, my running got stronger by the week and I was feeling loose, as I had in high school. I felt as healthy as ever and knew that now, nearing 40, it was time to become a track racer again. I couldn't wait.

CHAPTER 10

Comeback at 40: Back on Track

S eeking to become a miler again as I turned 40 years old, I began my 1996 season in January with a 4:08 in my namesake event, the Steve Scott Festival of Races, a road mile, in Santee, California. That was a 16-second improvement on my performance the previous year, when I was still rebounding from cancer. Many people in running were astonished at my progress. It was one thing to lick cancer and regain your health, quite another to regain athletic excellence as well.

To find so many people pulling for me was invigorating. Everywhere I went, runners and track fans would come up to me with good wishes. People I didn't even know offered me prayers. I got phone calls and letters from folks expressing a personal connection to my mission. Maybe all along I'd had more supporters than I'd realized. There seemed to be a collective excitement on my behalf—the recognition that my running renewal was more significant than anything I'd ever worked for and worthy of special recognition.

I must say there was never this much fuss over my dream miles. But I suppose people could relate to me. I'd gone through the transition from world-class miler to hanger-on, acquired a new coach, come through personal crises over family and financial issues, conquered cancer, and rebuilt myself into a credible athlete. I was like anyone in midlife trying to make a buck, guard my health, and keep my marriage together.

And, like the weekend warrior playing three-man basketball in the over-40 league at the grammar school gym, I was trying to stay in shape and remain youthful in running. The 4:08 showed me I was in good shape, and now I was poised to again pursue the ultimate signpost of running success: racing on the track.

Road miles are vastly different from track miles. On the road, there's plenty of room to maneuver, so you don't need intricate strategies to hold position, avoid getting boxed in by an opponent, or time your kick. All of your competitors are pretty much in view; on the road, there's little fear of someone coming from behind with a startling rally. It's also a lot easier to dash off in a straight line for four minutes or so than to negotiate four laps of a track. The dynamic of each lap of the track plays on your mind. You are forced to assess and re-assess. It's harder to relax on the track.

But the track is also where the passion is. And the passion of track racing is what I craved: to break from the start, my heart pounding, and furiously brush shoulders with anxious young men; to round the bend, pump the backstretch, inhale the sweaty aroma of competition; to hear the bell announcing the last lap, and feel communion with the crowd.

According to my coach, Irv Ray, although my 4:08 demonstrated fitness, I would need one more weapon for the track: speed. Road miles unfolded sedately, with the pace building gradually. The broad space compromised the effectiveness of a sharp burst of speed. But on the track, abrupt pace changes were the meat-and-potatoes of racing. In order to taste all the sweetness the track had to offer, I would need to fly.

However, I assumed the speed of my younger days was still attainable. I was Steve Scott—I was fast, wasn't I? Hadn't I run a 49-second quarter in lousy shoes on a cinder track at the age of 18? Hadn't I run a 52-second last quarter in a 3:48 mile at the age of 28?

If you don't practice running fast, however, you lose it. Irv asked me to do all-out 100-meter sprints on a daily basis. Irv's plan was for me to eventually run ten 100s in 12 seconds each. But I resisted, thinking my staple of longer runs would be enough.

I may have had some residual fears related to my illness. I didn't want to risk overdoing it, and sprinting the 100s seemed like overdoing it. Though I'd gotten past the cancer, it may have left a tiny scar on my psyche. I also suspected that I would not handle sprinting very well at this point and didn't want that weakness to demoralize me.

Speed aside, my training continued exceedingly well. Working out at my old college track at Cal-Irvine, I ran one workout that Irv calculated was "worth" a sub–4:00 mile. I ran a 57.6 400 meters, a 1:28 600, a 30-second 300, and a 57.6 400, with short jogs between each run. I did that workout by myself, with no training partner to break the wind. Irv called that session a "breakthrough" workout, but he still insisted I do the sprints to regain my native speed. I rationalized, if I'm making breakthroughs, why bother?

In addition to track training, I did weekly 10-mile runs—at 6:30 in the morning before going to work as a division manager at Soaring Eagle Ventures, makers of sports nutrition supplements. I'd taken the position that January. It was my first full-time job (I would leave after a year because of an ownership change), and I had to get used to the routine of a 9-to-5 day. I preferred training late in the day, but if I waited until after work that would interfere with family activities.

So 6:30 A.M. it was, and as I did the 10-miler or repeats of a 600-meter hill, I was reminded of my freshman summer at college when we had to be ready at that ungodly hour with spit-and-shine alertness for a long run. Now, running hard at daybreak could sometimes render me listless at work, and I'd walk around the office like a zombie.

But I lowered my 10-mile training times to 49 minutes while not pushing harder than 80 to 85 percent of maximum, and felt some of my old strength coming back. Being a 40-year-old with track racing aspirations was an experiment. While a number of studies showed that athletes could sustain their fitness with consistent training well into midlife, no one had yet put any aging world-class milers under the microscope.

I had little to go on other than trial and error. Irv's approach was very systematic, and that's what I needed: discipline; structure; someone to tell me to do this, do that; someone to grab me by the collar and pat me on the back. Someone to coax me out of bed at 6:30 in the morning for my 10-mile run.

Irv was also there to tell me if I was track-ready. But "being in shape" for the track made certain hypothetical assumptions; performing in competition was reality. Between those two poles was a vast, uncertain realm. We looked ahead and chose the Prefontaine Classic in Eugene, Oregon, on Memorial Day weekend, as the meet in which to return to the big-time. After all, Eugene was the Broadway stage of track racing.

For a reality check, I would first run a 1,500 meters in a small meet at Irvine in early May, the day before I turned 40. The 1,500 was my first track race in almost three years, and I was glad to see a few of my former college teammates show up to root me on. As I'd neared 40 and made appearances at certain events for probably the last time, I felt a big piece of my life slipping away. It was not easy for me to face the music and move on.

Encountering this next phase of my racing life, I had to make one concession to age. I learned at 40 that I could no longer sustain hard running on a daily basis. I needed a few days to recover from hard workouts, a discovery that was crystal clear in the 1,500-meter race at Irvine. All I could run was 3:51, equivalent to a 4:09 mile. As Irv pointed out, I'd done some very hard training that same week and probably was not fully rested. Then again, after three years away from the track, what could I expect?

Recovery time had been an important issue with 40-and-over runners like Rod Dixon of New Zealand, a cohort of John Walker's. Dixon, the 1972 Olympic bronze medalist in the 1,500 meters (and a 1983 New York City Marathon champion), ran 4:13 as a masters miler before calling it quits. He thought he should have run faster.

Eamonn Coghlan, my rival on the indoor circuit, had cited recovery time as a critical age consideration when he first attempted sub–4:00 at 40 in 1993. Running in Madison Square Garden before crowds that worshipped his every stride, Coghlan got close that winter. I admired his determination. Despite a painful upper-leg injury, Coghlan returned for the '94 indoor season at 41 and finally nailed his historic 3:58.15 on the fast 200-meter indoor track at Harvard. Runners everywhere, especially midlife runners, rejoiced.

When my cancer was diagnosed three months later, I seized Coghlan's milestone as my inspiration. While Eamonn might be the smarter, craftier runner, I always felt I had more pure athletic ability. Plus, Eamonn did not put together a solid outdoor performance, and running the first sub–4:00 at 40 on an outdoor track was still open to me. The masters outdoor world record for the mile was 4:02.53 by Britain's David Moorcroft, set in 1993. I thought that at some point in the future I might have a shot at that.

But at 40 I could not worry about records when all I wanted was to get my feet wet again in the arena in which I had made my life's work: the track. Bring on Eugene, America's Oslo, and the Prefontaine Classic.

Was I ready for a major track event? How would I react to all the emotion I anticipated in Eugene? The spring season seemed to rush by, and now the moment had come when the track world was buzzing with my comeback. The *New York Times* and other papers had written me up. Fortyish runners could relate to a workhorse like me still trying for a goal associated with youth. And they kept saying I was not only 40 but a cancer survivor. People derived hope from anyone who could thwart cancer. I knew I was a beacon. My speed may have been untested, but if you wanted inspiration, I was your man.

Hayward Field in Eugene, Oregon, served up all the excitement I needed to feel tingly as I entered the arena for the Pre mile. I had run at Hayward many times—at the 1976 and 1980 Olympic Trials, at the U.S. Nationals, at previous Pre Classics. Running there was like getting a big fat hug. Eugene, which bills itself as "Track Town USA," was a track sub-culture in a nation that gave its primary attention to so many other sports. The University of Oregon was renowned for its runners—especially its 35-year history of

4-minute milers—who were splashed all over the pages of the Eugene *Register-Guard.*

Eugene was "Bislett West": a true-to-heart American version of Oslo and its sparkling Bislett Games. Eugene distance-running legend Steve Prefontaine had in fact been so impressed by what he saw of track in Scandinavia that he brought the idea of Finland's spongy, wood-chip running trails home to Oregon. Soon after Prefontaine's untimely death in a car crash at age 25, the Prefontaine Classic was created with Pre's "athletes-first" attitude in mind. In 1996, it was elevated to Grand Prix I status, as one of 18 meets worldwide comprising the IAAF circuit. Athletes from at least two dozen nations competed, and the meet was covered on network television.

Eugene especially loved and nurtured its distance runners— from the milers to the marathoners. It was from this wellspring of local passion that the behemoth Nike had sprung a quarter-century ago. One of Nike's early stars, Mary Slaney, still lived in Eugene, and we'd appeared at the press conference before the meet. Mary was pushing 38 and trying to make the Olympic team in the 5,000 meters, a new women's event in the Games. When reporters asked Mary about her age, she said she had not lost her desire to participate and excel. Then reporters asked me about my age, and I told them much the same thing as Mary.

In fact, age was a constant theme throughout this Olympic year. Carl Lewis was turning 35. Lynn Jennings, running the 5,000, was 36. Ruth Wysocki, a good friend of mine from the San Diego area in the 1,500, was 39. Be that as it may, not all of what Mary and I told the press in Eugene was true. It was easy for us athletes long in the tooth to delude ourselves. We were surely not as capable as in our younger days, our best days, when we could win at will, not think a negative thought, feel the track as a big space as great and promising as life itself. But, knowing nothing else, it was natural to deny the inevitable, encroaching . . . end. Yet, the window was still open just a little and I was determined to breathe the fresh air for as long as I could.

Raceday was chilly and overcast with the threat of rain. Not good racing weather for a sun-worshipper like myself. But the raw conditions did not stop fans from filling the wooden forest-green seats at 9:30 on a Sunday morning. A record crowd of 13,804 bundled up in Pre sweatshirts and U. of O. parkas and brought thermoses of coffee and soup. Young children in blankets were held tightly in their mothers' arms. Concessions did a brisk business in obscure track books.

The cloudy skies could not dim the celebration as Eugenians ate up every event, from the sprints to the pole vault, and waited expectantly for their favorite race: the mile. As I did my warmup on the periphery of the field, people called to me with "Go, Steve," and I felt my heart tug with the realization that simply being in Eugene, rejoining the fraternity of track racers, was a triumph.

With 18 men in the lineup, the Prefontaine mile was ridiculously crowded. The field featured Steve Holman (the greatest threat to my American records), Kenya's Martin Keino (22-year-old son of Kip Keino, starting to nibble at Olympic contention), veteran world indoor champion Marcus O'Sullivan (doing his best outdoor running in a long while), and 18-year-old Michael Stember of California (trying to become the first high school runner in 29 years to break the 4-minute mile).

My introduction drew Eugene's best whooped-up cheers. All weekend, fans said how terrific it was to have me back, and on the starting line at Hayward Field—a spot that was almost holy in its track symbolism—the embrace I felt from the crowd was an affirmation. The young thoroughbreds would compete for victory. The Eugene reception told me I'd already won just by showing up. I wanted to grab that feeling and make it last.

When the gun sounded, I cut to the inside of the track and slipped toward the back of the field. With so many runners, it was a very busy race and I kept glancing around to make sure I wouldn't be jabbed by someone's elbow. The pacesetter hit the first quarter in 56. My split was a quick 60, but I didn't feel in a smooth rhythm. Three laps to go.

Now the field strung out. Far better at racing opponents than running strictly for time, I needed to maintain contact and feel the breath of competition on my neck. As crowded as it was, I felt like I was running alone. The leaders scooted past the half-mile in 1:55. My time was 2:01. If I could just run 2:01 for the second half, I'd have a 4:02 in my pocket. That would give me a world record for masters. But I had no right to expect such a heady performance. What was I doing at 2:01 for the first half?

For one thing, I kept hearing, "Go, Steve." When you hear your name, you move. I did want to satisfy the crowd and at least acquit myself as a runner who belonged. At this point, I was also in 17th place, and the only runner behind me was the high school kid, Stember. I had to keep up. "Just maintain," I told myself. "Just maintain."

I had almost forgotten how a hard race could hurt. But it was a good hurt. It was a hurt that pressed my chest, deadened my legs, and made me a little unsteady—a familiar hurt that served as an initiation back into the fraternity of the track. The miler's hurt was acute, but I did not consider it suffering. It was a privilege to feel this particular distress again because I could tell myself, "Yeah, you can take it." After everything I'd gone through, I felt an exalted power to persevere.

The rabbit discarded, Holman rushed through the three-quarter post in 2:55. He was chased by Keino and another Kenyan, David Kibet, the eventual winner. Stember and I kept company at the rear of the field. Sensing my fatigue, Stember bolted out of his slumber and made a bid to pass me on the homestretch with 100 meters to go. I offered no resistance. Dueling a high school kid, or anyone for that matter, in the closing stages of the Pre mile seemed beside the point.

When I crossed the finish in 4:10.43, the crowd cheered and I delighted in the appreciation. The 40-something folks got a kick out of seeing me run with the big boys half my age. People seemed anxious to offer a handshake, not only for my coming back and putting out but, in a way, for the breadth of my career—for being a barnstorming miler from the old days who'd seen it all and was still kicking up dust.

Most of the media attention was properly placed on the Olympic contenders up front in the 3:50 neighborhood. But a few reporters hunted me down for an interview, and as I gathered my belongings on the edge of the track and told my story one more time, kids pressed against the outer fencing, extending program and pen for my autograph. I happily obliged.

As a miler in midlife, I was not yet prepared to become a spectator. I found myself anxious to continue my pursuit of a sub–4:00 mile into 1997 and beyond. With the lessons of my 40th year, together with the perspective of a cancer survivor, I think I finally gained the maturity I lacked as a younger athlete. The goal is not finite. It is simply always changing, like life. We must go on.

The Last Sub-4:00 — and Beyond

When I look back on my career, I am most proud of the character I've shown as an athlete who never grew tired even when near-miss status seemed to follow me. I may be the American mile recordholder with times that no other Americans have come close to in more than a decade, but without a world record or an Olympic gold medal I'm still just "Miss Congeniality" in the international pantheon of miling. In American mile annals, Jim Ryun is said to be Babe Ruth while I'm considered Lou Gehrig (or, in today's roster, Cal Ripken)—known for my durability and decency but not on anyone's list of the "greatest." I guess all things considered, that's not so bad. But I did feel a little patronized at a 1996 banquet in New York when Sebastian Coe (who wasn't even there), Herb Elliot, and Roger Bannister received star treatment while I was introduced as "the nicest guy in the sport."

I've always reached out to people in the sport, and I've always appreciated my fans and supporters, even before cancer hit and their encouragement became so important to restoring my health. I've taken an interest in all track and field events, not just the mile, given autographs to every last spectator, gone to bat for up-and-coming runners, tried to be honest with the media, and showed a smile and a handshake to all.

More than anything, as my career draws to a close, I'd like to be known as the miler who raced under any circumstances—who competed with honesty, took on all opponents, ran sick or hurt, never quit on a field, and came back year after year with consistency, passion, and a heart full of desire.

As far as I'm concerned, passion defines the best of us. My mom had passion all those early mornings, jogging against the tide of convention and dragging me out of bed to do the same. My dad had passion as a kind of country doctor who took a personal interest in his patients. My coaches, from Bob Loney in high school, through Len Miller and now Irv Ray, gave me their passion for excellence. I think Kim and I, at least in the passion we've brought to our separate pursuits, have given Corey, Megan, and Shawn the foundation to reach heartily for their best at each stage in their young lives. Through the separations and periods of counseling, we have always retained the true feelings of love that brought us together.

In his quiet way, without breastbeating or fanfare, my old buddy John Walker exemplified the passion of the track. In the fall of '96, as I did my final training for Fifth Avenue Mile, word came out of New Zealand that Walker, 44, had been diagnosed with Parkinson's disease. I was stunned and tried to reach John. Somehow we did not connect, but I knew he was the same tough Kiwi. Commenting on his illness in an Auckland newspaper, John was in perfect character, conceding little:

I struggle to do things that I had always taken for granted, like brushing my teeth. I should live a reasonably normal life with only a very gradual deterioration over the years. There are a lot of people worse off than me.

Considering my relationship with John and my own bout with cancer, we were inevitably linked in press accounts. In an interview with a columnist from the *Times* of London, I reviewed what I'd gone through and then talked about Walker and our memorable races together. The columnist wrote this about us:

They haunted the commercial circus of grand prix races in Europe, living out of suitcases and subjecting their bodies to more demands than any before them had dreamt of. They were the first of a new breed.

In September '96, in New York for the Fifth Avenue Mile, I felt part of a completely different new breed—the midlife (or mid-youth, as marketers called it) miler who kept going, challenging the myths of age. At this point, I had no sense of my capability but was unconcerned since my only duty was to hold Eamonn Coghlan's hand through a jog. I had run Fifth Avenue many times, winning it twice, but considered it a boutique event, a no-pressure, post-season event to end the season. This time, all I'd expected for my trip East was a lot of public relations work on behalf of the sponsor and no more than a brisk jog with my old nemesis.

Organizers from the New York Road Runners Club had initially asked Eamonn and me to run more or less side by side in the "Champions' Mile," essentially a tribute in which we would barely break a sweat and smile for the cameras. Eamonn had retired from competition, was doing some modest fitness running, and had gained 15 pounds.

As the week went on, my competitive bones were tickled with excitement and I approached meet officials with the idea of me racing a mile in addition to doing my turn with Eamonn. At the least, it made good marketing sense for the sponsor, Discover Card.

The Fifth Avenue Mile had grown to 20 separate races run adjacent to Central Park, and finally officials agreed that I could compete in the master's mile race for men 40 and older, to occur 29 minutes before my run with Eamonn. That would give me only 25 minutes rest between the two miles. Eamonn like that. There was a lot of buzz about my double, especially since the two open-race favorites had begged off at the eleventh hour. Overnight, Svetlana Masterkova of Russia, the 1996 Olympic gold medalist in the 800 and 1,500 meters, complained of the flu. And Fermin Cacho of Spain, the '92 Olympic champion in the 1,500, said he twisted an ankle on a training run. I was the only name runner left. Me and Roger Bannister. The first sub–4:00 miler, now 64, was on hand to pose with Eamonn and me.

We made appearances around town and enjoyed poking jabs at one another at a press conference. Eamonn was the master of the mike and scored points with his sweet put-downs. It was all in good fun. Turning serious, he also wished me well in my pursuit of the sub–4:00, recognizing "how far I'd come" since the illness.

Over that summer, I'd hit the track hard. Three days a week I was doing speed, and the other days I cut my distance work to a few miles. On the track, I ran either 100-meter sprints, or five 200-meter sprints, or three 400s alternating all-out 50s. Once I got the hang of that, my times improved. At first, I was hitting 13.7 for my 100s. Within weeks, I was down to 12.2. These were flat-out sprints from a standing start with 3-minute recovery jogs. My speed seemed to be coming back.

None of the other masters entrants had credentials anywhere near 4:20 so I knew I'd have the race to myself. I started out hard, told myself not to pay attention to split times, and came up with a delightful surprise: 4:06.57. And that was despite easing off at the end to save some strength for the other run coming up. The last thing I wanted was to be caught short against Eamonn.

The 4:06 showed my speed program was on the money. I felt good all the way through the run, unlike my races the previous spring where I'd felt drained on the last lap. My confidence was high. All the elements for sub–4:00 at 40-something were in place.

I walked back to the start, jogged a little, felt fine, and lined up with Eamonn. After covering the first quarter in 65 seconds, a 4:20 pace, Eamonn turned to me and pleaded, "Let's slow down. I can't do this." We cooled it to the 1,500 mark, where, feeling frisky, I turned to Eamonn and said, "C'mon, let's go." That old dog had something left and I had to put my legs in gear to hold Eamonn off. Though it was meaningless, I made sure I leaned nominally ahead at the finish. I guess it was all those elbows I took from Eamonn on the indoor circuit.

The crowd along Fifth Avenue gave me a rousing cheer, and reporters hurried after me. It felt great to be appreciated, especially in New York where Eamonn had ruled for a decade. How about that—a 40-year-old miler stealing the day? Overwhelmed, I raced back to my hotel, training flats in one hand and crystal vase award in the other, to pack and hustle to the airport for the trip home.

Still wet from my shower, I just made my flight. Though exhausted, I felt stimulated and alive, bursting with energy. I would have raced down the aisle of the plane if I could. Once again, running touched the depths of my soul, and I couldn't wait to get home and share the experience with Kim and the kids.

My thoughts during the flight drifted back to my days as a high school neophyte and then dream miler. It made me feel hopeful to look back, to let both the good times and desperate struggles resonate in my mind. From the kid who practically had to be pulled by his ear to run, to the man who is still trying to make breakthroughs despite tough odds, I thought of myself as a pretty lucky guy. I've come to realize that racing the mile has more to do with love and sharing than medals and records.

I view my career as a journey, an adventure—25 years of heading out the door every day to find rapture and illumination (and greater and greater strength) in every run. I shot for the moon and the stars all at once; it was the only way I knew. Falling short on occasion did not deter me. I grew with each challenge and felt every pool of sweat was well worth the struggle. Being a mile racer has enriched my life and made me a better person.

During my career, I avoided shouting out loud about the wonder of the mile, but I have always felt a degree of exaltation as a runner. I believe that with the talent I was given, God conferred on me a certain privilege that I had to live up to. That's a big responsibility, and I took it seriously. Clearly, the task of being the best runner I could be governed my life. You could do a lot worse.

What is the essential running talent, really? It's the gift of speed in the muscle combined with the deployment of oxygen as the body pushes, pushes, pushes. . . . After that, it's all about hard work. You have to want to win badly. You have to be a kind of daredevil. There are too many risks every time you step on the track. A bad loss lingers.

But above all else you must love running, and I have. With every mile I raced and every mile I trained, I felt I was pursuing something virtuous—a level of excellence that was hard and pure and gave me a personal grandeur. Maybe I didn't have what it takes to be a company man, but I was fortunate to find a solo pursuit that was above the ordinary and ultimately put me in touch with something wonderful and profound: my truest self.

As hard as the miler's life has seemed at times, I would not trade even one of my sub–4:00 miles for comfort or security. I could never live without testing myself and, after a quarter-century of taking the starting line, I'm not ready to hang up my spikes yet. I still feel like Scottie the Miler, a kid at heart, racing around the track, remembering the old days when running felt warm and fresh.

Career Performances

STEVE SCOTT'S 136 SUB–4:00 MILES

This list does not include 1,500-meter races in equivalent sub–4:00 times, or road miles.

1977

Indoor:

DATE	MEET	SITE	TIME	PLACE
Jan. 15	Sunkist	Los Angeles	3:59.7	3rd
Feb. 18	Jack in the Box	San Diego	3:56.5	2nd

Outdoor:

DATE	MEET	SITE	TIME	PLACE
Mar. 27	Meet of Champions	Irvine, CA	3:57.8	1st
Apr. 30	Penn Relays	Philadelphia	3:55.21	2nd
May 7	West Coast Relays	Modesto, CA	3:59.6	1st
June 14	Pre Classic	Eugene, OR	3:57.9	1st
July 4	DN Galan	Stockholm	3:56.0	5th
July 30	Phillips	Gateshead, Eng	3:58.1	4th
Aug. 26	ISTAF	Berlin	3:58.7	8th

1978

Indoor:

DATE	MEET	SITE	TIME	PLACE
Feb. 17	Jack in the Box	San Diego	3:57.1	2nd

Outdoor:

DATE	MEET	SITE	TIME	PLACE
Mar. 25	Meet of Champions	Irvine, CA	3:53.9	1st
June 27	Bislett Games	Oslo	3:53.8	3rd
July 3	DN Galan	Stockholm	3:52.93	3rd
July 12	International	Dublin	3:57.5	2nd
Aug. 18	ISTAF	Berlin	3:55.7	2nd

1979

Indoor:

DATE	MEET	SITE	TIME	PLACE
Jan. 20	Sunkist	Los Angeles	3:56.7	2nd
Feb. 9	Millrose Games	New York	3:58.6	5th
Feb. 16	Jack in the Box	San Diego	3:54.1	2nd

Outdoor:

DATE	MEET	SITE	TIME	PLACE
Apr. 27	Drake Relays	Des Moines, IA	3:55.3	1st
May 6	Pepsi Inv	Los Angeles	3:56.91	2nd
May 11	Manley Games	Kingston	3:55.1	1st
June 30	Brooks	Philadelphia	3:53.39	2nd
July 3	DN Galan	Stockholm	3:55.96	1st
July 10	International	Dublin	3:56.26	1st
July 17	Bislett Games	Oslo	3:51.11	2nd

1980

Indoor:

DATE	MEET	SITE	TIME	PLACE
Feb. 15	Sunkist	Los Angeles	3:53.0	2nd*
Feb. 16	Brooks Astrodome	Houston	3:54.20	1st
Feb. 22	Jack in the Box	San Diego	3:59.3	5th

Outdoor:

DATE	MEET	SITE	TIME	PLACE
May 11	Pepsi Inv	Los Angeles	3:53.1	1st
May 17	California Relays	Modesto, CA	3:58.2	1st
June 1	Brooks	Berkeley	3:56.3	1st
July 7	DN Galan	Stockholm	3:53.59	1st
Aug. 17	Nikaia	Nice	3:54.10	1st
Aug. 22	Van Damme	Brussels	3:52.7	2nd=
Aug. 25	Invitational	London	3:52.92	2nd
Aug. 27	International	Dublin	3:53.8	1st

1981

Indoor:

DATE	MEET	SITE	TIME	PLACE
Jan. 2	Runner's World	Daly City, CA	3:59.6	1st
Jan. 10	E Tenn St Inv	Johnson City, TN	3:54.50	1st
Jan. 30	Sunkist	Los Angeles	3:53.7	1st
Feb. 6	Millrose Games	New York	3:55.0	4th
Feb. 13	Maple Leaf Games	Toronto	3:56.83	2nd
Feb. 14	Citizen Games	Ottawa	3:59.3	2nd
Feb. 20	Jack in the Box	San Diego	3:51.8	2nd*
Feb. 21	Examiner Games	Daly City, CA	3:55.3	1st
Feb. 27	USA Nationals	New York	3:57.3	1st

Outdoor:

DATE	MEET	SITE	TIME	PLACE
Apr. 25	Drake Relays	Des Moines, IA	3:58.54	1st
May 10	Pepsi Inv	Los Angeles	3:52.50	1st
May 16	California Relays	Modesto, CA	3:55.2	1st
May 30	Jumbo Elliott Inv	Villanova, PA	3:52.26	1st
June 13	Brooks	Berkeley	3:56.97	1st
July 11	Oslo Games	Oslo	3:49.68	3rd*
July 14	International	Dublin	3:54.75	1st
Aug. 19	Weltklasse	Zurich	3:53.98	8th
Aug. 21	ISTAF	Berlin	3:55.98	2nd
Aug. 28	Van Damme	Brussels	3:51.48	3rd

1982

Outdoor:

DATE	MEET	SITE	TIME	PLACE
Jan. 14	International	Melbourne	3:55.91	1st
Jan. 18	International	Sydney	3:58.82	1st
Jan. 30	International	Auckland	3:54.87	1st

Indoor:

DATE	MEET	SITE	TIME	PLACE
Feb. 5	LA Times Games	Los Angeles	3:58.3	4th
Feb. 12	Millrose Games	New York	3:55.37	1st
Feb. 19	Jack in the Box	San Diego	3:55.0	4th

Outdoor:

DATE	MEET	SITE	TIME	PLACE
May 16	Pepsi Inv	Los Angeles	3:52.68	1st
June 12	Kinney	Berkeley	3:54.1	1st
June 26	Bislett Games	Oslo	3:48.53	1st*
July 7	Oslo Games	Oslo	3:47.69	1st*
Aug. 25	International	Koblenz, Ger	3:49.72	1st

1983

Outdoor:

DATE	MEET	SITE	TIME	PLACE
Jan. 22	International	Auckland	3:56.29	1st

Indoor:

DATE	MEET	SITE	TIME	PLACE
Feb. 4	LA Times Games	Inglewood, CA	3:57.44	1st
Feb. 11	Foot Locker	Daly City, CA	3:57.5	1st
Feb. 18	Michelob	San Diego	3:54.5	2nd
Feb. 19	Knights of Col.	Cleveland	3:58.42	3rd
Feb. 25	USA Nationals	New York	3:58.99	2nd
Feb. 27	Olympic Inv	E Rutherford, NJ	3:52.28	3rd

Outdoor:

DATE	MEET	SITE	TIME	PLACE
May 15	Pepsi Inv	Los Angeles	3:53.16	1st
May 28	Jenner Inv	San Jose, CA	3:55.37	1st
June 12	Kinney	Berkeley	3:52.53	1st
July 9	Oslo Games	Oslo	3:49.49	1st
July 13	International	Cork, Ire	3:50.99	1st
July 23	International	London	3:51.56	1st
Aug. 17	ISTAF	Berlin	3:49.21	1st
Aug. 31	International	Koblenz, Ger	3:50.01	1st

1984

Indoor:

DATE	MEET	SITE	TIME	PLACE
Jan. 20	Sunkist	Los Angeles	3:57.69	1st
Jan. 27	Millrose Games	New York	3:59.38	1st
Feb. 17	Michelob	San Diego	3:58.0	4th

Outdoor:

DATE	MEET	SITE	TIME	PLACE
May 13	Pepsi Inv	Los Angeles	3:52.99	1st
May 26	Jenner Inv	San Jose, CA	3:57.71	1st
July 14	Kinney	Berkeley	3:56.40	1st
July 21	Pre Classic	Eugene, OR	3:54.44	1st
Aug. 17	ISTAF	Berlin	3:53.66	1st

1985

Indoor:

DATE	MEET	SITE	TIME	PLACE
Jan. 18	Sunkist	Los Angeles	3:56.35	2nd
Jan. 19	E Tenn St Inv	Johnson City, TN	3:55.92	4th
Jan. 25	Millrose Games	New York	3:56.61	5th
Jan. 27	Bally	Chicago	3:57.33	2nd
Feb. 1	Toronto Star	Toronto	3:59.66	2nd
Feb. 2	Times-Herald	Dallas	3:58.92	1st
Feb. 15	Michelob	San Diego	3:58.7	3rd

Outdoor:

DATE	MEET	SITE	TIME	PLACE
Mar. 2	International	Auckland	3:53.74	1st
May 11	S & W	Modesto, CA	3:58.60	1st
May 18	Pepsi Inv	Los Angeles	3:58.20	2nd
May 25	Jenner Inv	San Jose, CA	3:56.5	1st
June 23	Foot Locker	Berkeley	3:58.43	1st
July 27	Bislett Games	Oslo	3:49.93	4th

1986

Indoor:

DATE	MEET	SITE	TIME	PLACE
Feb. 14	Millrose Games	New York	3:59.13	5th
Feb. 21	LA Times Games	Los Angeles	3:59.59	3rd
Feb. 23	Michelob	San Diego	3:56.8	2nd

Outdoor:

DATE	MEET	SITE	TIME	PLACE
May 17	Pepsi Inv	Los Angeles	3:57.05	2nd
May 31	Jenner Inv	San Jose, CA	3:58.19	1st
June 10	Jerome Inv	Burnaby, Can	3:57.87	1st
June 30	Ulster Games	Belfast	3:58.12	2nd
July 5	Bislett Games	Oslo	3:48.73	2nd
July 15	Nikaia	Nice	3:52.13	1st
Aug. 8	Grand Prix	London	3:54.04	1st
Sept. 10	Grand Prix Final	Rome	3:50.28	1st

1987

Indoor:

DATE	MEET	SITE	TIME	PLACE
Feb. 22	Michelob	San Diego	3:56.7	2nd

Outdoor:

DATE	MEET	SITE	TIME	PLACE
May 16	Pepsi Inv	Los Angeles	3:59.08	1st
July 4	Bislett Games	Oslo	3:57.33	5th
Aug. 21	ISTAF	Berlin	3:52.36	2nd

1988

Outdoor:

DATE	MEET	SITE	TIME	PLACE
June 6	Pepsi Inv	Los Angeles	3:53.6	1st
June 25	Michelob	San Diego	3:56.06	1st
July 2	Bislett Games	Oslo	3:50.09	5th
July 5	International	Cork, Ire	3:55.49	1st

1989

Outdoor:

DATE	MEET	SITE	TIME	PLACE
July 17	Girobank Games	Belfast	3:58.09	2nd
July 22	New York Games	New York	3:53.83	2nd
Aug. 16	Jack in the Box	Los Angeles	3:57.1	5th

1990

Indoor:

DATE	MEET	SITE	TIME	PLACE
Feb. 16	LA Times Games	Los Angeles	3:59.78	4th
Feb. 23	USA Indoor	New York	3:57.35	1st

Outdoor:

DATE	MEET	SITE	TIME	PLACE
May 20	Jack in the Box	Los Angeles	3:57.22	2nd
Sept. 7	Grand Prix Final	Athens	3:56.34	8th

1991

Indoor:

DATE	MEET	SITE	TIME	PLACE
Jan. 20	Northeast Inv	Allston, MA	3:59.1	1st
Feb. 1	Millrose Games	New York	3:57.77	3rd
Feb. 8	Vitalis Inv	E Rutherford, NJ	3:59.63	4th

Outdoor:

DATE	MEET	SITE	TIME	PLACE
May 11	S & W	Modesto, CA	3:59.51	1st
July 1	BNP	Villeneuve d'Ascq, Fra	3:54.13	3rd
July 6	Bislett Games	Oslo	3:58.00	13th

1992

Indoor:

DATE	MEET	SITE	TIME	PLACE
Feb. 15	Sunkist	Los Angeles	3:58.54	1st

1993

Indoor:

DATE	MEET	SITE	TIME	PLACE
Feb. 20	Sunkist	Los Angeles	3:59.8	3rd

=tie
*American Record

SUMMARY OF PLACINGS:

First	71
Second	32
Third	12
Fourth	9
Fifth	8
Eighth	3
Thirteenth	1
TOTAL	**136**

SCOTT'S PERSONAL BEST PERFORMANCES

800 meters	1:45.05	Byrkjelo, Norway	July 4, 1982
1,000 meters	2:16.40	Nice, France	Aug. 23, 1981
1,500 meters	3:31.76	Nice, France	July 16, 1985
Mile	3:47.69	Oslo, Norway	July 7, 1982
3,000 meters	7:36.69	Ingleheim, Ger	Sept. 1, 1981
5,000 meters	13:30.39	Eugene, Oregon	June 6, 1987

SCOTT'S AMERICAN RECORD PERFORMANCES

Indoors:

Mile	3:53.0	Los Angeles, CA	Feb. 15, 1980
1,500 meters	3:36.0	San Diego, CA	Feb. 20, 1981*
Mile	3:51.8	San Diego, CA	Feb. 20, 1981*
2,000 meters	4:58.6	Louisville, KY	Feb. 7, 1981*
3,000 meters	7:39.94	E. Rutherford, NJ	Feb. 10, 1989*

Outdoors:

1,500 meters	3:31.96	Koblenz, Ger	Aug. 26, 1981
2,000 meters	4:48.72	Nice, France	Aug. 14, 1982
2,000 meters	4:54.71	Ingleheim, Ger	Aug. 31, 1982
Mile	3:49.68	Oslo, Norway	July 11, 1981
Mile	3:48.53	Oslo, Norway	June 26, 1982
Mile	3:47.69	Oslo, Norway	July 7, 1982*
3,000 meters	7:36.69	Ingleheim, Ger	Sept. 1, 1981

*Record still stands through 1997 season

SCOTT'S USA NATIONAL CHAMPIONSHIP TITLES

Indoors:		*Outdoors:*	
1979	Mile	1978	1,500 meters
1981	Mile	1979	1,500 meters
1984	Mile	1982	1,500 meters
1990	Mile	1983	1,500 meters
		1986	1,500 meters

SCOTT'S OLYMPIC PERFORMANCES

1980	Olympic Team, 1,500 meters (U.S. boycott)
1984	10th, 1,500 meters
1988	5th, 1,500 meters

I N D E X